Women, Men, and Power

Hilary M. Lips
Radford University

Mayfield Publishing Company
Mountain View, California
London • Toronto

Library of Congress Cataloging-in-Publication Data

Lips, Hilary M.
    Women, men, and power / by Hilary M. Lips.
        p.   cm.
    Includes bibliographical references and index.
    ISBN 0-87484-916-0
    1. Power (Social sciences) 2. Women—Psychology. 3. Men—Psychology.
    4. Sex role. I. Title.
HM136.L528   1990
305.3—dc20   90-41065
                                                                        CIP

Manufactured in the United States of America

10   9   8   7   6   5

Mayfield Publishing Company
1240 Villa Street
Mountain View, California 94041

Sponsoring Editor, Franklin C. Graham; managing editor, Linda Toy; production
editor, Carol Zafiropoulos; manuscript editor, Colleen O'Brien; text design, Jeanne
M. Schreiber; cover design and production artist, Jean Mailander. The text was
set in 10 1/2/12 1/2 Janson Text and printed on 50# Glatfelter Spring Forge by
Thomson-Shore.

Contents

CHAPTER SIX   *Dominance: The Structure of Power*   93

CHAPTER SEVEN   *Power, Sexuality, and Reproduction*   115

Preface

The old saying that "the hand that rocks the cradle rules the world" sums up, in a few words, the built-in contradictions in the cultural messages we have received about gender and power. Women do not appear powerful, but *really* they are, the message says. Men appear to rule the world, but *really* they do not. Rock the cradle, women, but do not rock the boat.

Sayings like this have beguiled women and men into mistrusting our own perceptions, our own experience, of power. But surely this message is a relic of the past? Perhaps so, in its assumption that women's major role is to mother children. Yet the modern cultural messages continue to conceal, rather than reveal, the power relationship between women and men: the song lyrics that claim that love conquers all, the movies that show couples walking, flying, riding, or jogging off into the sunset, the advice columns that remind us piously that good relationships require sacrifice. Women, in particular, often seem to be the targets of the message that, if they just love someone enough, everything will work out fine. What this message obscures is that individual relationships occur against a back-ground of intergroup relationships, and the groups to which women and men belong differ in power. When women and men seek intimacy in special relationships with each other, differences in men's and women's access to power tend to subvert this intimacy or turn it into a charade. When women and men seek to be friends or colleagues with each other, they find that the equality supposed in those relationships is constantly challenged by learned gender-related patterns of dominance and submission. As long as we do not acknowledge the role of power in these relationships, there is little hope of changing them for the better.

My task in this book is to explore the structured inequality of power that exists between women and men and the interpersonal and group processes through which that structure operates. My perspective is that of a feminist and a social psychologist. From my feminist perspective, I view power as a central aspect of gender relations: Women have less access than men do to most kinds of power, and most stereotypic male-female differences result from this imbalance. From my social-psychological perspective, I view the wider social context as crucial to understanding interpersonal relationships. In addition, I see both interpersonal and intergroup relationships as reciprocally reactive: The maintenance of any relationship requires, in some way, the cooperation of both parties, and within a relationship each party—even the most oppressed—has some power and makes some contribution to the way things are.

The book begins with an overview of the many aspects of power, then continues through five chapters that examine frameworks used to analyze power and gender: cultural images of power, the power motive, strategies of interpersonal influence, feelings of effectiveness and control, and the stable power structures of dominance. The next four chapters deal with gender power relations in specific contexts: sexuality, families, the workplace, and political action. The epilogue presents some projections for the future.

The fact that this book is finished at all reflects the help and encouragement of many people. I am grateful to the University of Winnipeg for granting me sabbatical time to be used partly for work on this manuscript, and to the University of Arizona's Southwest Institute for Research on Women for making me welcome as a visiting scholar while I worked on it. Especially, I thank the other members of the Center for Gender Studies at Radford University; their support and enthusiasm have kept me going on this and a variety of other projects. I appreciate the insights and suggestions provided by the following people on all or part of the manuscript: Susan Arpad, California State University, Fresno; Meredith Bombar, Elmira College; Patricia Faunce, University of Minnesota; Jeanne Kohl; Rosemary Krawczyk, Mankato State University; M. Chris Paxson, Washington State University; Jane Prather, California State University, Northridge; Claire Renzetti, St. Joseph's University; Virginia Sapiro, University of Wisconsin, Madison; and Carol Wade. I received invaluable help and encouragement from many people at Mayfield, especially Frank Graham and Carol Zafiropoulos. I am grateful to the many friends, colleagues and students whose willingness to sit and talk with me about gender and power was so important in developing the ideas for this book. And I thank Wayne Andrew, who endured much, helped me at every opportunity, commiserated, kept me laughing, and celebrated with me when it was finished.

Hilary M. Lips

To the ferociously creative women and men, some of whom I am fortunate to count as friends, who have the courage to face down old habits and hardened ideas and reconstruct their social world, beginning with their own relationships.

CHAPTER ONE

Power: Its Many Faces

In September 1988, women ran the 10,000-meter race in the Olympic
Games for the first time in history. In the same month, the Chinese
military announced the appointment of its first five female generals;
Barbara Harris, a middle-aged black woman from Pennsylvania, became
the first woman to be elected a bishop in the Episcopal church; and the
first American woman, Stacy Allison, reached the summit of Mount
Everest.

Those of us who keep track of "firsts" for women may lift our coffee
cups in quiet toasts of appreciation as we read the accounts in our
morning newspapers of these small victories. Some of us may reflect with
satisfaction that such firsts are becoming increasingly commonplace.
Hovering around the edges of that satisfaction, however, are familiar
nagging questions: Why are there still so many "firsts" for women? Why
is it taking so long to seem simply normal for women to try anything they
please and to achieve recognition and status in the whole variety of
human endeavors? Members of minority groups raise similar questions:
Why, only now, a first Hispanic American secretary of education, a first
African–American astronaut, a first Canadian member of parliament who
dares to publicly identify himself as gay? That such "firsts" are considered
significant demonstrates the extent to which positions of status, influence, and opportunity have been withheld from the groups these pioneers represent.

The excitement that still greets women's entry into each new arena
of achievement or public recognition signals that such breakthroughs for

women, while celebrated by many, are *not* commonplace. In fact, they represent a sharp discontinuity from the expected. The discontinuity represents more than a smashing of stereotypes or a shedding of gender roles. Men's entry into traditionally female arenas is not greeted with the same hoopla. There are no front-page headlines for the first man elected president of a regional nursing association or the first male secretary hired by a large corporation. The arenas controlled by women and men are not equivalent; although a woman's entry into a previously all-male field is almost always considered a step up, a sign of unusually high ability (or unusually good luck), a man's advance into a previously all-female field will gain him little special notice from the world at large.

The different reactions accorded to women and men who break from the expected pattern are a strong reminder that there is more to the social construction of gender than separate, complementary roles for females and males. There is, in fact, a hierarchy, or increasing levels of power and influence, in which the sphere of activities dominated by one group (males) is frequently accorded more importance and status than the sphere of activities dominated by the other (females). The existence of such a hierarchy does not have to be divined through complicated investigation; the most cursory look at the economic facts of life for women and men reveals a pattern in which men's activities are valued more highly than women's. Women still earn only about 70% of what men earn. The average salary for a female clerical worker—an occupation that accounts for much of female employment—is $12,220 (U.S. Department of Commerce, 1989). The average working man in the United States earned $22,516 in 1987, while the average working woman earned $15,756 (U.S. Department of Commerce, 1989). Raising children, the work most firmly associated with women, receives virtually no economic acknowledgment; employers in the United States still feel that they are doing women a favor by granting a few weeks of unpaid maternity leave. Women and the work they do have been economically marginalized; later in this book we will see that this marginalization extends beyond economics to many aspects of culture. The hierarchical aspect of sex (which refers to biological femaleness or maleness) and gender (which encompasses not only biological sex but also socially constructed femininity or masculinity) is further complicated by the interaction of sex and gender with such factors as race, ethnicity, social class, sexual orientation, and age.

A recognition of the hierarchy that underlies *gender roles*—patterns of behavior culturally associated with women and men—leads inevitably to the question of power. The issue is an uncomfortable one in the context of gender, for a variety of reasons. Traditionally, relationships between women and men are supposed to be characterized by attraction, and often love—who wants to spoil that by talking about something as chilling as power? In addition, the stereotype that has been assigned to women precludes power; women are not supposed to be interested in power or to behave in powerful ways. Finally, women—who have been on the outside looking in when it comes to power—have developed strong conflicting emotions, often characterized by distaste, toward the idea of power. Discomfort with the idea of examining the connections between gender and power has led to one of two responses: a refusal to discuss it, or an attempt to define power in a more palatable way. Refusing to discuss power will not make it go away. As Elizabeth Janeway (1981) noted in *Powers of the Weak*, "though one may decline a position of power, one can't escape the effect of the process" (p. 15).

DEFINITIONS OF POWER

Popular Definitions

My bank offers a "power checking" account. Bookstores are flooded with volumes on such themes as "power lunching" and "power dressing." The essence of power, as offered to the public in these forms, allows the consumer to appear important—and to use that image of importance to influence others. Power, at least in some circles, is clearly not a dirty word but rather a glamorous, sought-after commodity. Paradoxically, the popular media message is that to get more power, one needs to behave as if one already has it.

To a social psychologist, such a message is not as paradoxical as it first appears. It has been demonstrated over and over again that the way people behave toward others is shaped by their impressions of those others. If we think a person is "important," we will behave differently toward that person than if that person appears to be a "nobody." Social power is, to a large extent, in the eye of the beholder. Those who wish to *be* more powerful learn quickly that one important route to that goal is to *act* more powerful.

Built into this understanding of power is the assumption that there is only so much of it to go around. Those who want deference and exaggerated respect from others must act and appear more worthy of such behavior than others. If everyone is perceived to be equally important and equally powerful, there is no reason for one person to defer to anyone else. From this perspective, it is in the interest of the powerful to keep the powerless in a subordinate position. While not everyone views power in this way, those who do are naturally motivated not to share their higher status with others.

Traditional Social Science Definitions

Dictionary definitions of power include "the ability to do or act," "physical strength or force," and "control, influence, or authority" (*Random House Dictionary*, 1980). Only the last of these has been incorporated into traditional social science definitions of power, which emphasize influence and control. Social psychologists have defined power as the capacity to affect the quality of the other person's outcomes (Thibaut & Kelley, 1959) and the ability to get another person to do what one wants her or him to do, despite initial resistance (Cartwright & Zander, 1968). Power has also been defined by social scientists as control over resources, including human resources, and of core social institutions—control that makes possible both the effective initiation of action and decisions and the use of effective sanctions (Sherif, 1982).

Like the popular definitions, the preceding definitions treat power as a commodity—something that a person or group collects and has. But some social observers argue that power is not a commodity, not something we have, but something we *do* (Janeway, 1981). Viewed in this light, power is something that exists only in the context of a relationship; indeed, it is part of the process of that relationship. Power is the process of bargaining and compromise in which priorities are set and decisions made in relationships. Both parties, even if one dominates the other, contribute to the process. Janeway observes, in fact, that the process of growing from a dependent childhood to a self-sufficient adulthood involves largely learning how to respond to, predict and control events, to bargain, to negotiate with others, and to rebel—all part of the process of achieving power, of taking more and more power into one's own hands. We cannot think of power as a "thing" that only the powerful possess; it is a process in which we all engage as long as we are part of a network of human relationships.

The image of power is often seen as a double-edged sword. Power exercised by an individual can be labeled as either good or evil, depending on the context.[1] In its positive sense, power enables the holder to achieve goals perceived as valuable. This condition of power as good—that of being productive of valued ends—cannot stand alone as a criterion for judging power. For power to be thought of as good, it must also be achieved and exercised in ways deemed worthy of respect. Thus, in general, to command admiration for one's power, one must be seen as having achieved power through legitimate means. For example, the power of a government official may be seen as evil if it is suspected that

[1]I am indebted to my former colleague, Leslie Campbell, who, while she was teaching philosophy and women's studies at the University of Winnipeg, worked with me to elaborate these ideas in an earlier book, *Women, Men and the Psychology of Power* (Prentice-Hall, 1981).

the position of power was obtained through political patronage or cronyism. Similarly, although the power of an athlete is usually praised and celebrated, some Olympic athletes have found to their sorrow that athletic power becomes the object of contempt if it is discovered that the athlete's ability has been increased through use of steroids.

Besides the manner of its achievement, the way in which power is exercised affects its ethical evaluation. The frequently heard phrase "abuse of power" testifies to the importance of this consideration. Although a person may have legitimately gained a position of power and may use it to further valuable ends, that power will be judged negatively if its exercise is seen as undemocratic, tyrannical, ruthless, devious, or manipulative.

In general, three central considerations are relevant to people's evaluation of power: the *source*, or means by which it is gained, the *manner of its employment*, and the intended *effects* of its use.

Because people often differ in their evaluations of particular kinds and uses of power it is not surprising that power as an abstract concept causes conflicting reactions. Power is seen as evil if its source, manner of use, or goals are considered illegitimate; it is seen as good if it is considered deserved, well used, and productive of valuable effects. One of the reasons why power over others is sometimes viewed with suspicion is that a power-holder can be tempted to increase personal power rather than use power to help others or accomplish worthwhile things. And one of the reasons why female holders of powerful positions are often viewed in a negative light is that their very femaleness renders them, in the eyes of some, unfit for or undeserving of power.

Power as Social Structure or "Discipline"

While traditional views of power emphasized the intentional exercise of one individual's will over others, recent theoretical writings emphasize a different and broader view (Parker, 1989). According to this newer perspective, power is built into a social system in such a way that its exercise is almost independent of the will of a particular individual. Individuals, more or less unaware of the structure of power that surrounds them, participate in, maintain, and are limited by that power structure.

For example, an academic discipline such as psychology contains and is contained by a power system. This includes a method of discourse, a use of language that defines what is important and what counts as truth, what research methods are legitimate, who is qualified to speak for the discipline, and so on. There is no squad of psychology police, no ultimate authority, making sure that psychologists do not step out of line in the research questions they ask and in the way they investigate these questions. Yet psychologists keep one another in line on these issues through their efforts to be good members of the discipline by the way they evaluate others' work and censor their own ideas. The discipline of psychology itself becomes a system of power relations that transcends the dominance of one individual over another *within* that system. Of course, individual, intentional acts of dominance and individual power relationships go on within any system and often reflect it. A system of power does not just happen but is shaped in the first place by the actions of individuals pursuing their own goals.

Gender power relations, as explored in this book, can likewise be described as disciplinary power—a system, or structure, of power that transcends particular female–male relationships and the intentional acts of dominance, or attempts at equality, that occur within those relationships. It is the presence of this system, sometimes labeled "institutionalized sexism," that often makes it difficult for women to be viewed as powerful, that makes the exercise of power by a woman seem at best extraordinary and at worst illegitimate.

Participation in the accepted system of gender power relations, which we can hardly avoid as members of society, allows for the occurrence of many forms of routine oppression of women by men. Such oppression is mindless and unintentional, often unrecognized by either the perpetrators or the victims, but supported by the overall system of gender power relations. The automatic assumption that a woman in an office is a secretary; the failure of male groups to listen to women speak; the description of a female painter as "the best *woman* artist of the decade"— these are routine oppressions visited on women, often by well-meaning men—and other women. All of these examples show how institutionalized power relations between women and men affect and are perpetuated by an accumulation of individual behaviors. Thus, to understand gender power relations, it is crucial to realize that there is more to them than the intentional dominance of individual women by individual men.

FEMINIST DEBATES ABOUT POWER

The feminist movement strives to enhance women's status and to promote equality between the sexes. One of the basic assumptions underlying this movement is that power differences exist between women and men. For nearly a century and a half, feminists have raised questions and generated debates about power. They have identified power structures where none were recognized; for example, they oppose the idea that women's family roles in relation to men are shaped only by love and biology. They have also questioned what the proper approach to power should be: Is it "feminist" to strive for "power over" others, or should women try to define new approaches to power, approaches that do not depend on hierarchies? In what circumstances is it appropriate to assign or accept authority and leadership of one person or group over others? If women simply work their way into existing power hierarchies instead of challenging the notion that power must come from the top down, will any basic changes in human relationships really result?

During such arguments, feminists have at times divided power into two types—"bad" power (power over others) and "good" power (the capacity to achieve one's goals); between, as Elizabeth Janeway explains in her book *Powers of the Weak*, "a limiting power to compel and a liberating power to act" (p. 87). They sought to gain the "good" power while denying the "bad" power.

The hazards of disclaiming any interest in "bad" power are many, for power hierarchies can develop even where they are least intended. Yet, reflecting on the experience of being on the bottom end of the power hierarchy, of feeling powerless, can produce, among those of us who yearn for a more egalitarian world, a tendency to disclaim any desire to have "power over" other people. We argue that each person should have control over his or her own life; and we shrink from the notion of one person or one group controlling another. In our rush to do away with the concept of "power over," we have sometimes set up, in our own groups, political structures in which permanent leadership has no place. Sometimes these experiments have been successful; at other times they seem to have paved the way for what Jo Freeman (1973) calls the "tyranny of structurelessness."

When no rules about leadership or the management of power in a group exist, timid souls may find themselves watching in helpless, horrified fascination as the group in which there is no official leader becomes dominated by an unofficial leader: the person with the loudest voice, the least compromising opinions, and the highest tolerance for conflict. In such cases, it is the very refusal to deal with the issue of "power over" that leads to a situation in which one person exercises virtually uninhibited power over others in the group: The absence of an "official" powerholder does not mean that no one person is exercising power over the others.

The lesson here can be carried over to male–female relationships, both personal and collective. If men have the loudest voices and feel more comfortable than women do in conflict situations (as the research to be discussed later in this book suggests that they often do) and there are no rules to manage interactions, men will easily tend to dominate women. If women and men of good will, caught up in a vision of their shared commitments and common humanity, turn away in discomfort from an acknowledgement of the presence of "power over," whether individual or socially structured in their relationships, the result may well be that men's power over women will continue in myriad subtle ways, even among people whose stated goal is equality between the sexes.

Clearly, "power over" cannot be ignored. Feminist efforts to seek power without emphasizing control over others have lifted the veil from some other faces of power. One is the power of resistance, explored by Janeway (1981) under the label of "powers of the weak" and the psychology of response to oppression. Janeway, as we have seen, describes power as part of the process of social interaction. She notes that the weaker members of a relationship have at least one source of power that the stronger do not: an understanding of the power relationship from the bottom, and a sensitivity, born of necessity, to the shades of differences in that relationship. The weak, she argues, study the powerful in order to survive; they understand, in certain ways, the motivations of the powerful. The powerful, on the other hand, rarely study the weak. Some would argue that many members of weak groups are too burdened by their oppression to spend much energy studying the powerful.

Janeway points out that the continuation of the power relationship depends to some extent on the cooperation of the weak. Therefore, the weak can exert power by doubting and questioning the status quo instead of quietly accepting it. They can share their doubts with one another, and work together to bargain with the more powerful for a more beneficial arrangement. Such tactics do not exactly represent the "power over" face of power; they might more accurately be characterized "power from under." Nonetheless, they *are* tactics of influence over others that limit and compel the behavior of others.

Another face of power favored by feminists is the power to achieve goals, individually or collectively: for Florence Griffith-Joyner, finding the strength, self-confidence and determination to break the speed record for the women's 200 meter run; for students at Garfield high school in Los Angeles, providing one another with support and courage in collectively challenging the stereotype that poor Hispanic students from an underfunded school would never be able to pass the national advanced placement test in calculus.

A popular feminist term in recent years is *empowerment;* as individuals become increasingly empowered, they experience a growth and development of their sense of autonomy and a trust in their own abilities (Moglen, 1983). This change represents an increase in "good" power— the capacity to achieve one's goals. But even this face of power can be problematic: Too narrow a focus on achieving one's goals, by either an individual or a group, might be considered an abuse of power because it can result in the diversion of crucial resources from others or in reducing others to invisibility. For example, many feminists are concerned that the pursuit of the goals of mainly white middle class women in the feminist movement has contributed to the relative invisibility of nonwhite and poor women.

It must also be noted that empowerment cannot be completely isolated from the less savory "power over." Why? Because an empowered person or group, filled with the exhilaration of new strength, is more likely to challenge the existing hierarchy of "power over." The challenge, coming as it does from a new confidence in one's own meanings and metaphors, may be more transformative and ultimately disturbing to the established system than would any change coming from within the hierarchical framework.

Witness the images generated by a group of United Church women, newly empowered by a workshop at a Canadian national conference: They envisioned themselves as salt, ready to irritate and confront established systems, as turning the world upside down, as baking a whole new loaf instead of "accepting a slice of the ecclesiastical pie," and as "leaven instead of the whole loaf" ready to "attack oppressive systems from the bottom instead of flailing endlessly at the top" (Sinclair, 1984). As these newly empowered women set out to transform their church system, they will inevitably eventually have to use some version of "power over" others—forcing, bribing, bargaining, or cajoling—in order to get others to stop doing some things and to start doing others. When it comes to the power to change things, the difference between power over and power to achieve is not always clear.

At a 1988 workshop on "What is Power?" at a Canadian national women's conference, a Native American woman exploded in frustration after listening to speaker after speaker talk about the ins and outs of gaining political power. "I would like", she proclaimed angrily, "to see how you women would talk about power if you were naked, stripped of your clothes and your positions and your possessions. My Indian sisters in prison, who have been taken far from their families and who have had all outward signs of their dignity stripped away from them, have more power than any of you—because they have found an inner strength to endure that none of you have found."

This woman dramatically identified an aspect of power—"power from within" (Starhawk, 1982)—that is often ignored in the feminist debates, except by people interested in feminist spirituality. This understanding of power focuses on the individual value of every person and the inner strength that comes from that innate value if the person recognizes it. It cannot be measured necessarily by the amount of change a person manages to accomplish or by the number of people whose behavior she or he controls; indeed, the idea of measuring it at all is almost ludicrous. Yet, some argue, it is a potential that all human beings have—something that keeps us sane in insane times and that allows us, once in awhile, to endure against overwhelming odds, and to make unpopular choices in the face of negation by the power structure that surrounds us.

Traditional western religions have argued that inner strength comes not from within but from an external god. Both emerging feminist theologies (Ruether, 1983; Starhawk, 1982) and the spiritual traditions of certain Native American groups (Allen, 1986) emphasize that inner strength comes from persons' connecting with one another and with their environment.

The feminist debates have been extremely useful in expanding our notions of what power is, why it is important, and how an individual or group might achieve it. Yet, in terms of the individual, the debates have succeeded only in highlighting, not in resolving, the uneasiness about power; the seeming contradictions between the limiting, oppressive power of one person or group over others; and the liberating, energizing power of discovering one's own strength or the collective capacity to act. The contradictions cannot be resolved because, in a way, all of these forms of power are different faces of the same thing kept in a tenuous balance by the relationships in which they are embedded.

For example, in a family, all members relate to one another in terms of power as well as, or instead of, affection. These power relationships can be oppressive when, for instance, they express male dominance. However, oppression is only one face of power. Parents hold power over their children; in good circumstances, this power is used not oppressively, but protectively, is held in check by love for the child, and is gradually relinquished as the child matures and negotiates more independence. The limiting "power over" that a parent uses with respect to a child is not necessarily bad—although the newspapers are filled with tragic stories in which it has become so—but rather can and often does operate to ensure the child's survival to adulthood and even the child's own empowerment. But it can become oppressive, ugly, and even life-threatening to the child if love and sensitivity to the child's needs are missing, or if the parents, trapped, desperate and feeling powerless with respect to everyone and everything except the child, lash out unthinkingly or without restraint, abusing their power.

Such abuse of power, like other abuses of power over others, can be limited only by the presence of a surrounding community that takes responsibility for regulating the process of power. There is no escape from this conclusion. We cannot eliminate power over some people by others, because influence is a necessary part of our web of interactions with others. We must, instead, maintain a community responsibility to ensure that power over others is limited and balanced.

INSTITUTIONALIZING POWER

In some ways, our social world is less a community than a collection of institutions that regulates various aspects of its members' lives. There are schools, churches, military establishments, businesses, political parties, families—all with control over certain resources, all with long traditions of doing things a certain way. That certain traditions of relating to others have become institutionalized may make them appear natural rather than contrived. This apparent naturalness is a source of power for those who would maintain things as they are. Even if no one wants to maintain things as they are, however, institutionalized power relations help to maintain a general system of power, such as gender power relations, because they help to make the system invisible, like water to a fish.

As noted earlier, the first step in resisting someone else's power over oneself is to doubt and question the arrangement; but if that power is institutionalized, the doubting and questioning become more difficult and dangerous. How easily can we question the myth that it is natural for a wife to submit cheerfully to her husband's "God-given authority" when that myth is enmeshed in the precepts of such inviolate institutions as family and religion? How easily can we question the myth that men are more fit than women to govern, when male dominance of political parties and major political office rests on a history of laws that has excluded women from political participation by denying them the right to vote or the eligibility to run for office until well into this century?

Institutions are remarkably difficult to change; power, once entrenched in the way an institution is structured, can be modified, if at all, only with intense, prolonged, painful effort. More than 19 centuries after the apostle Paul's declaration that women were unfit to preach, the Catholic church continues to rationalize the exclusion of women from the priesthood (and also from the hierarchy of authority in the church). Seven decades after winning the right to vote, women hold only two seats in the United States senate. Years after the civil rights marches and anti-poverty campaigns of the 1960s, almost a third of African–Americans— a majority of them single mothers and their children—live below the poverty line.

Clearly, infiltrating an existing institution is slow and difficult. Those who seek social change often debate the wisdom of throwing all of their energy into this type of endeavor. Some argue that when outsiders, such as women, reach a *critical mass* (large enough numbers to have power through those numbers) in an institution, the institution itself will begin to change; others argue that relying on a critical mass theory of institutional change allows women to forego the development of a conscious strategy—except increased access to institutions—for change (Douglas, 1987). The reason a more conscious strategy might be important is that the values and structures built into existing institutions, in fact, may be hostile to the changes in power relationships sought by the infiltrating minority. For example, traditional hierarchical power structures may encourage the limiting, compelling "power over" and be destructive of the empowerment face of power. With this possibility in mind, feminists often strive to create organizational forms that emphasize equal participation more than authority.

Those who would change their own place in the system of social relationships that describes power would do well to consider the advisability not only of infiltrating and changing existing institutions but also of creating their own institutions. We have all heard the jokes about how hard it is to dismantle a committee after its original purpose has been accomplished, of how, for instance, the Department of Veterans' Affairs seems to expand its bureaucracy in inverse proportion to the number of veterans it serves. That lesson has not been lost on those who work to create organizations dedicated to research or advocacy for women, to gain secure funding for journals devoted to women's writing, and to institutionalize women's studies programs in universities, in women's caucuses in political parties, and in professional associations.

As Jill Vickers (1988) notes, the changes needed to transform the power relationship between women and men will not be completed during our lifetime. She argues that to secure the changes that have been accomplished and thus leave the next generation of women with a legacy of progress, it is necessary for women to institutionalize their collective power. This means setting up actual organizational structures that protect women's interests rather than relying on the hope that social attitudes, once changed in favor of gender equality, will remain stable.

PERSONAL, COLLECTIVE, AND INSTITUTIONAL POWER

Early in my teaching career, a student followed me to my office one day to ask a question about the lecture. As I sat behind my desk, waiting for her to articulate her question, I noticed with surprise and disbelief that she was trembling with nervousness. The disbelief stemmed from my inability to see myself as an intimidating person; in fact, in those days, I felt that it was I, rather than my students, who was intimidated. But I had reckoned without the institutionalized power that the university gave me, a professor, over her, a student. Her fear had little to do with me as an individual, and a lot to do with our respective institutional roles.

When a female secretary argues with her male boss, her power in the interaction is conditioned by more than just her personal skills at persuasion and the strength of her position. The results of the argument will depend not only on how empowered she is, on the strength of his personal disposition to exert power over others, on her willingness to use the power of resistance, or on the inner strength of either one of them. Rarely, if ever, is the power process between two individuals defined solely by their individual qualities. In this case, the secretary's (and the boss') power is also affected by the power relationships of the groups to which the two people belong: female/male, perhaps old/young, poor/rich, nonwhite/white. It is shaped as well by the way their work relationship is institutionalized in formal and informal rules, expectations, and access to resources: Do secretaries in this company generally have any right to question a boss' decision? How acceptable is it in the business world for a boss to accept advice from a secretary? Has the secretaries' collective power been institutionalized in the form of a union? An understanding of the power relationship between the secretary and the boss, like the understanding of any power relationship, requires an understanding of the participants' respective personal, collective, and institutional power.

This book explores the ways in which relationships between women and men may be shaped, not just by something as vague as gender roles, but by differences in their personal, collective, and institutional power. We will see that the three are not easily disentangled; for instance, members of the two gender groups may learn differing approaches to personal influence because of their groups' differences in collective power, and these differences in personal power may in turn help to maintain differences in institutional power. We will see that these different levels of power reinforce one another and are closely enough linked that changes in one can set off changes in the others. For those who are interested in changing the power process in female–male relationships, the trick is to discern, for a particular situation, how power is operating at various levels, and at what level intervention would be most helpful.

CONCLUSION: THE FACES OF POWER

Women are frequently described as less powerful than men, and a cursory examination of the respective economic positions of the two gender groups certainly indicates that less importance is attached to women's than to men's social and work roles. It is clear that gender roles are not simply different but differently valued. The struggles to do away with the hierarchy that defines men as more powerful than women have encouraged a focus on the meaning of power.

A variety of definitions of power have been in common use: control over others, capacity to achieve goals, strength to resist influence. While the definitions have different emphases, the common thread that runs through them is the capacity to make things happen as one wants them to, to have an impact on one's world. Add to this the notion of inner strength—the possession of the inner resources not to crumble, even when things don't happen as one wants them to—and we have a fairly complete definition of power from an individual perspective. To this perspective we must add the awareness that power also operates as a structured system or discipline that transcends the individual acts of dominance that may take place within it.

While debates have been waged over the rightness of particular faces of power, we can conclude that all the faces are necessary aspects of the process of human relationship. This does not mean that power cannot be abused; it is the presence of a responsible community that guards against such abuse by circumscribing the processes of power.

Power operates between women and men on personal, collective, and institutional levels, all of which are interconnected under the umbrella of a system of gender power relations. To understand female–male power relationships, all faces and levels of power must be examined.

The following chapter begins that examination by focusing on the way that images of femininity and masculinity fit with images of power, and how those images are conditioned by our participation in the disciplinary power of the gender relations system.

CHAPTER TWO

Images of Power
and Powerlessness

One February morning in 1989, newspapers featured an arresting image on the front page: A woman in bishop's clothing. The woman was black and middle-aged. The article said that she had been divorced, and that she had written "liberal" things about such topics as homosexuality and American policy in Central America. But the most striking thing about her was that she was joyful, for she, Barbara Harris, had just been consecrated as the first female bishop in the Episcopalian church, the first, in fact, in the 2000-year history of any of the "catholic" branches of Christianity. The shock value of the image of a woman—a black woman, at that—arrayed in full bishop's regalia, miter on her head and staff in her hand, was obviously not lost on newspaper editors who gave this picture so prominent a place. As a society we are still not accustomed to seeing women, especially women of color, wearing the accoutrements of power; we are still jolted by the confluence of our images of power with our images of people who are not supposed to have it.

So upsetting was the prospect of the elevation of a female to the rank of bishop that the Reverend Harris' initial election had touched off months of debate, with some church members arguing, even during the ceremony, that her consecration would be a sacrilege. Boston's Roman Catholic cardinal refused an invitation to attend the ceremony, saying that it had "serious ecumenical implications because it departs from a

I am indebted to Leslie Campbell for some of the ideas in this chapter.

15

common tradition in regard to sacramental orders" (Diamond, 1989, p. 2A). Traditionalists insisted that because the first apostles were men the position of bishop should rightfully go only to men. This argument, backed by the full power of the church, has successfully kept women out of the Roman Catholic priesthood. And until Barbara Harris, had worked to keep the few Episcopalian women priests from rising in the hierarchy. In this instance, the conservative forces were insufficient to exclude Barbara Harris, despite their appeals to truth and tradition, but there is much to be learned from their desperation to do so—and from their tactics.

The first important thing to note about this story is the intense personal discomfort experienced by certain individuals when confronted with the idea of a female bishop. The second is the scarcity of comparable images of powerful women in our culture. The third is the way that those resisting the inclusion of women in the priestly hierarchy have used a supposedly objective "truth" as the basis for their position. In this chapter, we will come to see that these three things are interconnected.

First, many people are genuinely uncomfortable with images of female power because these images do not conform with their own *schemas*, or mental frameworks, for power and for femininity. Second, the reason individuals find the images of femininity and power incongruous is that the culture's dominant collective knowledge or set of accepted myths portrays femininity and power as falling on opposite sides of a duality, and either gives no prominence to powerful women (even though there have been many of them) or includes them only as examples of distortions of what is natural. Third, the shape of this collective knowledge—what we sometimes think of as truth—is strongly influenced by authorities in positions of relative power who say they are objective but who have a (sometimes unacknowledged) vested interest in the status quo. These three processes work together to ensure that only "appropriate" images of power are absorbed into and expressed in our culture's accepted mythology. Together, they make it difficult for images of female power to be viewed with comfort and approval.

THE INDIVIDUAL DILEMMA: VISIONS OF POWER THAT DO NOT FIT

Powerful Images

The term *power* calls forth a host of stereotypic images. For example, the Judeo-Christian image of god is of a being who is supernatural and all-powerful: present everywhere, seeing and knowing everything, able to change anything. Some of the awe that people accord to supernatural power is also accorded to individuals believed to have a special link to that power: priests, prophets, evangelists, gurus, faith healers, witches, sorcerers, mystics. Another image associated with power is physical strength and skill. The champion boxer, the hockey star, the world-class runner, the discus thrower—all are surrounded with an aura of power. In the areas of politics and business, individuals who hold formal authority or who control vast resources are seen as powerful. Still other people are viewed as powerful because of a certain personal magnetism or charisma that allows them to charm others. Another image called up by the notion of power is that of the expert: the individual who understands what others do not, who has access to information that is beyond the reach of others.

Although the above images are stereotypic, or perhaps because they are stereotypic, they provide an outline of the schema of power that predominates in our culture and that organizes the way many of us think about power. Thinking is a complex process with which we make sense of the information that surrounds us, impose some mental order on it, and also have our minds changed by it. Schemas play a part in this process. According to cognitive psychologists, a schema is a mental structure, a kind of outline that we hold in our minds of an idea or concept. A schema develops as we learn about a concept and begin to think about it. Once it has begun to form, it filters the information we are constantly taking in, keeping or absorbing what seems to fit the schema, ignoring or rejecting what does not, sometimes subtly changing itself in response to new information. For example, when a child is introduced to the concept *family*, she or he may begin to form mental rules for distinguishing when a group of people is or is not a family. These rules form a pattern, or outline—a schema—against which to assess whether or not new groups encountered are families. The schema itself may change gradually over time as the child encounters more and more instances of groups defining themselves as families that did not fit the original schema. However, what will usually happen when the child encounters an instance of a family that does not fit the current schema is that the information will be ignored or quickly forgotten because it cannot easily be integrated into the family schema. In other words, the family that deviates significantly from the child's family schema may not be classified as a family at all.

Psychologists use the term schema as an attribute of the thought processes of particular individuals. Many schemas, however, are shared among the members of a culture, since they are constructed from the information that surrounds most of us. They are not necessarily shared across groups exposed to different information and experiences; for example, European-Americans and African-Americans, for whom the role of women has historically been somewhat different, may have over-lapping but far from identical schemas for the concept of *femininity*.

Most of us probably have a schema for the concept of power. Indeed, early studies of the shades of meaning that people attach to words and concepts show that one of the three major dimensions people use in characterizing a variety of images is potency, or power (Osgood, Suci, & Tannenbaum, 1957). Power, it seems, is an important component of people's evaluation of roles, activities, and other people they encounter. But whether an individual sees a particular behavior or a particular person as powerful, and how well she or he remembers a particular instance of powerful behavior, or a powerful person, depends to a large extent on whether the behavior or person in question fits that individual's schema for power. If we have learned through our culture that powerful leaders do not compromise, we may characterize as powerless or weak a politician who tries to negotiate a peace settlement or an employer who works hard to reach a mutually agreeable wage settlement with employ-ees—even if those actions require great risk-taking and stamina. And if we have learned that women do not generally wield most kinds of power, we may find it difficult to call to mind the instances of women's powerful behavior that we have observed: We have not integrated the information into our existing schemas for power (or for women).

Gender and the Images of Power

In reviewing stereotypic images of power, most readers will find that the examples of powerful people brought to mind are male. The image of God in Christian, Jewish, and Moslem religions is definitely male, as are most of the people thought to hold spiritual power by virtue of a special link to God. Examples of people who are physically powerful are also generally male, despite the widespread media attention given to such exceptions to that rule as Olympic athletes Jackie Joyner-Kersee, Florence Griffith-Joyner, and tennis star Martina Navratilova. In politics and business, when most people think of a president, prime minister, chairperson of the board, bank manager, or corporate chief executive, they think of a man, even though women sometimes hold these positions. And in the realm of expertise, masculine images still hold sway. It is men—mostly white men—who are pictured knee-deep in printouts in computer advertisements (Marshall & Bannon, 1988); the typical image of a scientist is still a man in a white lab coat; and female physicians, lawyers, professors, auto mechanics, plumbers, and accountants are still trusted less than their male counterparts. Perhaps only in the realm of power based on attractiveness, charisma, and personal magnetism do female power images compete with male ones: A beautiful, charming woman is said to be able to "wrap a man around her little finger."

Both sexes generally attribute more power to males than females, although women show this pattern less strongly. In one study in which university students were asked to list the most powerful person they knew, 91% of the males and 69% of the females named a man (Lips, 1985). The template for this tendency to see males as powerful more often than females may be laid down in the family: About one quarter of the male and female respondents in the study cited their father as the most powerful person they knew, but only 16% of the females and 2% of the males named their mothers.

The high proportion of male to female powerful images is not at all surprising when considered in the light of research on gender stereotypes. A large body of research in psychology has shown that men and women are often thought of as opposite sides of a duality: Men are strong, independent, worldly, aggressive, ambitious, logical, and rough; women are weak, dependent, passive, naive, not ambitious, illogical, and gentle (Broverman, Vogel, Broverman, Clarkson, & Rosenkrantz, 1972; Edwards & Williams, 1980). The most positively valued masculine traits have to do with activity and competence; highly valued feminine traits emphasize warmth and expressiveness, qualities not generally associated with power.

Portrayals of women and men based on the stereotypic notions of masculine strength and feminine weakness bombard us through the media. In any given week we can find numerous examples of tough guys on television: cool (but caring) cops, steely eyed and stubble-faced detectives, gung-ho Marines. Where are the tough gals? New York policewomen Cagney and Lacey, now gone from the screen, were the only reliable representatives. We are surrounded with the message that masculine males can be powerful, but feminine females cannot, or that women's only effective source of feminine influence is beauty and sex appeal. When the media does present an exception to the rule of the powerless woman, she is often portrayed as a tragic, bitter figure, like Dian Fossey in the film "Gorillas in the Mist," or as an evil, twisted character, like the other woman in the film "Fatal Attraction."

These media messages have such a self-fulfilling quality that it is difficult to say how and when the stereotypes got started and how the cycle can be broken. Are women seldom elevated to positions of power because they are stereotyped as weak and passive, or are they stereotyped as weak because they are rarely seen in powerful positions? Both processes operate together, creating a vicious circle. As we will see later in this chapter, that vicious circle has a history that reaches back for hundreds, even thousands, of years.

Why the "Powerful Woman" Makes Us Uncomfortable

Our society's notions of power and gender are so intertwined that it is next to impossible to separate the two. Any major alteration of our thinking about the relationship between the two concepts requires a radical change in our schemas for both. In fact, a number of researchers and writers have argued that gender differences and power differences are irretrievably confounded with each other because females are automatically given lower status than males (Hacker, 1951; Henley, 1977; MacKinnon, 1987).

The almost automatic status differential between women and men is one of the keys to understanding why the image of a powerful woman causes discomfort in so many people. There is a tendency for people to attribute a relative *status*—position in a hierarchy of power relations within a social group—to others they encounter. This attributed status helps to guide their interactions with the other person: Should they defer to that other? Treat her or him as an equal? Assume superiority? Attributed status is based on both *achievement* (the role one performs and how well one performs it) and *ascription* (personal characteristics such as age, race, social class, sex, appearance). Research shows clearly that the status ascribed to females is consistently lower than that of males (Berger, Rosenholtz, & Zelditch, 1980). The effect is so strong that when women are seen to be invading a particular high-status occupation, the status of that occupation drops significantly (Touhey, 1974).

Since people use sex as an indicator of *ascribed* status, they are likely to attribute different statuses to males and females performing the same roles. A male flight attendant may be ascribed more status than a female flight attendant, a male police officer may be seen as having more authority than a female police officer, and a woman complaining about poor service in a store or restaurant may get a slower response than a man making a similar complaint. In each case, the person ascribed higher status, the man, is more likely to be listened to, to be treated with respect, and to be taken seriously. Moreover, the woman who holds a role that gives her high *achieved* status finds herself in a position of *status incongruity*: The high achieved status of her role conflicts with the low ascribed status of her sex. Others who encounter her may feel uncomfortable with this double status message. Why? First, it jeopardizes their carefully constructed categories for the roles associated with women and men, forcing them to do more mental work. Second, in the absence of old and familiar rules for relating to women and men, they feel awkward about relating to her—and everyone hates feeling awkward. Third, her violation of the unspoken rules of social structure by achieving too high a status for a woman may be seen and resented as an implicit threat to their own position in the status hierarchy.

Of course, sex is not the only source of ascribed status. Status ascribed according to sex can and does interact with status ascribed according to other characteristics such as race or sexual orientation. A man who is suspected of being gay may be ascribed less status than a female colleague, and white women may be ascribed more status than their nonwhite counterparts.

One of the reasons why power in the hands of a woman is sometimes regarded as sinister and dangerous is that women are seen to exert power in different ways than men. As discussed in more detail in Chapter Four, women sometimes rely on less direct forms of influence than men because they have less access to traditional avenues of power and have been encouraged to use feminine charms and wiles to get their way. When the successful use of power is covert or manipulative, we are likely to view the power wielder as duping others, and we judge the person's behavior as unfair.

Such supposed differences in the styles of power exertion do not, however, account for the negative reaction to and portrayal of women who are powerful—women such as England's Prime Minister, Margaret Thatcher—in the same way as men are powerful. Journalists often refer to Thatcher as "the iron maiden" and "Attila the Hen." Such epithets, even if they were masculinized, would not be applied to a man behaving in a similar fashion. Their use seems to represent an uneasy attempt to trivialize or make ridiculous the notion of a woman holding so much formal power. Although powerful male politicians are often caricatured, their masculinity is seldom called into question in public, whereas slurs upon the femininity of a powerful female politician are frequent. The masculinity of male politicians is, on the other hand, questioned only if they appear weak.

THE CULTURAL MYTHOLOGY OF POWER AND GENDER

It is all very well to note that individuals feel uncomfortable when images challenge their schemas for power or for gender and to say that status incongruity is the explanation for the discomfort. But why do people tend to ascribe lower status to females than to males? Why do so many individuals develop schemas for femininity that are incongruous with powerful behavior or position? Part of the reason is that for centuries many Western cultures have mythologized the images of male and female as opposing sides of a duality in which male was equated with strength, activity, aggression, and light; whereas female was equated with weakness, passivity, subtlety, and darkness. This mythology of dualism, of opposites, has become so much a part of our consciousness, and is reinforced so extensively that it is difficult to conceive of gender in any other way. Within the framework of this dualism, a woman seen acting in a powerful way is seen to be acting like a man, and thus, by definition, not like a woman. Therefore, women holding powerful positions or behaving in powerful ways risk being viewed as unwomanly or unfeminine. Because of the cultural habit of thinking dualistically, the concept of power just does not fit with the concept of woman. When the two concepts are forced together, the result is the contradiction of the unwomanly woman. Powerful women are subjected to extremely pejorative labels: castrating bitch, ball-breaker, iron maiden, witch.

The responses of the dominant patriarchal culture to powerful women have tended to be first violence and hostility, then indifference and dismissal. Powerful women have been and are frequently rejected, vilified, insulted, threatened, and attacked. Once women cease, through absence or death, to be a threat to the dominant order, their contributions, their very existence, is ignored. Many historical examples of this pattern exist. Let us look briefly at two of them: the persecution of witches, and the hostility, neglect, and trivialization directed toward female scientists.

The Powerful Woman as Witch

Beginning in the 13th century, a ruthless persecution of witches resulted in the torture and execution of between one and nine million persons. Most (85%) of the alleged witches put to death in these proceedings were women (Dworkin, 1974); feminist theorists have compared this persecution to the Nazi holocaust (Raymond, 1978; Ruether, 1975).

Accusations that brought women to trial for witchcraft fell into three main categories: sexual crimes (copulation with the devil or causing a man to be impotent), being organized (meeting in groups), and possession of magical powers affecting health. Feminist historians have argued that many of those accused and condemned were simply peasant women who had power—power to heal through their knowledge of herbs and their skill at midwifery (Ehrenreich & English, 1973). That these women were practising healing at a time when the medical profession was becoming a respected field of masculine endeavor is cited as one explanation of the resentment they aroused. Because they commanded respect among the peasantry, these skilled women angered authorities in the medical field and worried and annoyed rulers in both church and state. As Ehrenreich and English say, "The real issue was control: Male upper class healing under the auspices of the Church was acceptable, female healing as part of a peasant subculture was not" (p. 11).

Mary Daly (1978) cites the abandonment in the 16th century of the legal distinction between "good witch" and "bad witch" as evidence of the patriarchy's resentment of all female powers, even those directed at good purposes. The women accused of witchcraft, Daly argues, were a threat to the growing (male) professional hierarchy because they were independent, uncertified knowers and healers, possessors of unlegitimated learning. Another scholar claims that the witch trials served to register society's fear and intolerance of single women—a group that lived "without family and without patriarchal control" (Midelfort, 1972; p. 196).

It appears, then, that women healers and nonconformists were seen as dangerous because their power threatened established male authority in the state, church, and medical fields. However, women were viewed as dangerous for a second reason: their sexuality. Remember that women have been stereotypically depicted not only as weak, but also as mysterious, and that sexuality and personal attractiveness are the only sources of power routinely attributed to women. The image of the witch combined the notion of mystery with that of a devouring female sexuality, and the result was disconcerting and frightening to men. Men's fear of female sexuality (and their own) led to the depiction of the witch as a woman who lusted after the devil and who derived pleasure from magically removing males' sexual organs.

The extreme fear and hostility toward women thought to have supernatural powers that characterized the witch craze is not natural but cultural. Many cultures have differed from the Judeo–Christian ones in their reactions to such powerful women. In some societies, women claiming supernatural powers have been respected as sorcerers. For example, MacCormack (1977) describes the secret, sacred society of women in the Sherbo and Mende cultures in Sierra Leone in West Africa. Initiates into the society learn to take control of their reproduction and sexuality and to heal various illnesses. Women in commanding roles in this sacred society are treated with reverence and respect, and they exert significant political force. Other examples can be found in Native American societies. In the ancient Navajo culture, the shaman or chanter—the most powerful religious figures—could be either male or female (Downs, 1972). Among the Cherokee, the head of the Women's Council, known as the Beloved Woman of the Nation, was thought to express the voice of the Great Spirit speaking through her (Allen, 1986). Likewise, in some traditional Latin American and Caribbean religions, women have consistently been attributed spiritual power and have played leading roles. However, these examples of female power are ignored or trivialized by the dominant white culture because they do not fit that culture's notions of womanhood. In many cases, such as that of Native American societies, traditions emphasizing female power have been ruthlessly stamped out.

Women in Science: Interlopers and Outcasts

Not only in the realm of spiritual power, but also in that of the worldly power based on learning and knowledge, women who dared to tread on male authority have been made to pay dearly. Often, they have been viciously punished for invading male turf, and they have been rendered largely invisible in the history of science through the neglect or underrating of their contributions.

Like the women accused of witchcraft, women who ventured into the world of science often risked humiliation, ruin, and even death. For example, Hypatia, a 4th-century Alexandrian woman who achieved eminence in mathematics and astronomy, was, according to one historian, the most famous woman scientist until Marie Curie (Alic, 1986). She made important contributions to the development of algebra and geometry and was also a designer of scientific instruments. Hypatia was a pagan, a rationalist, and an influential political figure in an era when Alexandria was increasingly ruled by Christians. Refusing to convert to Christianity or to change her outspoken views, she was finally ambushed and brutally murdered by a gang of fanatical monks in the year A.D. 415. Centuries earlier, in classical Athens, women had risked death if they tried to practice medicine. In about 300 B.C., one woman, Agnodice, disguised herself as a man in order to study medicine and midwifery, then returned to Athens, still dressed as a man, to set up a practice. The other physicians, jealous of the success of Agnodice, charged the new doctor with corrupting the women patients. To blunt this accusation, Agnodice revealed herself to be a woman, whereupon she was immediately prosecuted for being a woman physician. She would have been condemned to death had not the women of the city joined forces to save her life by protesting that they would all die with her if she were executed (Alic, 1986).

Even when they have not risked death, women scientists have often risked ridicule and the nullifying of their work. Frequently, women scientists have not been credited with their contributions and discoveries, either because their work was not viewed as appropriate for women at the time they did it, or because later scholars left them out of the historical record. Lady Anne Conway, a natural philosopher of the vitalist school, whose work formed the basis for many of the ideas now attributed to Leibniz, was one of the first to dispute the dualistic, mechanistic worldview of Descartes. She denied Descartes' distinction between matter and spirit, viewing them instead as interchangeable, and coined the idea of "monads" that was later adopted and made famous by Leibniz. While Leibniz is sometimes called the father of modern science, Anne Conway is all but forgotten. Her name was left off the title page of her book because it was unseemly for a woman's name to appear in such a place. While Leibniz repeatedly acknowledged her strong influence on his thinking, historians of science have chosen to ignore her (Alic, 1986).

Women have not been allowed easy access to influence in the world of science; the contributions of those who did make it past the barriers have been largely suppressed. As in the case of the witches, these women threatened not only the popular ideas about femininity and womanhood of their time, but also the established hierarchy of male expertise and male authority. The contradiction between the concepts of woman and scientist made it difficult for people to mesh these concepts into an acceptable whole; it has always been easier to ignore the exceptional women who did not fit the cultural schema for womanhood than to adapt that schema to include them. This difficulty was (and is) convenient for the existing scientific establishment.

Mythological Roots of Male Authority

As the above examples illustrate, the belief in male authority is a strong element in Western culture, and a threat to that authority is likely to provoke extremely negative reactions. The roots of this belief reach back into Western religious and mythological heritage.

An awareness of Greek and Roman mythology and the Judeo-Christian tradition leads to the conclusion that in these streams of thought women are more likely than men to be portrayed as agents of evil. Eve in the biblical story of "The Fall," Delilah and Lot's wife in the *Old Testament*, and the Sirens in Homer's *Odyssey* share the same image—temptresses who test men's resolve, who lead men astray. Women, especially attractive ones, are thought to be dangerous and evil because men are distracted by them from the path of righteousness. In Christianity, since the highest achievement is to be in spiritual communion with a noncorporeal god, whatever distracted a man from contemplation of the godhead was viewed as despicable. Normal sexual desire caused men to be attracted—and therefore distracted—by women. However, instead of recognizing their own desires as the source of their distraction, men projected all the sexuality onto women, casting women as seductresses who lured well-meaning men into sin. This male perspective also accounts for the frequency with which the clergy have admonished women to dress modestly. As de Beauvoir (1952) says, "In a religion that holds the flesh accursed, woman becomes the devil's most fearsome temptation" (p. 110).

Christianity, in fact, institutionalizes a power relationship between women and men that is modeled on the one assumed to exist between humankind and a patriarchal god. In the *Old Testament* story of Adam and Eve, Eve is punished for her curiosity in eating from the tree of knowledge by being not only banished from paradise along with her partner, but also condemned to bring forth children in pain and sorrow and to submit to the authority of Adam, her mate. Thus, the would-be independent woman is subdued, and the power relationship in which a husband rules over his wife is not only legitimized but also mystified as holy and proper. A husband's dominance over his wife is likened to God's dominance over his people; moreover, women's tendency to try to subvert men's power through temptation is underscored. Present-day Christian marriage ceremonies continue to reflect this world view, with women often promising to obey their husbands or even, in some cases, to "submit to his God-given authority."

Mythological Traditions of Female Power

Not all religious and mythological traditions are patriarchal, however. If we go back far enough in time, even Western tradition derives from an earlier mythology that placed less emphasis on dominance and included female figures as the chief objects of worship (Campbell, 1959; Harrison, 1963). Whereas the existence of goddess religions does not necessarily mean that early societies were matriarchies, the myth of the goddess supported the notion of female powerfulness as a possibility. Goddess religions were based on the awe in which the processes of creating life were held; the goddess was the giver of form and life. The very body of the goddess was the earth; there are strong mythological traditions for the characterization of Nature as female and the use of the term Mother Earth.

The Mother Goddess held sway in various forms among the agricultural people of the Middle East and in Greece and Rome until about 1750 B.C. However, as more aggressive hunting peoples invaded these regions, they tended, as part of the conquering process, to supplant the Mother Goddess with male deities of their own. In one story set during the rise of Babylon, All-Mother Goddess Tiamat is blown to bits when the young male god Marduk sends winds into her open mouth. He then dismembers her and uses the parts of her body to create the earth and heavens. Interestingly, in the mother-goddess mythology, the mother-goddess herself is already the universe, so Marduk's act of creating the universe again from her body was superfluous. However, as the male god takes over, he usurps the role of creator (Campbell, 1988).

Much early Native American religion and mythology was centered on great goddesses who were the givers of life and power to human beings. The following examples are provided by Paula Gunn Allen (1986). The genatrix of the Hopi, Hard Beings Woman, creates the Hopi by breathing life into male and female effigies that become their parents. Thought Woman, of the Keres people, is a Supreme Spirit who is both Mother and Father to all people and all creatures. The life-giving power of these goddesses is not limited to fertility or maternity; it is the power to create or transform. For example, in Keres theology, the goddess is conceptualized as She Who Thinks rather than She Who Bears, and female thought is the origin of reality. Goddesses provided food and other resources for the people. In the Abanaki myth, First Woman, in order to feed the starving people, asked her husband to kill her and drag her body through a field until the flesh was worn from her bones, then bury her bones in the field and leave the field alone for seven months. When the people returned to the field, they found corn to eat and tobacco to smoke; because First Woman was sacred, her flesh and bones could generate life.

While the power of goddesses in Native American religions has not been limited to maternity, maternity itself is filled with powerful images in this mythology. The power to make life, which is not considered merely biological fertility but also the power of thought, is considered the primary power, the source of all other power and the model for all ritual magic. "Mother" is a term of respect and status; in some groups it is the chosen term of address for anyone, woman or man, who is carrying out ritual (i.e. who is transforming something from one state to another), and men as well as women are honored by the title of mother.

If the myth of patriarchy has not always and everywhere been in place, what accounts for the virtual obliteration of powerful female images in present-day Western religions? Some have argued that goddess worship declined when men made the discovery that they were partners in the conception of children and that a child could be identified as belonging to a particular man (Lipman-Blumen, 1984; Rich, 1976). Rich argues that this recognition was responsible not only for the demise of the great goddesses but also for the rise of the patriarchal family, with its emphasis on sexual possession, monogamy, and the economic dependence of women.

In many societies, however, the fall of the goddesses seems to have had more to do with the imposition of control by external sources than with any change in awareness about men's role in conception. Goddess religions were often characteristic of peaceful, harmonious cultures; imperialistic invaders favored fearsome warrior gods and imposed these on conquered peoples, beginning about 4000 B.C. As late as the 18th and 19th centuries, white colonial governments and missionaries in North America made strong and deliberate attempts to undermine traditional American Indian religions and the often gynocratic, or female-ruled, social structures that accompanied them. The Christian model of the patriarchal family and patriarchal government was imposed by white colonial officials' refusal to deal with female Indian leaders and through the forcible removal of Indian children from their homes and villages to distant boarding schools.

Whatever the major force behind the change, as male authority became more entrenched, goddesses began to change character and to lose status by gaining a more powerful husband or son. The goddess images of ancient times changed from benevolent earth-mothers (Demeter, Cybele, Artemis) to temptresses (Pandora, Hera) and destructive mothers (Gaea, Kali, Medea, Clytemnestra). In North America, the many goddesses of Native American religions have been largely replaced by a male-gendered "Great Spirit"; tribal female goddesses such as Spider Woman of the Hopi and the Cherokee's Goddess of the River Foam are replaced by male deities in many stories; others such as the Iroquois Sky Woman receive their powers from fathers, husbands or sons (Allen, 1986).

People have never allowed the goddess myth to be completely stamped out for long, however. It survives, disguised, in the reverence accorded to Mary as the Mother of God in the Christian tradition, in the almost androgynous vision of Jesus that is presented in the *New Testament*, in the present-day goddess religions of India, and in the current revival of goddess religions in North America. In some respects, the attachment to the goddess seems to represent a refusal to accept the dualism that characterizes patriarchal religious thinking. The goddess symbology in India represents a mystery that is beyond female and male, beyond all pairs of opposites. The female goddess, as the "giver of forms," knows that those forms come from a mystery that is beyond all categories of thought (Campbell, 1988). In an era when feminist theorists are rethinking, and working to deconstruct, the meaning of the dualistic oppositions used to define gender, it is interesting to note the revival of the goddess myth, which is grounded in a multiplicity of meanings and resists easy categorization.

THE RELATIONSHIP BETWEEN "TRUTH" AND POWER

I have argued that powerful images of women cause discomfort because, in the dominant white culture, they do not fit most individuals' accepted schemas for women or for power. A reason for this lack of fit is that the dominant mythology of Western culture emphasizes a dualistic mode of thinking in which femininity and masculinity are seen as opposites, with femininity at the weak, submissive, nurturant pole and masculinity at the strong, powerful, individualistic pole. As we have glimpsed in the preceding sections, there have been many women and men who did not fit neatly into this stereotypic vision of gender, and many cultures in which such a vision was not (and is not) the accepted view. Yet these instances tend to be, at best, treated as exceptions to the rule and, at worst, disregarded completely. Since they do not fit the accepted vision, they are not integrated into the shared knowledge of the dominant culture. How many North Americans are aware of the matriarchal societies that existed among the Iroquois and other Native American groups before the onslaught of the European invaders? How many students taking courses in the history of science have heard of Hypatia, or of her 19th-century counterpart Sofia Kovalevsky, the first woman to earn a doctorate in mathematics? And how many have heard of the dedicated, feminist Russian *male* scientists who placed their own careers on the line in order to support the right of Sofia and other women of her time and place to study science? How many students of abnormal psychology have been taught a thoughtless acceptance of the view that the witches were women who were "sick," who needed treatment rather than torture? How many strong, powerful, gifted women—writers, scientists, activists, teachers, athletes, political leaders—have been erased from, or never added to, the common body of shared knowledge and consciousness that we call culture?

The omission from our culture's "official" knowledge of so many examples that contradict its vision of gender and power points to a systematic, rather than a random, cultural blindness. It is a blindness that is an extension of the individual's difficulty with integrating information that is at variance with already developed schemas, already solidified stereotypes. It is a blindness that is perpetuated by power.

Power and the "Interpretive Community"

One of many examples of how the culture's official knowledge is protected from contradictions can be found in the field of literary criticism. Feminist students of English literature have noted with discomfort in recent years how few female authors are represented in undergraduate survey courses. Their complaints are often met by the retort, on the part of faculty, that few works by female authors are worthy to be called classics. Students interested in women's writing are directed to special "Women in Literature" courses.

Who is it that holds the power to decide the worth of a literary work? In a book that caused much comment among literary scholars, Stanley Fish (1980) presents a view that the critical judgment of works of literature—judgment, for instance, of what is and is not worthy of study or of being labeled good literature—is made and validated by an *interpretive community*. He argues that literature is an open category, containing what the interpretive community decides to put into it. A reader, as a member of the community, uses the shared assumptions of the community to determine what will count as literature. What his argument omits, and what Elizabeth Meese (1986) notes bluntly in her commentary on it, is that the interpretive community is neither neutral nor representative. Rather, the most vocal and influential members of the interpretive community—professors and literary critics—are most often relatively privileged, powerful, white males whose shared assumptions reflect the status quo. The interpretive community, in fact, acts as an authoritative community. Under the guise of maintaining standards, it effectively excludes from the category literature anything that threatens mainstream literary traditions. As Meese comments, the notion of an interpretive community can be seen as less benign than a neutral group of scholars and critics objectively applying common assumptions in their assessment of literary works. Rather, it can be seen as "the construction of a strong insider-outsider dynamic, a gender-based literary tribalism that comes into play as a means of control" (Meese, 1986; p. 7). A critic on the inside of the literary establishment has the power to dismiss and exclude the works of writers on the outside, and that power is often exercised under the guise of the objective application of shared standards. Yet those shared standards are based on the limited perspective of a quite homogeneous group, and a critic's point of view reflects, among other things, his or her training, membership in and identification with a social group, and the ideas that are in vogue at the time.

A critic who aspires to a perfectly objective or neutral stance aspires to the impossible. The pretence, or even the blind belief in, scholarly objectivity can mask a stubborn adherence to biases that have nothing whatever to do with standards of excellence and everything to do with the comfortable familiarity of thinking a certain way. What emerges as truth from the so-called objective judgments of the interpretive community cannot be separated from the power that that community represents. Thus, established literary scholars can write whole books about criticism without mentioning the works of women or minority writers, and nothing is thought amiss. A book that included only references to works by black female authors would, by contrast, be considered narrowly specialized.

Power and the "Transcendent Subject"

Clearly, what is considered important, worthwhile, or true is related to who is doing the considering. This principle is one we all acknowledge easily in our personal lives, but we have found it strangely difficult as a society to acknowledge it in the realm of formal scholarship and knowledge. We have clung relentlessly to the idea that advanced learning enables people to become *objective knowers* of reality; that scientists and other scholars can separate themselves from the reality they are observing, hover above it intellectually, and make disinterested judgments about it. Although this dualistic view of the separation of the objective knower and reality remains very prevalent, it has been criticized heavily in the natural sciences (Heisenberg, 1972), in the humanities (Derrida, 1978), and in the social sciences (Henriques, Holloway, Unwin, Venn, & Walkerdine, 1984). The criticism is based, in the first instance, on the sheer impossibility of separating the observer from the observed, of observing without influencing; and in the second instance, on considerations of power that are implicit in the idea of the knower as a *transcendent subject* (someone who is separate from the reality being studied).

The power considerations built into the notion of the knower as objective and transcendent are present on three levels. At the first level, the objective knower is in some way superior to, and has power over, that which is known. The knower is actively engaged in observation and study; the known (reality), is passive, subject to manipulation and interpretation. One can argue, as Catherine MacKinnon (1987) does, that when the world is apprehended from an objective stance, the world is *objectified*—a social perception that leads inevitably to dominance and control. Even when the known is another person or a group of people, as occurs in social and behavioral research, the relationship between the knower and the known, the researcher and the subject, is implicitly hierarchical as long as their connectedness is not acknowledged. This implicit hierarchy becomes explicit on the rare occasions when research is mocked or satirized by imagining the power relationships turned upside down: cartoons in which the white rats whisper conspiratorially to one another about how they are making the psychologists behave, or science fiction tales of human scientists becoming the guinea pigs for another species.

The second level at which power is implicit in the "knower as transcendent subject" view of knowledge and scholarship is more insidious than the first. It is built into the way those who claim objectivity for their own perspective accuse those with differing perspectives of being subjective—and thus, by implication, of producing insights that are less true, less valuable, less generalizeable. It is easy to think one is being objective if one is part of the mainstream, if one's perspective matches the dominant perspective; it is those who are part of the scholarly, scientific establishment, those who are members of dominant groups, who are most likely to make the claim that their perspective is objective or neutral. Those who challenge this establishment, those who are members of minority or outsider groups, are the most vulnerable to the charge of subjectivity and the denigration of their work that goes with it. Thus, feminist scholars who acknowledge their point of view are accused by traditional scholars of bias; departments of women's studies and minority studies are criticized by mainstream scholars as allowing politics to intrude on scholarship. The traditional, dominant perspective is assumed to represent objective truth; challenges to that perspective are labeled subjective. In this way, the official body of knowledge is protected against perspectives and insights that threaten to change its shape.

We see the third level on which power is built into the notion of the knower as separate from the known in the very dramatic way in which gender is distributed across these two categories. Traditionally, men, not women, have been the knowers. Women have either been the subject of study, the known, or they have been ignored. Historically, women who ventured into the territory of the knowers were swiftly and brutally punished, as in the case of the witches and the women who studied science. Although no longer executed for possessing dangerous or forbidden knowledge, women are still the recipients of many messages that imply they are inappropriate or inadequate as knowers. As Catherine MacKinnon (1987) notes, women come to the experience of learning with a specific history: "Women have been silenced as women: we have been told we are stupid because we are women, told that our thoughts are trivial because we are women, told that our experiences as women are unspeakable, told that women can't speak the language of significance . . ." (pp. 56–57). Such a history, she argues, means that women tend to enter the traditional academic situation—in which someone is discoursing authoritatively from the front of the room while others sit in silent receptivity—with feelings of intimidation and of being excluded that are specific to their gender. Because of women's historical exclusion from the formal processes of education, because of the stereotype that women are intuitive rather than logical, and emotional rather than intellectual, the dichotomy between the knower and the known has a particular significance for them.

Challenging Dualistic Thinking

The dualistic, oppositional approach that characterizes traditional thinking about the separateness of the knower from the known is not at all unique to that relationship. What many theorists argue is that the notion of an ego or subject separate from what it is apprehending is the foundation for a whole system of categorical, hierarchical thinking. Binarism, the habit of thinking in either/or oppositions is, in fact, deeply embedded in Western thought and has had a major impact on conceptions of gender and on the images of women and men. Among the pairs of opposites that cluster around the oppositional images of male and female are activity/ passivity, sun/moon, culture/nature, day/night, father/mother, head/ heart, intelligible/palpable, logos/pathos, high/low, and master/slave (Cixous & Clement, 1975). When critics have attempted to deconstruct— to open up, or rewrite—these oppositions in order to release their full meaning, they have concluded that these oppositions are implicitly hi- erarchical in the way they are understood. One of the terms in each pair is more favored, or is thought of as governing the other or as being more right than the other. What these critics argue is that the habit of *binary* (employing two alternatives only) thinking that pervades our Western thought and our images of femininity and masculinity is implicitly a habit of *hierarchical* (a ranked system of authority) thinking. If they are correct, then assumptions about power are built into the whole notion of female and male as opposites.

Feminist theorists are struggling to develop new ways of thinking that do not rely on the old dichotomies and that are not automatically hierarchical. For example, as Dawne McCance (1987) notes, they reject the dichotomy between subjectivity and objectivity (in which objectivity has been given more status than subjectivity). They prefer instead to speak of the *contextuality* of meaning (something cannot be understood without knowing its context). The rejection of such dichotomies and their implicit hierarchies involves a rethinking of many traditional West- ern images and myths. Given the linkages that have existed among these images in our religious and cultural traditions, it is but a short step, for instance, from criticizing the male/female hierarchy to criticizing the God/"man" hierarchy, the spirit/matter hierarchy, or the hierarchy of human beings over nature (Ruether, 1983). Feminist theorists are in- volved in the struggle to reinvent the images of female and male in such a way that they do not flow easily into dichotomies such as powerful/ powerless.

Language, Truth, and Images of Power

In many respects, how human beings think is constrained by the language available to express their thoughts. It is this particular insight that leads some feminist theorists to critique, and try to reinvent, lan- guage itself. These theorists argue that it is difficult to imagine radical new images of women and men or human relationships while working in a language that incorporates patriarchal (father/male)assumptions. They believe that women's self-expression is constrained by language that has been shaped by and reflects male-female power relationships. They pose the question, formulated thus by Luce Irigaray (1977; p. 78, quoted in

Wiemer, 1987): "How can women analyze their exploitation, inscribe their claims, within an order prescribed by the masculine?"

The most basic and common feminist critique of English language is that the male holds both the neutral and male positions. Through the use of the generic "he" to mean he or she, of "mankind" to mean human beings, of "man" to mean humanity, language creates the message that male is the norm, the neutral standard, while female is the Other, the special case. As Catherine MacKinnon (1987) notes, "This is another way of saying that the neutrality of objectivity and of maleness are coextensive linguistically, whereas women occupy the marked, the gendered, the different, the forever-female position" (p. 55). Current English usage so enshrines this notion of the male as the standard or neutral case and the female as special, or Other, that women may find it difficult in many contexts not to think of themselves as intruders, people whose presence is often tolerated by dispensation.

The language incorporates hierarchical, and more specifically, patriarchal assumptions in other ways as well. The practice of the husband/father's name being the surname for the family, the absence of words for certain kinds of relationships such as the "co-mothers" described in Marge Piercy's (1976) novel *Woman at the Edge of Time*, the use of sexual terms to insult and to express hostility—all reflect notions of male dominance. Some theorists have argued that women are always forced to filter their thought through the approved linguistic forms of the dominant group, so that women speak with a double voice: submerged feminine meanings beneath a more accessible public content (Showalter, 1982). Feminist literary critics have sought to discover these submerged meanings in the works of women writers, while contemporary feminist writers have struggled to find new forms of expression that do not reflect a patriarchal code.

It is difficult to say where the feminist critique of language may lead. These critics and writers, in trying to rediscover an authentic feminine voice beneath the text of patriarchy and to transform language and criticism to allow the expression of that voice, have set themselves an enormously challenging task. If the enterprise is successful, it will begin to transform the culture's official knowledge, and hence our dominant imagery, of gender and power.

CONCLUSION: THE INVISIBLE POWERFUL WOMAN

Given the congruence of individual and group forces described in this chapter, the virtual invisibility of the powerful woman in Western culture seems assured. The human individual's propensity to think in categories and stereotypes and to ignore information that cannot be integrated easily into those categories means that gender/power images that are incompatible with stereotypic ones will make little impact. The dualistic imagery of female and male as opposites, with female as weak and male as strong, which pervades the mythology of white Western culture, helps to ensure that individuals' stereotypes keep developing in a set pattern and remain fixed. The presence of authorities who claim neutrality while enforcing a specific perspective based on power and privilege lends further strength to the traditional notions about gender and power by essentially blocking from incorporation into official knowledge many instances that do not fit accepted standards or images. Thus, powerful women remain invisible, and those who do achieve visibility often retain an aura of illegitimacy or evil.

The negative image of the overtly powerful woman lies at the heart of many of the gender differences in power-related behavior (and theories about such behavior) that will be discussed in the chapters to follow.

CHAPTER THREE

Responsibility vs. Dominance? Women, Men, and the Need for Power

W hen would-be presidents or chief executive officers talk piously about basing their motivation for leadership on the desire to *serve*—their country, their company, their community —it is difficult for those of us listening not to feel at least a twinge of cynicism. Could they be leaving something out? Surely, the struggle to achieve political or executive leadership is motivated at least in part by a personal desire for power and influence? One psychologist who has spent years studying people's motivation to achieve power comments that the infrequency with which people ascribe their own actions to a desire for power suggests that power strivings are now being repressed and disguised in much the same way as sexuality was repressed and denied during the 19th century (Winter, 1973).

It is a truism that, whether they admit it or not, some people seem to need, even crave, power over others. Moreover, as discussed in Chapter One, all of us participate to some extent in the processes of power for these are the very processes of give and take in relationships. On the personal level of our examination of power, individual power motivation, or the need for power, is a significant topic, one that provides a piece in the puzzle of how power works. A focus on the power motive allows us to ask why individuals differ from one another in the strength of their power motive, whether the strength of a person's power motive is related to the way that person behaves, whether different groups (such as women and men) differ, on the average, in the intensity of the power motive.

DEFINING AND MEASURING THE POWER MOTIVE

Perhaps the two most commonly accepted definitions of the power motive are those of David Winter and David McClelland. Winter (1973) stresses *social* power, and thus defines the power motive as the striving "to produce effects (consciously or unconsciously intended) on the behavior or feelings of another person" (p. 10). McClelland (1975), taking a somewhat broader perspective, argues that "the *goal* of power *motivation* is to *feel powerful*, and that influencing others is only one of the many ways of feeling powerful" (p. 17). As we will see, a sense of power, when defined and measured by researchers, seems to boil down to the feeling that one is having an impact on the environment.

Psychologists interested in the study of human motivation have noted that a major difficulty in measurement is that people are not always aware of their own motives, of why they behave as they do. It is the (controversial) notion that people do not necessarily always know what they want or why they want it that has led to the measurement of motives through *projective tests* such as the Thematic Apperception Test (TAT), which is presumably able to detect and assess even unconscious strivings for power.

The TAT, developed by Murray (1937) to measure the achievement motive, involves showing a person an ambiguous stimulus and requesting that she or he make up a dynamic story about it. The stories are thought to indicate both conscious and unconscious motives of the storyteller. Winter (1973), building on the work of Veroff (1957), developed a revised TAT for the measurement of the power motive. A series of pictures is shown with a slide projector, and the viewers are then asked to write stories about what they see in each picture. Stories are scored using a standardized scoring system. (For a detailed description of the development and use of this scoring system, see Winter [1973]). The individual's score, based on the results for the entire series of stories, is called that person's level of need for power, or *n* Power.

The assumptions behind the use of projective tests are troubling: They suggest a god-like capacity on the part of the psychologist to use fairly ambiguous material to discern and render judgments about feelings that the individual taking the test does not know she or he has—without ever checking back with the individual about the correctness of the interpretation. Of course, the psychologist's interpretation is not meant to be whimsical, but rather is based on a scoring system that is meant to be evenly applied across stories and individuals (for example, whenever an instance of one person threatening another occurs in any story, it is scored as an indication of the power motive). Yet such a system can never be infallible, chiefly because it is next to impossible to anticipate all the variations in response that can come up. The scorer of a projective test must often make subjective judgments about how to interpret a particular story. Surely we are none of us (including psychologists) always aware of our feelings or honest with ourselves or others about our motives. Yet, just as surely, the more objective determinations by others of our feelings or motives are not always entirely correct and should not necessarily be automatically accepted at face value. On an individual basis, there is reason to be sceptical about the notion that projective tests can be used to read a person's mind. They can, however, provide a rough guide to understanding an individual's motives. If used properly, they may also provide an outline of group similarities and differences.

Researchers who use the TAT to measure the strength of motives assume that: (1) a motive can be more or less aroused in an individual depending on circumstances and therefore can be experimentally changed or manipulated; (2) the same motive is stronger in some people than in others; and (3) a person with a habitually strong motive will respond to the TAT in the same way as will a person whose motive has been deliberately aroused. So, the scoring system to arrive at *n* Power, or a person's level of need for power, was developed through a series of experiments in which some individuals were exposed to conditions thought to arouse the power motive and some were not.[1] The differences in story themes that reliably appeared between aroused and nonaroused subjects were thought to characterize high and low *n* Power. Taking that assumption further, these same differences in story themes were thought to characterize persons who were habitually high or low in *n* Power. The assumption is valid only if the methods used to arouse the power motive actually do arouse that motive (and only that motive).

Accepting, for a moment, the notion that the methods used by researchers to arouse the power motive have actually had the desired effect, the differences in the stories told by aroused and nonaroused individuals in these studies should reflect the presence or relative absence of the power motive. What kinds of differences in the stories they tell distinguish the aroused from the nonaroused? And, by implication, the highly power-motivated from the less highly power-motivated? According to Winter (1973), "Power Imagery is scored if some person or group of persons in the story is concerned about establishing, maintaining, or restoring his power—that is, his impact, control or influence over another person, group of persons, or the world at large" (p. 250).

---

[1]Some of the conditions used to arouse the power motive included being assigned the role of the psychological experimenter or viewing a demonstration of hypnosis (Uleman, 1966) and viewing a film of a United States presidential inauguration oath and address (Winter, 1967).

Specifically, a person concerned with power can be expected to use three general themes in the stories: showing power through powerful actions; doing something that arouses strong positive or negative emotions in others; or showing concern for reputation or position. The general theme of powerful actions can include forceful behavior such as assaults, threats, or insults; sexual exploitation; taking advantage of another's weakness; giving unsolicited help, support, or protection; trying to control another person by regulating behavior, or living conditions, or by seeking information; trying to influence or persuade another; and trying to impress another person or the world at large. Each story is scored according to the number of different power imagery categories it contains, and then the scores for all the stories are added up to determine the *n* Power score.[2]

The Power Motive in Women and Men

Almost all of the original research on *n* Power was done with men, a pattern which parallels early research on the achievement motive. The bias inherent in such an exclusive reliance on male subjects is more than simply inappropriate, it severely threatens the accuracy of the conclusions reached by the researchers. Male and female response patterns to a particular procedure may differ, as indeed happened in the research on achievement motivation when the researchers finally got around to studying women. When such gender differences appear, there has been a tendency in the male-dominated world of scientific research to define the male response pattern as the norm and the female response as deviant—and to either ignore or explain away the female response when drawing conclusions.

Simple logic tells us if on the average women and men differ in their response to a given situation, it makes as much sense to call the men's response deviant as the women's. And simple logic, carried one step further, allows us to see that an adequate model for the behavior in question would explain the way both women *and* men act, without resorting to labeling either one of them deviant. Over the years, research on the power motive has gradually moved from a phase in which women were ignored completely to one in which a single model—that of the interrelationship between the power motive and responsibility training —seems to account well for some of the differences observed between women and men. This model, discussed at length later in the chapter,

[2]A number of researchers have questioned the usefulness of the *n* Power score, arguing that it cannot be proven to measure actual need for power and that it is unreliable. For a discussion of these issues, see Winter (1973).

suggests that the expression of the power motive is shaped by the degree to which individuals are socialized to be responsibly nurturant in their relationships with others.

Levels and Arousal of the Power Motive

Most studies that do report *n* Power scores for both males and females suggest that there are no gender differences in the strength of the power motive under neutral conditions (Booth, Vinograd-Bausell, & Harper, 1984; Winter, 1988). Moreover, Abigail Stewart and David Winter (1976) have shown that *n* Power can be aroused in women using the same procedures as those that work for men—watching a demonstration of hypnosis or listening to excerpts of speeches by powerful men. (What about speeches by powerful women? This procedure appears not to have been tried.) These procedures produced the same increase in *n* Power scores for women as for men. Furthermore, the stories written by women in response to TAT pictures showed no other (nonpower) themes that were not present in the stories written by men (Winter & Stewart, 1978). Thus, these arousal procedures seem to have the same effect on the power motivation of both women and men, at least as far as that motivation can be measured.

Although the research shows that *n* Power can be aroused in women and men by the same experiences, one might think that particular experiences could be associated with *n* Power arousal for either sex. There has been very little research on this question, but one researcher (Stewart, 1975, cited in Winter & Stewart, 1978), speculating that the experience of providing food from their own bodies to dependent infants might arouse feelings of power in nursing mothers, studied the effects on fantasy of nursing a baby. The study revealed no differences in *n* Power between the nursing and control mothers, however. Other experiences unique to women or men have yet to be investigated. Would women respond with increased *n* Power scores to accounts of pregnancy and birth? Would women's or men's *n* Power scores be aroused differently in response to descriptions of certain kinds of sexual scenes? At present, this territory remains unexplored.

Correlates of the Power Motive

If a person is highly power-motivated, what does this imply about his or her behavior? In other words, what kinds of behavior correlate with (are related to) *n* Power? The behaviors that have been investigated in this regard fall into two categories: leadership and *profligate impulsive* (reckless, destructive behavior). Early research suggested that males and females high in the power motive were equally likely to engage in leadership behaviors. In both women and men, high *n* Power is associated with acquiring formal social power through leadership roles or offices, or through careers such as business executive, teacher, psychologist, or member of the clergy, which involve direct, legitimate, interpersonal power over others (Winter & Stewart, 1978).[3] For both women and men, *n* Power has been positively linked to prestige and visibility. For college students of both sexes, the power motive is associated with the possession of such prestige items as television sets and tape recorders. For males and females in several economic groups, the power motive is also related to the number of credit cards carried (McClelland, 1975; Winter & Stewart, 1978). Like highly power-motivated college males, female college students high in *n* Power tend to do things to command attention and make themselves more visible: writing letters to their college newspapers and putting their names on their room doors (Winter, 1988).

It is in the area of profligate impulsive behaviors, such as drinking, aggression, and sexual exploitation, that the correlates of the power motive seem to differ for men and women. With respect to drinking alcohol, McClelland, Davis, Kalin & Wanner (1972) demonstrated that drinking increased the level of men's power motive. For women, as for men, the power motive is related to drinking history and to consumption of alcohol in a simulated social drinking setting (Wilsnack, 1974). However, there is no evidence that women's *n* Power scores increase after social drinking. It is supposed that men's drinking correlates with *n* Power because alcohol may free the man to feel powerful through fantasy, but such an explanation does not speak to the findings for women. Research also links *n* Power to drug use, physical and verbal aggression, and gambling for men, but not for women.

One particular area of profligate impulsive behavior in which *n* Power appears to predict very different behaviors for women and men is that of male–female relationships. Men with strong power motives have difficulty in their relationships with women and tend to hold an exploitative view of such relationships (Winter & Stewart, 1978). High *n* Power men tend to have more sexual partners, to prefer wives who are dependent and submissive, and to read pornographic magazines (Winter, 1973). In one study, when male college students were asked to draw male and female figures, the highly power-motivated men tended to emphasize female breasts in their sketches and to draw bizarre, distorted female (but

---

[3]Direct, legitimate power involves having the authority to influence others openly (discussed in more detail in Chapter Four). Winter and Stewart note that the important aspect of the careers that correlate with *n* Power seems to be the opportunity to direct others on an individual, immediate basis.

not male) figures (Winter & Stewart, 1978). High power motivation has been linked with the tendency by male (but not female) college undergraduates to physically abuse their intimate partners (Mason & Blankenship, 1987). McClelland (1975) reports that highly power-motivated men tend to be separated or divorced from their wives. In marriages that do endure, the husband's *n* Power tends to be inversely related to the wife's career level (Winter, Stewart, & McClelland, 1977).

In a study of dating heterosexual couples, Hope of Power[4] among the men was negatively related to their own and their partner's satisfaction with the dating relationship and positively related to the tendency to anticipate problems in the relationship (Stewart & Rubin, 1974). Men's Hope of Power was also negatively related to their love and liking for their partner. Finally, a two-year follow-up showed that couples in which the man scored high on Hope of Power were much more likely to have broken up and much less likely to have married than couples in which the man scored low in Hope of Power.

Converging evidence, then, suggests that high *n* Power men exhibit difficulty and exploitation in their relationships with women. For women, however, most studies have not shown a link between the power motive and difficulties with or an exploitative approach to relationships. In the study of dating couples mentioned above, women's Hope of Power scores were not related to their own or their partner's reported satisfaction with the relationship or to their measured love or liking for their partners. Similarly, there was no relationship between a woman's Hope of Power score and the tendency for the couple to break up. In a followup study of women whose *n* Power had been measured when they were in college 10 years before, the relationship of power motivation to difficulty in relationships was found to be reversed from that usually found for men: Power-motivated women tended to stay in one relationship, to avoid extramarital affairs, and not to be divorced (Stewart, 1975).

Fear of Power

The avoidance side of the power motive involves sensitivity to power and power relationships combined with a negative feeling about them. It

---

[4]Winter and Stewart (1978) note a distinction between two aspects of the *n* Power score: *Hope of Power* and *Fear of Power*. These concepts represent the approach and avoidance sides of the power motive. Hope of Power implies a tendency to hope for and seek power; Fear of Power is the tendency to fear, mistrust, and avoid power. An individual's overall *n* Power score, which represents the total concern with our motivational importance of power, can be broken down into these two categories. Winter and Stewart find, however, that Hope of Power is usually highly correlated with *n* Power, while Fear of Power is not.

may include both a negative reaction to others holding power as well as discomfort with one's own power. Research evidence suggests that Fear of Power derives from the experience of powerlessness. For males, at least, being the youngest member of a relatively large family is connected with high scores on Fear of Power. Comparable data for females are not available, leaving some interesting questions to be answered.

Fear of Power is related to a variety of behaviors for both women and men. Winter and Stewart (1978) report that college students high in Fear of Power tend to view power or authority with distrust or suspicion, and they are protective of their own autonomy and independence. Such students spend time alone, prefer less-structured aspects of academic life (seminars over lectures, papers over exams, freedom of choice over rigid requirements), disregard academic deadlines, and deny the influence of peers over them. They also carefully guard information about themselves. Such individuals use their power to help others: lending their possessions, sharing their knowledge, equalizing the power or resource differences between the helper and the helped. They do poorly in situations calling for strong action and appear more comfortable and effective when acting to help others than when acting for personal gain. Whereas some of the behaviors that accompany Fear of Power seem similar to those displayed by women in studies of experimental games and small task groups described later in this chapter, it remains to be seen whether this avoidance side of the power motive is useful in understanding differences in the ways women and men handle power.

GENDER, ROLES, AND THE POWER MOTIVE

The pattern of findings showing that power motivation was linked to impulsive, irresponsible, and exploitative behaviors for men but not for women was attributed initially to gender roles. Authors speculated that social pressures to conform to the feminine or masculine roles (wherein, for instance, aggression and sexual exploitation are considered to be more masculine behaviors) led to differences in the ways women and men expressed their needs for power. This explanation, while seemingly self-evident, is too general to be very useful in predicting the behavior of power-motivated individuals. Furthermore, it has been called into question by studies suggesting that profligate behavior does not necessarily affect people's judgments of women differently from their judgments of men. Winter (1988), using written descriptions on which the gender label could be changed from "John" to "Joan," tested reactions to descriptions of people whose behavior was described as either profligate or neutral. He demonstrated with several different groups of respondents that there was no tendency for described behavior that fit the profligate theme—aggression, drinking, gambling, high risk-taking, interest in pornography, a swinging sex life—to have any more adverse effects on college students' ratings of women than of men on such items as "influence," "would vote for," "popularity," "amount of dating," "psychological problems" and "dangerous to others." In these studies, the profligate person was often seen as less powerful than the neutral person, and the woman as less powerful than the man; however, the drop in perceived powerfulness that occurred from the neutral to the profligate style was no greater when the person described was female than when that person was male.

The above studies, while casting doubt on the gender roles explanation for male-female differences in the behavior that correlates with the power motive, do not rule out the status aspect of gender as an explanation for this phenomenon. After all, the profligate woman is still rated as less influential than anyone else, and power-motivated women may perceive that, unlike men, they cannot afford the drop in influence and prestige that accompanies the profligate style. Every businesswoman on her way up the promotion ladder recognizes clearly that, whereas drunkenness at the office party may lower her male colleagues' reputations, their position is more solid than hers is to begin with. For her, having a few drinks too many at the party is a risk to her reputation—and her power—that she dare not take.

Responsibility and the Power Motive

What, besides the status aspect of gender, might account for the gender differences in the correlations between the power motive and impulsive, exploitative behavior? Recent research has uncovered a promising lead: socialization for responsibility (Winter, 1988; Winter & Barenbaum, 1985). A clue that responsibility training might be an important moderator of the way the power motive is expressed in women's and men's behavior comes from the cross-cultural work of Whiting and Whiting (1975). Studying children in six cultures, these researchers identified several behavior clusters that varied across the cultures. Winter (1988) later noted that two of these behavior clusters—egoistic dominance (physical and verbal aggression, rough play, attention-seeking) and responsible nurturance (giving help and support, prosocial dominance, and physical contact)—were much like the two ways (profligate vs. leadership behavior) that people express the power motive. The Whitings' research showed that children who had younger siblings scored more toward responsible nurturance, while those without younger siblings tended more toward egoistic dominance. Furthermore, a tendency toward responsible nurturance was also associated with early responsibility training in the area of household chores contributing to the family's welfare. Egoistic dominance, on the other hand, was associated with early socialization that emphasized individual achievement.

Winter (1988), reflecting on these cross-cultural findings, theorized that responsibility training might be the key to explaining why highly power-motivated men were so much more likely than highly power-motivated women to behave in profligate, impulsive ways. While the overall level of power motivation would determine a person's tendency to engage in any kind of power-related actions, responsibility training (or the lack of it) might channel that tendency into either responsible leadership behaviors or egoistic dominance. As children, females generally receive more responsibility training than males do, regardless of the presence of younger siblings. Thus, as adults, women should be more likely to express their power needs in socially responsible than in profligate ways, while men should lean toward the profligate impulsive forms of expression. However, for both women and men, the expression of the power motive should be moderated by responsibility training, indicated by such variables as having younger siblings, or having children.

Winter tested his idea by examining the data from several studies of power motivation to see whether there was indeed a relationship between having younger siblings or having children and the way power-motivated adults behaved. The results suggest support for the link between responsibility training and the expression of the power motive. Among women with younger siblings, *n* Power is associated with such responsible leadership actions as holding office, but no association between power motivation and leadership behaviors is found among women without younger siblings. Furthermore, among women without younger siblings, *n* Power *is* linked to the same pattern of profligate impulsive behaviors often found among power-motivated men. A similar pattern apparently exists for men: Among a sample of male college students, the link between *n* Power and office-holding was present only for men with younger siblings, whereas the link between power motivation and physical fights, a carefree attitude toward the future, and a cluster of profligate variables was present only for men without younger siblings.

Having children of one's own, like having younger siblings, is related to the way the power motive is expressed. For both women and men, *n* Power is more strongly linked to responsible leadership behaviors among those with children than among those who do not have children. These findings suggest that socialization for responsibility is an important variable in determining how the power motive will be expressed, and that the gender difference in the way that *n* Power relates to profligate impulsive behavior may be an outcome of the differences in the way females and males are socialized with respect to responsibility. This conclusion receives further support from work by Winter and Barenbaum (1985), who devised a TAT-based measure of responsibility. Using this measure, they found that among college students and middle-class adults who were high in responsibility, power motivation predicted responsible social power actions. Among people who scored low on the responsibility measure, however, power motivation was associated with a variety of profligate, impulsive behaviors.

A reasonable conclusion from the above research is that it is responsibility rather than gender that determines how a person will express power motivation. However, certain aspects of responsibility seem to be correlated with gender, so perhaps it would be more accurate to say that responsibility is *the aspect of gender* that is important with respect to power motivation. Gender itself is largely a social construction, a product of the way we differentially socialize females and males as children and adults and the rules and reward structures we, as a society, maintain for feminine and masculine behavior. Orientation toward responsible nurturance is one of the major differences in the social expectations set out for female and male behavior. As Whiting and Whiting (1975) showed, in a variety of cultures girls are more likely than boys to be socialized toward caring for others. Certainly in our own society the expectation that women will be ultimately responsible for the care and nurturance of children and other family members has abated little in the face of the women's movement, the large-scale migration of women into the paid workforce, or the increased availability of daycare and parental leave.

Interacting in Power Situations: Further Clues about Responsibility and Dominance

Several different streams of research converge to suggest that responsibility is a stronger theme in the reactions of women than men to situations that involve making judgments about or exercising power. Research on strategies in experimental games, reward allocation, and moral reasoning indicates that, in situations where conflicts among the interests of several people require the negotiation and compromise characteristic of the processes of power, women are more likely than men to use responsibility to others as a criterion for behavior. Power motivation has not been explicitly examined in these areas, but the findings, like those discussed above, suggest that responsibility orientation is one key to the difference in the ways women and men treat power.

Strategies in experimental games   Task-oriented games carried out in a laboratory provide an opportunity for researchers to observe a variety of power-related behaviors: seeking visibility and prestige, forming alliances, aggression, competition, cooperation. Within such situations, as in real life, power can be exercised in a variety of ways. It is often possible to have as much impact on others through cooperation as through competition, by sharing resources as by accumulating them for display or status, or by working with others to get a task accomplished as by insisting on one's own way. Early research on three-person games showed that women and men differed, on the average, in their approach to working with others and accumulating points (Bond & Vinacke, 1961; Komorita & Moore, 1976; Vinacke, 1959). Men formed coalitions, or alliances, with others only when doing so would help them to win the game and to maximize their own gains. Women, on the other hand, formed alliances even when they could have won the game alone and were less likely than men to take advantage of weak partners. They seemed to feel a sense of responsibility toward one another and were concerned with achieving the best outcome for all players so that each player would have a share of the final prize. These differences hold in later research for both same-sex and mixed-sex groups. Worthy of note is the fact that women do as well as or better than men in terms of total points earned, despite using a strategy that Vinacke called an "accommodative" rather than an "exploitative" one.

Dividing the spoils: reward allocation   Early research with small groups showed that when groups of men completing a task were asked to distribute a reward among themselves, they tended to base the distribution on equity: the allocation of payments on the basis of how well each participant had performed or contributed to the task. When women were asked to divide up rewards, they were more likely to favor an equal distribution, regardless of differences among themselves in how much each person had contributed to the work at hand (Sampson, 1975). There are several possible interpretations of this gender difference; one that has received a good deal of attention is the idea that women and men have different interaction goals when they work together in groups. Men, according to this hypothesis, tend to be narrowly task-oriented; women are focused not just on the task but on their relationship to the other participants. A focus on the task alone leads men to choose a reward system that emphasizes only contributions to the performance of that task; a focus on relationships leads women to safeguard the feelings of all participants by de-emphasizing differences in task input even when that means accepting smaller individual rewards.

Support for the *interaction goals hypothesis* comes from many studies. Particularly interesting is an investigation by Carles and Carver (1979), who demonstrated that females were more generous in their reward allocations to a partner when they knew that person's identity and personal attributes than they were when they had no such information. Males, on the other hand, were less generous when they had personal information about their partner than when they did not. Questionnaires completed by the participants in this study revealed that the men felt more competitive when their partner was made prominent to them as a person, whereas women felt less competitive under these conditions.

Despite the research support for the notion that women and men tend to differ in their interaction goals when working in task groups, the explanation for the frequently observed gender differences in reward allocation may be more complex. As Arnold Kahn and William Gaeddert (1985) note in their review of the field, much of the research that shows these gender differences has used same-sex groups, thus confounding sex of allocator with sex of recipient; and there is some research that shows that everyone, female and male, tends to be more generous in allocating to women than to men. This issue remains to be sorted out by future research.

In the meantime, several other possible explanations for gender differences in reward allocation have been suggested. The most persuasive of these is the *status hypothesis:* the notion that equity and equality represent, respectively, the allocation strategies used by people who have high and low status (Meeker & Weitzel-O'Neill, 1977). A low status person is less likely than a high status one to be taken seriously in a group; such an individual's participation, if seemingly too assertive, may be viewed as self-serving. A low status person must work hard t convey good intentions and competence in order to gain legitimacy in the group. Such a motivation, rather than a responsible orientation toward relationships in the group, may explain women's tendency to allocate rewards equally, since women are typically considered low in status compared to men. Similarly, competition among high status group members may explain men's tendency to allocate equitably, particularly in same-sex groups.

The interaction goals and status explanations may actually work together. People (in this case, men) who have been socialized to believe in their own high status, and to value that status, are likely to be motivated to maintain and improve that status, a motivation that is very likely to affect their interaction goals. On the other hand, people (in this case, women) who have not been socialized to think in terms of guarding their status may be freer to include a variety of motivations, including concern for relationships, in their interaction goals. It is also quite possible that both equity and equality approaches to allocation are consistent with the expression of power motivation. Women and men, while both concerned about their impact on a situation, may focus on different aspects of that impact. Men may show a tendency to seek impact by winning over others in terms of resources or status. Women may seek impact by becoming well liked and forming friendships. Either interaction goal could reflect the presence of the power motive as well as of other factors.

Moral reasoning: responsibility vs. rights   It is easy to see that questions of morality are not independent of questions of power: All one must do is notice how easily people holding powerful positions develop arguments to justify (literally, to make right) their own decisions or behavior, even if such decisions or behavior seem outrageous and reprehensible to everyone else. Research on people who hold power over others shows that the "power-over" relationship tends to be associated with the powerholder's taking credit for the achievements of those over whom she or he has power, belittling those people, and trying to distance herself or himself socially from them (Kipnis, 1972; Kipnis, Castell, Gergen, & Mauch, 1976). A study of spousal relationships and of housewives' relationships to their maids found that the more power one spouse feels she or he has over another, and the more power a woman feels she has over her maid, the less those powerholders trust and respect the person over whom they hold the power (Kipnis et al., 1976). The processes that allow the powerholder to become contemptuous of and distant from subordinates is a cyclical one: The more successfully a powerholder distances herself or himself from subordinates, the easier it is emotionally to belittle them and to justify holding power over them and treating them badly. "I have a right to withhold raises from my employees this year," a person in such a position might argue. "They did not work hard enough to meet the production goals we set."

The notion of rights is a familiar one in discussions of moral reasoning. Psychological research on the development of the capacity for moral reasoning has, until recent years, focused on elaborating the developmental stages through which individuals move in their capacity to assign and weigh individual rights in a moral conflict (Kohlberg, 1984). Every introductory psychology student knows the story: Heinz's wife is dying. The sole drug that can save her is obtainable only from a pharmacist who charges a price too exorbitant for Heinz to afford. What should Heinz do, and why? Respondents ponder the conflict, and their answers reflect struggles with such questions as "Does Heinz have a right to steal the drug?" "Does the pharmacist have a right to charge this price?" Based on (mostly male) respondents' answers to questions about a series of such moral dilemmas, Kohlberg developed a hierarchy of moral developmental stages. Individuals at the bottom showed a morality of self-concern, a tendency to think only of their own rights and needs in a conflict situation (Heinz should steal the drug because he needs his wife).

Individuals near the top showed a principled morality—a morality that recognized the rights of the various parties in a situation and assigned weights to those rights: The pharmacist has a right to make a profit, but not at the expense of depriving Heinz's wife of the opportunity to recover. Her right to health and life outweighs his right to profit from the drug. Such reasoning is reminiscent of an equity approach to reward allocation; the reasoner must decide who deserves what, whose needs take priority. It sounds righteous but cold; is this truly a complete picture of the pinnacle of moral development?

Psychologist Carol Gilligan was convinced that Kohlberg's picture of moral development left something out. Part of her conviction stemmed from the knowledge that Kohlberg's research had relied on male respondents. Would females reason the same way? Her own research (Gilligan, 1982) led her to conclude that earlier studies had missed a whole dimension of moral reasoning: responsibility and care. It was this dimension that she discovered when she attended to the voices of girls and women as they struggled with moral dilemmas. It was important, these females argued, that Heinz had a responsibility to his wife, because of their relationship, to do everything he could do to help her. On the other hand, some noted, Heinz had to think this through carefully: If he landed in jail as a result of stealing the drug, who would care for his wife? If this dimension of responsibility and care had been part of the moral reasoning expressed by Kohlberg's male subjects, it had not been noticed. Thus, Gilligan suggested that females were more likely than males to emphasize issues of responsibility and care in their moral decisions.

Other researchers have rushed in to test Gilligan's hypothesis about gender differences in moral reasoning. They have found, in general, that both women and men use each of the two orientations. If there is a more consistent tendency for females to emphasize responsibility and for males to emphasize rights, it has not been demonstrated unequivocally. In one study, the interview responses of 25 female and 25 male college students to three moral dilemmas were coded according to the orientation used (Rothbart, Hanley, & Albert, 1986). The results showed that both the rights and the responsibility orientations were widely used by both women and men, but that women were more likely to emphasize the responsibility orientation. This study also revealed that the content of a particular moral dilemma had a strong relationship to the type of moral reasoning used, suggesting that situation, not simply gender, affects the way people make decisions about what is right. When subjects were confronted with the Heinz dilemma about whether or not a husband should steal a drug to save his dying wife, more than 76% of them gave responses based on the justice/rights orientation. A moral dilemma about how a person makes decisions about physical intimacy with another person elicited predominantly care/responsibility responses from 78% of the subjects. In the end, gender accounted for far less variance in subjects' responses than did the content of the dilemma.

Another study examined the self-reports of female and male undergraduate students about moral dilemmas they themselves had experienced (Ford & Lowery, 1986). Once again, this study revealed the use of both moral orientations by both genders; however, females were more consistent in reporting a responsibility orientation, while males were more consistent in reporting a rights orientation. For both sexes, the more important the conflict in their life and the more difficult they perceived the decision to be, the more likely they were to report a care orientation toward that conflict. Women rated their conflicts as more important and difficult than did men.

Additionally, the study showed that males who were more feminine, as measured by a paper and pencil test of gender role orientation, were more likely to report the use of a responsibility/care orientation than were less feminine males. Femininity or masculinity, in this context, refers simply to how closely an individual's responses to questions on a test match the average responses for females or males respectively. Thus, we can assume that the more feminine males in this study answered questions more closely to the way the average woman would than did the less feminine males; that is, their responses showed that they shared, to some extent, the preferences and interests of the typical woman. Since socialization has been shown to be a major determinant of these preferences and interests, it is a safe assumption that many of the more feminine males in this study had been subjected to less rigid masculine role socialization pressures than had their less feminine counterparts. That the more feminine males were more likely than less feminine males to emphasize a responsibility and care orientation to morality suggests that socialization to what dominant North American culture has defined as the masculine role may tend to mute the responsibility dimension of morality; and/or that socialization to the feminine role may tend to enhance it. This conclusion would be consistent with the findings, discussed above, that females are generally socialized more in the direction of responsibility and nurturance than are males.

This section began with the assertion that issues of morality and power were linked. Gilligan's work, and that of the researchers who have further explored and tested her ideas, suggests new perspectives on that link. Perhaps the more that people have been taught to emphasize responsibility and nurturance the more likely they are to develop a morality that emphasizes connectedness more than separateness, safeguarding relationships more than safeguarding status differences, finding the best outcome for all concerned rather than enhancing the power of one party at the expense of others. Perhaps such individuals are less likely than others to feel they have a moral right, because of their position, their hard work, their contribution to society, to impose suffering on others.

Ten years ago, in an article reviewing years of research on aggressive behavior, Eron (1980) made a strong recommendation which, within our cultural context that assumes male superiority, was absolutely stunning: Boys should be socialized more like girls. Girls, he argued, tended to be taught to constrain their aggressive feelings to particular situations rather than expressing them at will, and to be caring in their orientations toward others—invaluable lessons for a society to teach its children if it is serious about reducing the amount of aggression. This aspect of his article is not frequently cited; perhaps the recommendation was both too radical and too simple. Yet, research since his article appeared, including the research on justice and morality described here, has tended to converge in support of his conclusion: training people to be competitive and aggressive helps to create a culture where power is expressed as dominance; training people to be caring and nurturant may help to shape a culture where power is expressed as responsibility.

Before we accept socialization as a solution to the dominance versus responsibility question, let us remember the findings that suggest the importance of the situation, of social structure, to the expression of power. The housewives who held power over their maids in the Kipnis et al. (1976) study had no doubt been socialized toward traditional feminine values of responsibility and care. But when placed in positions of power with respect to other women, their maids, they fell into the same pattern of negative attributions, dominating, controlling behavior, and maintenance of social distance that male powerholders often do. Clearly, while socialization issues are important, the situational impact of holding power over others is too strong to be overlooked. If it were not so strong, it would be rare indeed to see women exploit and dominate other women or mistreat their children; and it would be unheard of that an oppressed minority, finally gaining the upper hand in a political situation, would then engage in the same abuses of power that drove them to rebel in the first place. But such instances are not actually rare; they are, in fact depressingly predictable.

To reduce the danger that allowing one person power over others will result more in exploitation and dominance than in responsible service, administration, and caretaking, we must acknowledge, not minimize, that danger. Individuals must be socialized toward responsibility, true, but they must also be educated about power. Individuals need to understand the effects of holding power over others in order to recognize these effects in themselves and others; and institutions must be ever cautious in their acceptance of "power-over" relationships and ever vigilant in monitoring such relationships.

CULTURE AND THE EXPRESSION OF THE POWER MOTIVE

Although many people may be motivated by a similar need for power, the expression of that need can take many forms. The popular stereotype of the power-motivated person as one who gives orders, accumulates and keeps vast personal wealth, and strives for high personal visibility and fame is too narrow. To predict or understand how a power-motivated person will behave, one must have some knowledge of that person's cultural and social context.

McClelland's (1975) analysis of traditional Indian society shows how a culture can be structured so that the major acceptable way to express the power motive is through giving. According to McClelland, who achieved these insights by analyzing Indian documents and children's stories, a person in traditional India is thought to accumulate merit and status in proportion to the amount she or he gives to others. One demonstrates moral superiority by being interested in giving rather than receiving. The paradox that one must first accumulate resources in order to give them away causes some conflict, and attempts to gain wealth or position are often rationalized by the thought that this will allow the individual to be more generous. Giving to another also creates or preserves a status difference between the giver and the receiver or between two givers: The more generous giver is superior. Thus, there may be covert contests for dominance in a relationship, waged through mutual attempts to outgive the other. McClelland cites the conflict that sometimes occurs in India between a new wife and her husband's mother. The mother has achieved her moral status, and thus her power over her son, through a constant display of giving and self-sacrifice on his behalf. When the new wife moves into the household, her own display of giving and self-sacrifice toward the husband challenges the mother's status. A fierce power struggle may ensue, with both women trying to gain control through displays of superior moral merit.

Another aspect of the traditional Indian system of power-through-giving is that one cannot win recognition by seeking it, but only by being modest and self-effacing while hoping that someone will notice and commend one's humility. One seeks power by pretending not to seek it. If one does not extract an expression of appreciation or gratitude for one's humble generosity, then one has not successfully exerted power. This stands in sharp contrast to another culture's version of gaining power through giving: the once traditional Sun Dance ceremony of the Blackfoot Indians of North America, described by Maslow (1971). This ceremony, designed in part to allow individuals to display power and achieve status by showing off their generosity, included the ritualistic giving away of all accumulated possessions by the rich men of the tribe. During the ritual, the givers are described as strutting and boasting about their wealth and as anything but self-effacing about their generosity.

Knowing something about how power needs are expressed in various cultures should promote caution in the easy labeling of certain power styles as masculine or feminine. For example, in North America it is common to try to gain power through acting generous and humble; a case in point is the parent who exerts control over children by sacrificing so much for them that the children are forever bound by a mixture of guilt and gratitude. This control through martyrdom strategy is often labeled manipulative and is stereotyped as a feminine power mode. Yet McClelland's research indicates that this approach to power is just as prevalent among men as women in Indian society, and thus suggests that culture rather than gender shapes the ways in which power is sought.

We have seen that many behaviors can lead to the experience of power; however, most of the emphasis has been on individual expressions of the need for power. Casual observation suggests that many people have apparently satisfied their need for power, not by enhancing their own individual influence or prominence, but by other means: helping to empower their community or their family, working collectively to make a political impact or to create social change, even identifying with the power-related accomplishments of others and gaining vicarious satisfaction from them. Perhaps these methods of satisfying power needs are most characteristic of those who have few opportunities for individual power; perhaps they are more characteristic of some cultures than others. The research on power motivation, emphasizing individual power as it does, does not tell us. It appears, however, that the notion of power motivation could usefully be expanded beyond the individual need for personal influence or effectiveness to acknowledge the possibility that power motivation can be satisfied by such things as vicarious power and collective power.

CONCLUSION: POWER MOTIVATION IN WOMEN AND MEN

The power motive can be defined as the need to feel that one is having an impact on one's environment. To a certain extent, this motive can be aroused by external events and its presence assessed with a projective test. Individuals differ in the strength of their power motive, but collectively, women and men show equally strong n Power under arousal conditions and similar correlates of n Power. Having a strong power motive is associated with both responsible leadership and profligate impulsive behaviors. While responsible leadership behaviors are associated with high power motivation in both men and women, research shows that power-motivated men are more likely to show the exploitative, impulsive behavior pattern than are power-motivated women. Research suggests one plausible explanation for this finding: Women are more likely than men to have been socialized toward responsibility and nurturance. Perhaps it would benefit society, as some writers have suggested, to socialize boys more in the way that girls are socialized. However, socialization is only part of the explanation for the differing ways that individuals act out their need for power; the social situation, especially the degree to which an individual holds power over others or has responsibility for others, also plays an important role.

Even the most cursory examination of our own and other cultures indicates that an individual's power goal of having an impact can be reached in a variety of ways. Depending on the situation, a person can achieve feelings of power by winning, by gaining respect and liking, by accomplishing an important task, by giving away possessions, or even by being pointedly self-sacrificing and modest. Thus, a power-motivated person can express this motivation in many ways.

The following chapter explores in detail the variety of power styles that women and men may adopt in their efforts to make an impact on their interpersonal environments.

CHAPTER FOUR

Interpersonal Influence: Resources, Tactics, and Gender Politics

N ewspapers have been peppered in recent years with stories of sexual harassment. The theme of the stories is almost always the same: A female worker brings a complaint against her male supervisor,[1] claiming that he forced his sexual attentions on her by threatening, explicitly or implicitly, to fire her if she did not cooperate. Whether involved in resisting the "bargain," or participating unwillingly and unhappily in this exchange, the woman has become stressed, demoralized, angry, and often ill. Her desperation to keep her job may inhibit her from making a fuss. Although her public silence has helped her to keep her job—something she wants and needs very much—she feels as if she has been rendered powerless. This is an extreme example of lopsided interpersonal influence: one person getting an unwilling other to behave in a particular way.

The most common examples of social influence are not as imbalanced or as sinister as the one above. We are almost always engaged in either trying to exert influence on the people with whom we interact or responding to pressures of influence directed at us by others. How can I get my students to read the material more carefully? How does my coworker always manage to manipulate me into taking public positions with which

---

[1]The male harasser/female victim example is not a baseless stereotype. North American studies indicate that females are by far the most frequent victims of sexual harassment at work, and males are by far the most frequent harassers (e.g., Gutek & Nakamura, 1983; Tangri, Burt, & Johnson, 1982).

I am not comfortable? How does my niece get her teachers to pay attention to her? These are the processes of power in which we all engage; our social interactions are virtually filled with these processes. In fact, as noted in Chapter One, social psychologists have typically defined social power as the ability to get others to do what one wants them to do, despite resistance. Furthermore, they measure power in a particular interaction by assessing the range of behaviors through which one person can move another.

POWER, RESOURCES, AND SOCIAL EXCHANGE

People's capacity to entice others to their way of thinking or behaving is based on *resources*. An entire theory—social exchange theory—has been developed to explain the ways in which one person's ability to influence another depends on the first person's control over resources that the other wants (Homans, 1974). These resources can be tangible, such as food, shelter, objects, sex, money, job advancement, awards, honors, grades; or intangible, such as love, approval, acceptance, emotional support. In a power-based social exchange, each individual gets and gives something that she or he wants or needs. As long as each person has something the other wants, neither has complete or ultimate control over the other. For example, an employer might offer to trade extra time off later for an employee's agreement to put in overtime this weekend. The employer is the boss, but as long as she or he needs the services of the employee, the boss is not in a position of perfect control over that employee.

The Principle of Least Interest

While the occurrence of an exchange of resources indicates that both parties have some control over each other's outcomes, it does not mean that the power of the parties in the exchange is equal. The potential for inequality of power in a social exchange is illustrated dramatically in the sexual harassment example at the beginning of the chapter. The victim in this case feels she had little choice but to participate in the exchange because of her strong need for the resource over which her supervisor had control: her job. The harasser, while wanting to take sexual liberties with his employee, is most likely not as desperate to achieve that outcome as she is to keep her job. If he were as desperate or more desperate than she, the power relationship would be somewhat different: She could, if she chose, take the upper hand and threaten to quit, or even use the promise of sexual cooperation to extract for herself rewards such as promotions and salary increases. It is each party's need for the resources or outcomes controlled by the other that determines the balance of power.

According to social exchange theory, the importance of need in determining who holds the most power in a particular interaction is described by the principle of least interest (Waller, 1938). This principle holds that the party who is least dependent on the other for reward has the greater power. The more the victim of sexual harassment wants to keep her job, the less power she has in any given interaction with a harasser who can fire her.

Unless one is considering an exchange between two strangers who will in all probability never see each other again, it is not particularly useful to consider a single exchange in isolation. In a relationship, the person who has the greater power is the one who needs the least out of the exchanges taken as a whole; that is, the person who needs the relationship least has the most power. This generalized power difference between two people sometimes has an impact on specific exchanges—an impact that could not be predicted merely by examining the immediate costs and rewards to the participants.

This point is well illustrated by considering parent-child interactions. In a particular interaction, such as a parent trying to convince a child to eat vegetables, the parent may try to trade a resource that she or he controls—the privilege of eating dessert—for the child's cooperation. The child, on the other hand, may be trying to trade a resource that she or he controls—the threat of a screaming fit that would ruin everyone's dinner—for being allowed to leave the vegetables on the plate. Who wins out in this particular interaction depends on how badly the child wants dessert relative to how badly the parents want peace and quiet. When examining power in this situation, it is wise to remember that the parent-child conflict takes place in a relationship context in which the child is more dependent on the parent for a variety of outcomes, such as food, clothing, shelter, entertainment, love, and approval, than the parent is on the child. The young child who begins to carry out the ultimate threat to run away from home usually faces this reality before she or he has gone more than a few blocks. The parent also has what Lacey (1979) calls "agenda control." This means that the child may be able to choose between eating or not eating the vegetables, but it is the parent who decides when dinner will occur, and even whether it will occur at all. Although the child may have the power to win in a particular *social exchange* with the parent, an awareness of possible far-reaching consequences may stop the child from using this power. In judging power in ongoing social relationships, it is important to consider both the specific exchange and the general power differences between the parties.

The social exchange theory describes power as a matter of negotiation: Both parties rationally weigh the costs and rewards of various outcomes that can be brought about by the other person and decide whether to change their behavior. Also included in the equation may be the perceived possibility of obtaining rewards elsewhere, as well as each individual's judgment about whether the rewards the other can provide are deserved. This scenario probably places too much emphasis on rationality; many influence-related decisions are made in the heat of the moment, and the payoff system rationally constructed by the social scientist may often fail to predict the outcomes of social exchange. For instance, the person who holds what John Thibaut and Harold Kelley (1959) call "fate control" over another—the sense, for example, of having the final decision about that person's promotion—may exercise that power without carefully considering the ways in which the controlled person can make life miserable once it is known there is no hope of ever getting promoted. The bitterly resentful employee may blatantly sabotage a project that is crucial to the employer—even though this action means almost certain professional ruin for that employee.

The very degree of frustration that most of us encounter in trying to influence or control the behavior of others is a signal that the process is not based completely on rationality. It also suggests that, even when being rational, individuals frequently disagree on the perceived value of various outcomes in an exchange. Ultimately, regardless of the degree of control we have over another person's outcomes, we have no power with respect to that person unless she or he values those outcomes.

The Psychology of Winning at Any Cost: Social Control As Its Own Reward

There are times when attempts to control another's behavior appear completely irrational and go beyond the bounds of anything that can be described as social exchange. In such situations, the need for control over another, or others, becomes paramount. It obliterates any inclination to bargain, compromise, or make the best of a situation. To take a tragic and all too common example, an estranged husband or boyfriend may murder his ex-partner rather than allow her to start a new life without him—even though the costs of exerting this form of ultimate control are too staggering, rationally speaking, to compensate for anything that might be gained. The men who do this often say they were motivated by love, as in the case of the man who scaled the outside of an apartment building to break into his former girlfriend's apartment, killed her, and cut her body into pieces because he "couldn't stop loving her." It takes no special training in psychology to see that such an action has nothing whatsoever to do with love and everything to do with an inability to give up control. An individual who is willing to kill a former lover, and often himself as well, not because she is actively interfering with him in any way but simply because she has left him, is an extreme example of the psychology of winning at any cost. This person is not exerting control in order to achieve a particular goal; control *is* the ultimate goal. We have seen in Chapter Three that some degree of need for power is normal among men and women and that the sexes do not differ, at least on paper-and-pencil measures, in their level of power motivation. For both women and men, the exertion of power, the very process of exerting control over another, can be experienced as a reward in itself rather than as a means to another goal. We have also seen that the experience of power over another or others can be addictive and dangerous for both men and women.

Yet, as described in Chapter Three, men seem ready to sacrifice more in terms of relationships in order to get control or to win. Men appear far more likely than women to try to exert ultimate control through violence by doing so much damage to the other person that no further social exchange is possible. It is far more often men than women who stalk and kill their former lovers, far more often men than women who become skilled at extracting information and compliance from other human beings through torture, far more often men than women who pursue political goals through acts of deadly terrorism. Are these differences simply a matter of opportunity? Of training? Such questions have puzzled psychologists for years and there are no unequivocal data on which to base answers. We may speculate that part of the answer lies in the gender difference in training toward responsibility and nurturance, discussed in Chapter Three. Perhaps, also, women's attempts at control are equally strong but take a different, less obvious, form. As discussed in the next section, there are a wide variety of factors that affect why and how individuals use power.

THE INTERPLAY BETWEEN POWER RESOURCES AND INFLUENCE STRATEGIES

The process of power as a series of implicit or explicit negotiations and exchanges rests on resources. The would-be influencer is in a poor position if she or he has nothing to offer in return for compliance. A first step in analyzing the power in any set of relationships is an examination of the way resources are distributed.

Resources as Bases of Social Power

More than three decades ago, two social psychologists, John French and Bertram Raven (1959), defined the basis of interpersonal power as the relationship between two persons that was the source of one person's power over the other. They listed five possible bases on which one person's power with respect to another might rest: reward power, coercive power, legitimate power, referent power, and expert power.

Reward power   One person's power in relation to another may be based on his or her perceived ability to reward the other. The larger and more important the rewards one person can give another, the more likely is the second person to do what the first asks, or to try to please that person. If person A's affection and approval, or the ability to grant a promotion or a raise, is important to person B, this forms a basis of reward power that A has with respect to B. It is critical that the rewards A controls are important to B and that B actually views A as controlling those rewards. It is not A's ability to dole out rewards but B's perception of that ability that is a source of power for A in trying to influence B.

Coercive power   Power in relation to another person may also rest on the threat of punishment for noncompliance. To the extent that person B regards person A as willing and able to administer important negative consequences, person B will be motivated to avoid those consequences by doing what A wishes. If I am terrified of your anger, or if I see that you can withhold an important letter of recommendation for me, this aspect of our relationship gives you an important source of power with respect to me.

The emotional consequences of reward power and coercive power can be quite different (Homans, 1974). The person who feels coerced is often frustrated and angry; the person who has been rewarded may feel a happy sense of accomplishment. Homans suggests that those who use coercive power must always guard against the anger of the coerced—a major cost incurred by users of coercive power. He also notes that whereas the giving of a reward indicates that the power user has exerted power successfully, the administration of punishment indicates that the power user has *not* exerted power successfully: The punishment is meted out for *non*compliance. In such a case, the person's power base of coercion has not been converted into power because the desired behavioral response did not occur—the coercion did not work. On the other hand, the carrying out of a threat on one occasion may strengthen the hand of the coercive power user by indicating that she or he is not bluffing and thus raising the level of fear on the part of the other person.

Legitimate power   This most complex basis of power stems from the values that an individual holds about how she or he should behave and who has a right to influence her or him. Using these values, one person can exert power by invoking some code of behavior that is accepted by the other. For example, one friend may convince another to provide help by reminding her of a previous promise to do so; that is, one has a legitimate right to expect help if it has been promised. However, legitimate power based on a promise is effective only if the promiser thinks it is important to keep her word. In a similar vein, a husband may try to influence his wife to cook dinner every night when they both return home from their jobs—by pointing out that cooking dinner is part of the expected role of a wife. This influence attempt will work only if the wife agrees that cooking dinner every night *is* part of her role as wife. Acknowledged authority is also a type of legitimate power; within the framework of the job, an employer is seen as having a legitimate right to demand certain behaviors from an employee. In a variety of ways, one person can use legitimate power with respect to another by arguing that, for whatever reason, she or he has a legitimate right, acknowledged by both persons, to expect the desired behavior.

Referent power   This power base depends on the other person's liking for or identification with the power user. If a daughter wants badly to be like her mother, this desire gives her mother a source of power in relation to her. Because the daughter wants to be like her mother, she may assume her mother's attitudes or behaviors, regardless of any rewards and punishments from the mother for such imitation. Similarly, a person may conform to the standards of an attractive reference group without being directly rewarded by the group for doing so. The person being influenced is often unaware of the referent power being exerted by a person or group. Presumably, although French and Raven (1959) do not suggest this, someone other than the reference person can exert influence based on referent power by reminding the target person of the behavior that is necessary to become like the important person or group: Someone who knows little about tennis may influence the behavior of an aspiring young tennis player by telling her or him that Martina Navratilova or Steffie Graf follows a certain dietary or exercise regimen.

Expert power   One person's power with respect to another may be based on that person's presumed knowledge or expertise in a given area. In health matters, many of us are particularly receptive to influence attempts directed at us by a person who has earned a medical degree. We assume that such a person's opinion is likely to be informed and accurate. It is often this perception of expertise, rather than the content of the advice, that gives doctors, lawyers, accountants, plumbers, and other experts a source of power in dealing with their clients.

Informational power   The five bases of power listed above are all *source-dependent*; that is, their presence and strength depend on qualities the target person sees in or attributes to the person who is the source of the influence attempt. Raven (1965) notes a sixth power base, which is not source-dependent. Informational power is based on the content of the influence message rather than on the person who delivers it. If someone influences you by presenting an argument that sounds logical, reasonable, and informed, you have responded to informational power. It follows that a person who has access to many facts and arguments and who is articulate in presenting these has a large source of informational power.

Even with a clear understanding of the six bases of power listed here, it is seldom possible to isolate a single power base from which a real-life influence attempt stems. More commonly, an attempt to change someone's attitude or behavior rests on a combination of power bases. For example, the sexual harasser in the opening example is most obviously using coercive power ("You'll never get anywhere in this company if you don't cooperate with me"); he may also be using some reward power ("I can make more opportunities available to you"); and legitimate power ("You are overreacting. You have no right to make such a big fuss over my being friendly to you"). An ability to identify the combination of bases on which a particular influence attempt rests allows for a beginning answer to the question "Why does one person have power with respect to another?"

Strategies of Power Use

An analysis of the bases of power helps to answer the question of why one person has power with respect to another; a different analysis is required to address the question of how such power is exerted. Given potential power with respect to another person, how will the power-holder try to exert influence? Researchers have identified several dimensions along which influence strategies may vary.

Johnson's three dimensions of power use   Social psychologist Paula Johnson (1976) argues that the exertion of influence can vary according to three dimensions: *directness-indirectness*, *competence-helplessness*, and *personal-concrete*. She suggests that not only do these dimensions aid in the general understanding of power use, but that they may provide a key to understanding the differences sometimes observed in the ways women and men use power.

The directness-indirectness dimension refers to the openness of an influence attempt. A direct influence strategy is one in which the influencer does not try to disguise his or her attempt to use power. In contrast, an indirect strategy is covert. The indirect influencer is sneaky; she or he tries to influence without being noticed. These differences show up, for example, between the person who tells his friends he would rather go out for hamburgers than pizza, and the one, who, while claiming no preference, subtly steers the group toward Burger King.

The competence-helplessness dimension distinguishes between the exertion of influence through strength and competence or through weakness. It is easy to see how power use can be based on strength and competence: A person who is physically strong can easily order a weaker person around; and an acknowledged expert should have little trouble influencing someone who feels ignorant of a particular subject. But power exerted through weakness is less obvious. A weakness-based influence style, while less visible than power exerted through strength, is very commonly used. It is used *indirectly* by people who "simply can't" learn to drive and have to be chauffeured everywhere; by people who are so persistently incompetent at any task they are asked to perform against their will that it becomes easier not to ask them for help; or by those who exact guilt and compliance from others with refrains such as "Don't stay home with me just because I'm lonely and miserable. It's not important that I'm unhappy; it's important that you go out and have a good time."

Helplessness is used more *directly* by people who simply ask for help, citing weakness, illness, or incapacity as justification. Often, as Johnson points out, helplessness is a style based on legitimate power. When someone is helpless or ill, others may feel that that person has a right to make certain requests that would otherwise be perceived as illegitimate.

Johnson's third dimension refers to the idea that the *resources on which the exertion of influence rests* can range from the concrete to the very personal. Concrete resources, such as money, knowledge, and physical strength, are relatively independent of particular relationships and so can be used to back up influence attempts in many situations. Personal resources depend for their effectiveness on a specific relationship context. Liking, love, and approval are personal resources. They work as resources only in certain relationships: If individuals do not care whether you like them, your personal resource of affection gives you little basis for influencing them.

Power strategies in intimate relationships   Some researchers have tried specifically to uncover the dimensions of power use that exist in intimate relationships. Toni Falbo and Anne Peplau (1980) examined the influence strategies reported by members of heterosexual, lesbian, and gay couples. They found two dimensions: *directness* (direct-indirect) and *interactiveness* (unilateral-bilateral). As in Paula Johnson's analysis, directness refers to the degree of openness or deviousness that characterizes an influence attempt. The interactiveness dimension refers to the amount of mutual engagement with the partner required in the influence attempt. A very unilateral strategy, such as one individual giving an order to another, refusing to speak to the other person, or just going ahead and doing what one wants, involves no mutual engagement at all; a bilateral strategy, such as arguing, requires a lot of engagement and interchange between two individuals.

Gender and Other Predictors of Influence Strategy

There is a persistent stereotype in Western culture that women and men use different methods to get what they want. Women are portrayed as relying on tears, sex appeal, and general deviousness; men as giving orders, shouting, threatening, and hurting people. Manitoba suffragette Nellie McClung summed up the feminine stereotype in 1915:

> The "womanly way" is to nag and tease. Women have often been told that if they go about it right that they can get anything. They are encouraged to plot and scheme, and deceive, and wheedle, and coax for things. This is womanly and sweet. Of course, if this fails, they still have tears—they can always cry and have hysterics, and raise hob generally, but they must do it in a womanly way. Will the time ever come when the word "feminine" will have in it no trace of trickery? (McClung, 1915, p. 75)

Hidden influence strategy   Many observers have found some truth to the stereotypic portrayal of feminine and masculine influence styles and have linked this pattern to the kinds of resources, or bases of power, controlled by women and men. Anthropologist Michelle Rosaldo (1974) argued that women in many cultures share a common lack, not of all kinds of power, but specifically of the legitimate power of authority. They wield considerable influence behind the scenes, often through their husbands, brothers, and sons, but this influence is both concealed and unacknowledged. The open exercise of power by women has been seen—and in large measure continues to be seen—in many cultures as disruptive and illegitimate. Our history is filled with examples of men reminding women of their great hidden power; the effect of these reminders is to keep women from competing for open positions of power and authority.

Jessie Bernard (1972) makes a similar point about hidden power when writing of marriage in North America. Women do not necessarily have less power than men in the traditional marriage relationship, she argues. Rather, what is necessary is that women *appear* to have less power—so the wife and husband often conspire to hide the wife's power. Again, cultural requirements dictate that the woman's use of power be kept in the dark. Women, because they are women and thus secondary in status to men, and because they are wives and thus commanded to be submissive to their husbands, have little access to authority, at least over their husbands, as a legitimate basis of power. If they are seen to give orders, they are viewed as acting illegitimately.

Structural resources and influence   Gender differences in influence styles may stem also from gender differences in resources other than legitimate authority. Paula Johnson (1976) argues that women's use of power tends to be more indirect, helpless, and personal, while men's is more likely to be direct, competent, and concrete—because women simply have less control than men do over concrete resources and less access to expertise as well as to authority. Research on both the stereotypes of women's and men's power use and actual observations and self-reports of influence strategies provides some support for her arguments. In one study, Johnson (1976) used a questionnaire that outlined a hypothetical situation—one student trying to get another to change opinions on a legal case—and listed 15 influence strategies that might be tried. For each strategy, the respondents were asked to indicate whether they thought the influencer was more likely male or female. Results showed that respondents expected certain kinds of influence strategies of men: coercion based on concrete resources, competent legitimate, expert, and direct informational influence. Strategies using personal reward and sexuality were seen as significantly more characteristic of females. Of all the strategies listed, only the latter two were more strongly expected of females than males.

This pattern, Johnson suggests, indicates that power—all power—is considered essentially a male domain. Men are expected to use the masculine power strategies such as coercion, but they may also use other strategies that seem appropriate. Women are expected to stick to the less aggressive forms of power and are considered out of line if they adopt direct, competent, concrete influence methods.

Not only are women and men expected to use power differently, they actually do use it differently, at least in the kinds of situations that have been studied by social psychologists. In one study, Johnson (1974) gave male and female group leaders an opportunity to choose one of six influence messages to persuade their group to work faster at a given task. Strong differences emerged between males and females in the messages they chose. Males frequently used the message based on expert power, the "do it this way because I know how" type of message. Females avoided that message; they often used the helplessness strategy—the "I need your help" plea—which males, without exception, rejected. The findings in this study also showed that any of the influence methods except helplessness tended to raise the self-esteem of the user. The use of helplessness was linked to a reduction in self-esteem.

It appears that the gender differences in influence styles may be correlated with differences in the amount and types of power bases, or resources, generally available to women and men. This conclusion is strengthened by research on couples that shows feminine influence styles to be characteristic of people, female and male, who do not feel powerful or who have control over fewer resources than their partners. In Falbo and Peplau's (1980) study of power in heterosexual, gay, and lesbian couples, the pattern for all three was for individuals who perceived themselves as having less power than their partners to report more indirect and unilateral influence tactics to get their way; those who saw themselves as having more power than their partners reported more use of direct and bilateral strategies. Among the heterosexual couples participating in the study, the women were more likely than the men to view themselves as having a power disadvantage.

Another study of the relationship between gender and power in intimate relationships shows even more clearly that stereotypically feminine influence strategies are correlated with a lack of control over resources. These researchers studied a cross section of adults in long-term cross-sex and same-sex relationships in order to determine the relative importance to influence styles of gender, gender-role orientation (femininity, masculinity), control over structural resources (money, education, age), physical attractiveness and dependence on the relationship (Howard, Blumstein, & Schwartz, 1986). They identified six types of influence tactics: *manipulation* (dropping hints, flattering, behaving seductively); *supplication* (pleading, crying, acting ill or helpless); *bullying* (threatening, insulting, becoming violent); *autocracy* (insisting, claiming greater knowledge, asserting authority); *disengagement* (sulking, leaving the scene); and *bargaining* (reasoning, offering to compromise).

Manipulation and supplication represent the stereotypically feminine "weak" strategies of indirectness and helplessness; bullying and autocracy are stereotypically "strong" strategies based on coercion and expertise, usually associated with males. The researchers predicted that the use of the weak strategies would be linked to being female, to femininity, to having less structural power than and being more dependent on the relationship than the partner. They found that having control of fewer resources, such as having less income or seeing oneself as less attractive than one's partner and being more dependent on the relationship were linked to the use of weaker power strategies, as was femininity.

Target gender as a predictor of influence   A particularly striking finding in this study emerged: There was no relationship between the influencer's sex and her or his influence tactics, but there *was* a strong relationship between influence tactics and the sex of the target of influence. Both females and males with male partners were more likely to report using the weak influence strategies than were females and males with female partners. In other words, people tended to use weak influence strategies on males more often than on females. These effects of the partner's gender were not explainable by differences in structural power; the target's gender had an effect over and above other measured sources of power and level of dependence. The authors of the paper conclude that there is power associated with being male that is "expressed in behavior that elicits weak strategies from one's partner" (Howard et al, 1986; p. 107).

The above study suggests that men's capacity to elicit deferent behavior cannot be completely explained by their access to such concrete resources as income or by their partners' dependence on the relationship. Why and how, then, do men elicit weak rather than strong influence strategies from their intimate partners? One possibility is the implicit threat of aggression—temper tantrums or physical violence—more associated with men than with women. People may be more fearful of provoking a man than a woman by using a strong influence strategy. Another possibility: The legitimate power that comes with being male in our society gives men an aura of confidence that reduces the likelihood others will try strong influence strategies on them.

Early childhood influences   Psychologists have observed that patterns of gender differences in influence strategies and males' resistance to influence begin early in childhood. Even among toddlers, girls paired with male playmates behave more passively than do girls paired with other girls or than boys paired with either girls or boys. Vocal prohibitions (such as "Stop! Don't do that!") are most likely to be ignored when addressed to a boy by a girl (Jacklin & Maccoby, 1978). Among preschoolers, boys make a greater number of influence attempts on their male and female peers than girls do, mainly because boys use a lot more direct requests and orders than girls (Serbin, Sprafkin, Elman, & Doyle, 1982). Between the ages of three and five years, boys become increasingly likely to use direct influence attempts, such as ordering a peer to "Give me the truck," announcing "You have to give me the truck," or specifying roles, as in "Pretend you're the doctor." Across the same ages, girls become more likely to use indirect requests, in which either the request is implied rather than clearly spelled out ("I need the truck"), or it is bracketed in polite phrases ("May I please have the truck?"). Furthermore, between the ages of three and five, boys become less and less responsive to peer influence attempts, particularly indirect requests, whereas girls' responsiveness to influence attempts remains stable. When girls do use direct influence strategies, they are more effective with other girls than with boys—an experience that helps to perpetuate both the high levels of same-sex play found in preschool classrooms and the development of increasingly gender-differentiated verbal social influence styles.

It is clear that girls learn very early that they are ineffective influencers with respect to boys; they seem to retreat toward the influence styles (indirect, polite) and contexts (other females) that do work for them. For girls who do not retreat into accepted styles, there are problems ahead. A study of first and second graders shows that reactions to power holders differ in female and male groups. Boys at the top of their dominance hierarchy were liked and accepted by their same-sex peers; powerful girls were disliked and rejected (Jones, 1983). The habits of deference to males and the norms that permit males but not females to be powerful in certain ways have their foundations in these early experiences.

Legitimacy as a predictor of influence strategy   The social norms that grant males more perceived legitimacy than women in many situations appear to play a key role in creating the gender differences in influence styles that sometimes appear. Consider an experimental study of influence strategies (Cann, 1979). The researcher placed women and men in a simulated work situation; they were to supervise workers in another room and were allowed to communicate with them by written messages. The supervisors were allowed to threaten and/or reward the workers and were instructed simply to influence them to increase production. Cann found that male and female supervisors did not differ in the methods they used in this simulation; both genders relied heavily on persuasion and reward. However, men made more attempts to influence than women did, and men were also more likely than women to view their own behavior as powerful and aggressive. At the end of the experiment, the women indicated a significantly lower desire than the men to play the role of manager again.

In Cann's study, which provided both women and men with equally legitimate positions of authority from which to exert influence, no gender differences in influence strategies were found. In the real world, however, such equality is seldom present. Men are routinely ascribed higher status than women. Husbands are regularly viewed as heads of households. Leadership positions in organizations—from businesses to armies to nations—are usually filled by men. These positions tend to reinforce men's higher status; men are often viewed as superior to and more informed, more intelligent, more capable, and more logical than women. Consequently, when a man is trying to influence a woman, he is often operating from a position of explicit authority or implicit superiority. A woman trying to influence a man is often working from a subordinate position. Even when women are given positions of authority over men, the incongruity in status and the conflict with social norms for using power are often enough to make everyone uncomfortable. Women may try to reduce the discomfort by being unobtrusive in their authority roles. This scenario fits the Cann study, where women supervisors expressed a lack of comfort in their roles and used fewer influence attempts than men did.

In most influence situations, the more legitimate power the influencer holds, the more direct she or he is able to be in making influence attempts. Whether the legitimacy stems from position, role, social norms, or previous agreements, one can be more open about a demand or request when feeling secure in one's right to make it. Since women (unless they are using legitimate helplessness) are so often backed by less legitimate power than men, their frequent reliance on indirect influence methods is not surprising. But what if the social situation were reversed? In a situation where women had legitimacy on their side, would men employ indirect influence techniques? Let's look at a hypothetical example: Over the past five years, a woman has worked to put her husband through graduate school. Now he has a good job; according to a previous agreement, it is her turn to pursue advanced training in her own field. The husband, happy enough with their pact when it was made five years ago, now is dissatisfied with the wife's plans. He feels they can now afford to have a family. He likes the image of himself as a successful professional, coming home at the end of the day to a happy wife, a clean house, and two or three adoring children. Yet, if he tries to influence his wife in this traditional direction now, the normal legitimacy that such a demand would have (after all, motherhood is a strongly socially endorsed ideal for women) would be lacking because of their original agreement. Therefore, the husband may adopt very indirect influence methods. While verbally reinforcing her plans and their agreement, he may at the same time begin to speak sadly and longingly of babies in her presence, joke pointedly with her mother about her daughter's lack of maternal instinct, and leave conspicuously on the coffee table the latest magazine article on the dangers of putting off childbearing. If confronted, he is likely to deny, with an air of injured innocence, any attempt to influence her. After all, fair is fair, and they do have an agreement.

If the above scenario sounds familiar, it may be because variations on it are being played out in countless North American families as women and men struggle to redefine their roles or to find an acceptable balance between the aspirations of both members of a couple. Women returning to school or paid work after many years of staying home to look after their families often speak bitterly about husbands and children who verbally support and reinforce their efforts, but who indirectly sabotage them in countless ways: by refusing to adjust the family vacation schedule to mother's new needs, by making a scene about how dirty the house is on the night before her crucial exam, by being totally incompetent at any housework they are asked to do, by insisting that PTA meetings and baking cookies for the class are still mother's jobs, and by, in innumerable ways, laying on guilt about neglected family responsibilities.

These are situations where legitimacy is ambiguous. The woman may feel tentative in her new role and anxious not to let her family suffer, even though she thinks she has made a legitimate decision. The man may be eager to be fair and reasonable but unhappy about the disruption in his lifestyle. The man feels he cannot assert his wishes openly because they are unfair and, hence, illegitimate. The woman, feeling that her actions are not only reasonable but also agreed to by her partner, is confused and angered by the double messages she receives from him. Such situations, if not dealt with constructively, lead to widening rifts between the partners.

The above example shows that the major determinants of influence style—and gender differences in style—are likely to be situational, and that one very important aspect of the situation is the perceived legitimacy of the influence attempt. Another crucial aspect of the situation, one that often interacts with legitimacy, is the relationship between the influencer and the person to whom the influence attempt is directed. In a family, for instance, a woman may feel that although her status gives her little legitimate authority in dealing with her husband, it does give her considerable authority in relation to her children. The influence strategies she uses with her husband and children may differ markedly.

The gender-related patterns of influence strategies that have been discussed here have been studied mainly for North American, white adults. When the scope of investigation is widened to include culture as well as gender, the findings underline just how strong is the effect of social norms on the way power is used. In a study examining power strategy use in intimate relationships of women and men in Mexico and the United States, the overall association of culture with influence strategies was much greater than the association between gender and such strategies (Belk, Snell, Garcia-Falconi, Hernandez-Sanchez, Hargrove, & Holtzman, 1988). Mexican women and men were more likely than their American counterparts to use bilateral influence strategies (strategies that require mutual engagement and interchange) with their intimate partners—a finding that may be due to the high level of community and cooperation that characterizes Mexican families. As noted in the discussion of legitimacy above, social norms have a strong effect on the strategies people use to influence one another.

Effects of Influence Strategies on Their Users

It is rare for a behavior to have only a single, intended consequence. Influence-directed activities may have consequences, not only in terms of gaining compliance, but also in terms of influencers' self-perception, satisfaction, and public image. The continual reliance on indirect forms of power may disguise influence potential only too well. As Johnson (1976) notes, even though indirect influencers may generally get their way, others, not seeing them as the source of the influence, may not view them or treat them as powerful. Despite indirect influencers' success at getting their way, they do not gain in status and may not even gain in self-esteem. The effective direct influencers, on the other hand, may reap rewards in respect, admiration, and increased self-esteem because they are regarded and treated as powerful.

Loss of others' good opinion   The use of helplessness to influence others carries dangers. The person who acts helpless and weak much of the time may be regarded with contempt or resentment, even by those she or he influences. The price of relying on this type of influence may be chronic low self-esteem. There are also dangers in too much use of competence and strength as a style of influence. The person who has never shown weakness may be disbelieved rather than helped if she or he ever does have to influence from a position of helplessness.

Loss of future power resources   The use of personal resources such as affection and approval as a main influence base may leave the influencer feeling somewhat insecure, since personal resources are effective only with certain people in certain relationships. If an individual is forced to deal with new people, or if the character of the relationship changes, power based on personal resources may literally evaporate. Power based on concrete resources is generally effective in a wide variety of situations, but there too the power stems only from the perceived value of the resources. A person to whom money is unimportant cannot be bribed.

Besides affecting how the influencer feels, the ways in which power is used may actually increase or undermine resources for future power use. It is dangerous, for example, to use threats or promises that cannot be fulfilled. The credibility lost on these occasions reduces the power of the influencer because it takes the teeth out of future threats and promises. It is also inadvisable to try to extend legitimate power outside the range for which it is prescribed. An employer who tries to dictate behavior in an employee's personal life may be seen as overstepping legitimate authority. This would have the effect of decreasing the employer's legitimate power and attractiveness. Also, it is possible that someone who exerts more power than is necessary to gain a desired degree of compliance will be disliked, leading ultimately to a decrease in power.

Stereotyping of influencer   Finally, the reliance by certain groups on particular power tactics may have long-range social consequences in terms of stereotyping and trust. The politician who promises lower taxes and the salesperson who insists that "that outfit is you" are acting so much within the stereotypes of how such people exert influence that sincerity is automatically doubted—at least by anyone inclined to be skeptical. People who become known as manipulators quickly lose the trust of their colleagues, and perhaps it is this tendency that is partially responsible for the stereotype that women do not trust other women. Women, who have traditionally had few of the resources provided by money, authority, or expertise have been taught to be indirect, helpless, and even seductive in their attempts to influence men. Such influence tactics by women are often effective with men taught to believe that deference and flattery from women are their due and who like to feel that women are dependent on them. However, when women use these influence methods on other women, they are simply not as effective, and they breed mistrust. Women who rely heavily on indirect, personal types of influence may prefer and seek out the company of men because they know how to operate successfully with them. This behavior may cause resentment among other women: It reinforces a stereotype of women as dependent and/or manipulative, thus undermining their own efforts to deal directly and competently with men; it implies that women are not worthwhile companions.

An understanding of the implications of using various types of power is crucial not just to an understanding of the relationships between women and men, but also to an understanding of relationships among women. Such knowledge is also crucial for comprehending male-male relationships; if men accept the strong, aggressive power stereotype, they may be unable to communicate with one another about doubts, uncertainties, vulnerabilities, and weaknesses.

CONCLUSION: GENDER AND INTERPERSONAL INFLUENCE

The ability of one person to influence another is most easily understood to result from the ability to control the other's outcomes. In any social exchange, each person has some control over the outcomes of the other. The principle of least interest predicts that the person who is the least dependent on the other for rewards—the one who needs the exchange or the relationship least—will have the most power.

Power to influence others can rest on one or more of the bases of reward, coercion, legitimacy, expertise, personal or reference group attraction, and information. Influence can be exerted in a number of ways, many of them hidden and not at all apparent at first glance. A belief exists that women and men use power differently, and some research supports this stereotype. However, it is increasingly clear that an extremely important factor in how influence is wielded lies in the social environment and the precariousness of the influencer's position in that environment. For instance, for both women and men, it is difficult to be direct and outspoken in trying to influence others if one has no accepted legitimate claim on their compliance. When women are trying to influence men, they are often in just such a precarious position.

There is reason to think that the type of influence style a person adopts has consequences not only for influence effectiveness, but also for self-esteem and social relationships. The strategies that seem to take the largest toll in self-esteem are the indirect, helpless strategies that are stereotypically attributed to women. If they are in the position to do so, women should break out of the mold of the "womanly" influence methods that build on their perceived incompetence and work instead to develop influence styles that reinforce their feelings and appearance of competence.

Even people who are equally effective at influencing others may differ in how powerful they actually feel, as discussed in the next chapter.

CHAPTER FIVE

Feeling Powerful: The Sense of Competence and Effectiveness

I n her autobiography, prolific mystery writer Agatha Christie (1977) describes the excitement she and her friends felt as young girls standing on the edge of adulthood and contemplating the future:

The real excitement of being a girl—of being, that is, a woman in embryo—was that life was such a wonderful gamble. *You didn't know what was going to happen to you.* That was what made being a woman so exciting. No worry about what you should be or do—Biology would decide. You were waiting for The Man, and when the man came, he would change your entire life. You can say what you like, that is an exciting point of view to hold at the threshold of life. What will happen? . . . The whole world was open to you—not open to your *choice*, but open to what Fate *brought* you. You might marry *anyone*; you might, of course, marry a drunkard or be very unhappy, but that only heightened the general feeling of excitement. (p. 131)

The experience Christie describes so eloquently is one of great possibilities but little power. The girl feels that her life is determined by fate, not by any actions she herself may take. It is a stance that will lead her to avoid making choices based on her own preferences, her own needs. It is a stance that will lead her to wait to see what happens to her rather than trying to make things happen. She does not immediately recognize it as such, but it is a feeling of powerlessness.

Observation tells us that holding power in some objective sense—controlling structural resources, having expertise and competence—is not always correlated with the individual's feelings of powerfulness.

Some people underestimate their own power, or literally give their power away in situations where they feel unable to use it. They defer to others out of habit rather than necessity. Other individuals feel more effective than they really are and make grandiose power plays that end in disaster. An understanding of the processes of power requires that we examine not just the obvious levels of power—its exertion through social influence strategies—but also the level that Minton (1967) referred to as "latent power"—individual feelings of power and readiness to use social influence.

There are many indications that gender is an important factor at the latent level of power. For example, when Eleanor Maccoby and Carol Jacklin (1974) reviewed the psychological research on male-female differences, they found that studies consistently showed that men and boys described themselves as more powerful and stronger than did girls and women. Similarly, psychological research using questionnaire measures of "locus of control" indicate that by college age and beyond, women, on average, describe themselves as feeling somewhat more externally controlled than men do; men are more likely than women to feel a sense of *internal* control—a belief that they control their own fate.

The implications of believing that one's fate is controlled by external forces rather than by one's own efforts are important. Research has shown that if, in a specific situation, a person is made to feel that she or he has no control over what happens, she or he will eventually stop trying to influence the situation. This phenomenon has been called "learned helplessness" (Seligman, 1975). Unfortunately, learned helplessness tends to extend beyond the specific situation in which it was learned. This happens when the person attributes a particular failure to a global, or general, rather than a specific, cause (Abramson, Seligman, & Teasdale, 1978). The individual is left with a feeling of ineffectiveness and an unwillingness to try to control outcomes in other situations. For example, someone who repeatedly fails in the attempt to find employment may attribute the failure to an inability to appear competent to others, rather than to difficulties specific to the particular unsuccessful attempts, such as a financial recession or too many people in that particular field. The person may gradually develop a lack of self-confidence. A decrease in self-confidence may overlap other areas, such as relations with others and decision-making. This effect is all the more probable if the individual believes that the inability to appear competent is not related to her or his qualifications or self-presentation, but rather to something arbitrary and unchangeable such as her or his sex, race, age, or appearance. In the latter case, the individual sees the outcomes as neither specific to the situation nor related to her or his own actions or achievement—a prime condition for the development of learned helplessness. Learned helplessness is, furthermore, a possible antecedent of depression—an affliction from which women are now known to suffer at higher rates than men (Nolen-Hoeksma, 1987; Weissman & Klerman, 1977).

SOCIALIZATION TOWARD HELPLESSNESS

The opening example of this chapter suggests that it is more convenient for male members of a society if young women are socialized to turn their fates over to others and to wait to see what happens rather than to exert too much active control over their own lives. Why might it be more convenient? For one thing, only the male half of the population has to make serious long-range career decisions while the female half simply accommodates to these decisions. This means less competition for men in sought-after positions, less of the pulling in different directions that strains two-career marriages, more likelihood that women will willingly adapt their lives, their work, their interests to the presence of children so that men don't have to. It means that society does not have to concern itself with daycare, parental leave, or the needs of dual-earner couples. Whether these concerns are acknowledged and articulated or not, they seem to underscore one of the major dimensions on which the socialization of females and males differs from childhood onward: Females, in contrast to males, are taught that their actions *do not make a difference.*

Childhood Learning about Control

Psychologist Jeanne Block (1984), summarizing a lifetime of research into the socialization of girls and boys, characterized the difference most aptly: Girls, she said, were subjected to a pattern of socialization that encouraged them to develop *roots*, boys were taught to develop *wings.* Girls, she said, were given few chances to master the environment, and their socialization tended toward "fostering proximity, discouraging independent problem solving by premature or excessive intervention, restricting exploration, and discouraging active play" (p. 111). Boys were encouraged to "develop a premise system that presumes or anticipates mastery, efficacy, and instrumental competence" (p. 131). A look at recent research supports Block's claim: Parents and teachers, often unwittingly, teach girls not to try things (because their efforts don't make any difference) and not to speak (because no one will pay serious attention to them). Boys, by contrast, are taught clearly that their outcomes are contingent on their own efforts and that their concerns are taken seriously by adults.

Parents   In one study (Frankel & Rollins, 1983), parents were observed while working with their six-year-old children on jigsaw-puzzle and memory tasks. The observers noted that the parents of sons and daughters used different strategies: parents of sons were more likely to suggest general problem-solving strategies and let the boy figure out how to apply them to the task at hand; parents of girls were more likely to suggest specific solutions rather than waiting for their daughters to work out the solutions themselves. With a daughter, parents were more likely to work cooperatively; with a son, they were more likely to remain physically uninvolved but to offer praise for good performance and scolding for inattention to the task. What the parents in this study seemed to be communicating to their children is that it is more important for the sons than for the daughters to learn to solve this particular problem and others like it, and that they do it, as far as possible, on their own.

Although parents in various cultural groups differ in the rules they attach to gender, it is not unusual to find that parents, particularly fathers, pay more attention to boys than girls; fathers emphasize cooperation and nurturance more for girls and achievement and autonomy more for boys. For example, Phyllis Bronstein (1984) showed, in a study of Mexican families, that when interacting with their school-aged children, fathers listened more to boys than to girls and were more likely to show boys than girls how to do things. These fathers treated their daughters especially gently, but they seldom gave them their full attention and were quick to impose opinions on them. They were communicating to their children that what boys have to say is more important than what girls have to say, and that boys are more capable than girls of learning new skills.

Teachers   The message that boys are to be taken more seriously than girls, that boys are more capable than girls, and that boys' actions are more likely than those of girls to have an effect is driven home not just by parents but by teachers; and in a society where schools reflect predominantly white middle-class values, it is these values that are enforced in the different treatment of girls and boys. Even preschool teachers, apparently unaware of the different treatment they hand out, pay more attention to boys and respond more to boys who act aggressive and to girls who act dependent (Serbin & O'Leary, 1975). These researchers also found that teachers actually teach boys more than they teach girls, with boys twice as likely as girls to receive individual instruction in how to do things. For example, when children in one classroom were making paper baskets, the teacher circulated through the room, helping each child with the task of attaching handles to the basket. With boys, she held the handle in place and allowed the child to staple it himself; with girls, unless the child spontaneously stapled the handle herself, the teacher took the basket and stapled it for her rather than showing her how to do it.

Feedback in elementary school classrooms is dispensed differently to boys and girls—and the differences reinforce feelings of mastery and control in boys and helplessness in girls. Teachers allow boys to talk and to interrupt them more than they do girls, thus ensuring that more time will be spent on boys' than on girls' questions and that children will learn that male concerns take first priority. Teachers interact with boys more than with girls and call on them more often for answers (Brophy, 1985). This pattern of greater teacher interaction with boys than with girls extends into high school and includes non-academic interactions (joking, informal talks) as well as academic (Becker, 1981). Boys receive more criticism than girls, but that criticism is usually directed toward disruptive behavior, sloppiness, or not trying hard enough rather than incompetence. Girls receive less criticism, but what criticism they do receive is directed toward their academic mistakes. For praise, the reverse is true: Boys tend to be praised for good academic performance, girls for neatness, good conduct, or compliance (Dweck, Davidson, Nelson, & Enna, 1978). (The above researchers noted, in fact, that even when girls gave the wrong answer, they were sometimes not given negative feedback about the incorrectness of the answer, but *were* given positive feedback about non-intellectual aspects of the answer such as their delivery.) When boys make mistakes, they are encouraged to keep trying until they get the answer right; girls are more often told not to worry about a mistake, and teachers spend less time with them suggesting new approaches or encouraging them to keep trying (Sadker & Sadker, 1985). Furthermore, teachers' judgments of girls' intellectual competence is predicted by girls' compliance to the teacher; however, teacher ratings of boys' competence is unrelated to compliance (Gold, Crombie, & Noble, 1987).

These findings add up to a pattern in which girls are rewarded for being good and boys are rewarded for trying hard. Boys learn that failure is simply a step on the road to learning something; girls learn that failure means they are incompetent. By first grade, girls and boys have learned different things about what is important in school: Boys' academic self-concept includes a strong focus on being able to learn quickly; girls are focused on the importance of obeying the rules and being honest (Entwisle, Alexander, Pallas, & Cadigan, 1987). Social psychologist Carol Dweck (1986) suggests that the end result of all this is that girls may be more likely to develop a "performance"-based achievement motivation, whereas boys may tend to develop a "learning"-based motivation. In other words, girls learn that it is important to demonstrate their ability by performing well; when this orientation is combined with low confidence, girls learn to avoid challenging tasks because failure threatens their own and others' opinions of their ability. Boys learn to think of their skills as improvable and to focus on that possibility of improvement as a goal. Because they are rewarded for trying, they learn, regardless of their confidence level, to appreciate challenging tasks, to respond to a difficult task with persistence, and to regard failure as a sign that they are not trying hard enough. In other words, boys learn that their efforts make a difference, that by trying harder they can master a difficult situation. Although girls generally get better grades than boys, boys approach most new academic tasks with more confidence than girls (Kimball, 1989). What boys learn, in effect, is that they are potentially powerful.

Race Makes No Difference

The role of teachers as (perhaps unwitting) enforcers of white middle-class conceptions of gender roles is demonstrated dramatically in a pair of studies by Jacqueline Irvine (1985; 1986). Among elementary school students, Irvine found that white girls received significantly less total communication from teachers than did white boys or African-American girls and boys. When she examined teacher-student interactions across grade levels, it became clear that African-American girls were being socialized by their teachers to join their white sisters in invisibility. In the first two grades, African-American girls did not receive less feedback from the teacher than did their male counterparts; by grades three through five, however, the African-American girls fit the pattern of inconspicuousness to the teacher that had characterized the white girls from the beginning. Irvine suggests that it is because African-American girls are not socialized to the passive and submissive behavior encouraged in white girls that they receive more teacher attention than do white girls in the early grades. However, as the African-American girls move from lower to upper elementary school grades, there is a significant decline in the total amount of teacher feedback they receive, in the amount of positive teacher feedback they receive, and in the number of opportunities they are given to respond in class. As Irvine (1986) notes, "Black female students present an active, interacting and initiating profile in the early grades but join their white female counterparts in the later grades in what appears to be traditional female sex role behaviors" (p. 20). It appears to be no exaggeration to say that schools socialize girls toward helplessness.

HELPLESSNESS VS. EFFECTIVENESS

The Structure of Self-Image

The socialization of an individual toward helplessness rather than effectiveness obviously affects not only that individual's behavior, but more importantly, her or his view of that behavior. As noted in the discussion of gender in the classroom, the key to developing a sense of mastery lies not so much in the amount of success or failure achieved, but in the interpretation of that success and failure. As children or adults, how we think about ourselves and our actions often has more impact on our experience than does the actual situation. We may sometimes act in a way that causes others to label us as powerful and competent at the same time that we feel weak and insecure. While the labels applied by others can have a powerful effect, the labels we construct for ourselves often prevail in the face of contrary opinions. Such self-image labels tend to be self-perpetuating; they form a framework within which we explain our actions. Any change in our power relationships presumes a shift in the kinds of images we form of ourselves and others and in the causes to which we attribute our and others' actions.

People frequently explain their successes and failures by invoking one or some combination of the following four causes: ability, effort, luck, and the difficulty of the task (Weiner, Frieze, Kukla, Reed, Rest, and Rosenbaum, 1971). These causes vary according to how internal to the individual, stable, and intentional they are seen to be. Ability and effort are considered internal factors, originating within the individual. Luck and task difficulty are external. Ability and task difficulty are relatively stable and unchanging. Luck and effort are unstable, subject to large fluctuations. Effort is an intentional factor, controlled to some extent by the individual. Ability, luck, and task difficulty are seen to operate without the person's choice.

Accepting one of the above reasons as an explanation for one's own success or failure has implications both for how one experiences the event and for one's self-image. It is difficult for someone to maintain a self-image of power and effectiveness if her or his successes are continually attributed to unintentional or external causes. Irene Frieze (1975) explains that a person feels maximum pride and security in an achievement if that achievement is seen to be the result of the internal, stable factor of ability; whereas success attributed to external factors brings less pride. She also points out that if lack of ability is seen as the cause of a failure, there is little tendency to try again because the person has little reason to believe that continued effort will change failure to success. Frieze argues that high self-esteem is theoretically associated with accepting internal, stable reasons for one's success and external or unstable reasons for failure.

As seen in the discussion of the ways parents and teachers respond to the achievement attempts of girls and boys, strong differences often appear in the way the two groups of children are taught to respond to failure—and these differences parallel those outlined by Frieze as associated with low and high self-esteem. Boys, in the pattern of high self-esteem, are taught to attribute, or assign, failure to lack of effort; girls, in the pattern of low self-esteem, are left to attribute failure to a lack of ability. It is not surprising that some studies suggest the presence of similar gender differences in attribution of, or accounting for, causes of success and failure up to college age (Kimball, 1989). Men are found to rely heavily on *ability* to explain success, and on unstable or external factors to explain failure; women appear to rely more on *effort* and on external reasons to explain success and on lack of ability to explain failure.

All this suggests that women and men, even under conditions of equal success, often do not experience success in the same way. Men have learned to claim credit for success and to view it as a source of pride. Women have learned to view success as less susceptible to their own control and, therefore, as less reliable and worthy of praise. A consideration of how success is interpreted by the individual allows us to understand how that person can maintain a self-image of weakness and powerlessness even when her or his behavior appears to others to be a demonstration of achievement, skill, and strength. That such an individual would, in North America, most likely be female, is a reasonable conclusion from the research on attribution patterns.

Changing Patterns of Attribution

Is it possible to change the pattern of attributing causes for success and failure? We know that thoughts, feelings, and behaviors are intertwined: A change in thoughts or feelings can alter behavior; a change in behavior can cause a shift in thoughts and feelings. One way to change patterns of attribution is to re-educate people in ways of interpreting their outcomes; and certain behavioral changes make new interpretations easier. If the object is for women to feel more effective and powerful, two specific types of behavioral change may be useful: increasing the use of direct styles of interpersonal power, and developing special abilities and competence.

Johnson's (1976) analysis of the advantages and disadvantages of different power strategies, discussed in Chapter Four, suggest that the *way* one exercises power is closely linked to how powerful one feels. She argues that the indirect power user does not receive credit for the influence that she or he exerts because that power is hidden. Thus, the indirect influencer, while quietly effective, continues to be viewed and treated by others as powerless. This individual's powerless image in the eyes of others has ramifications for her or his *self*-image: It is difficult to feel powerful when those around you regard you as a jellyfish. It seems obvious that the person who wishes to feel more powerful must try to be more open or direct in influence situations. The sensible way to begin is by being especially open and direct in situations where one is relatively sure of being effective. Openness also includes taking proper credit, in public, for the successful use of influence. The individual who argues convincingly to sway a committee to a particular point of view, and who is later congratulated on being brilliantly persuasive, is well advised to accept the compliment rather than pooh-pooh it. In many situations, modesty is the enemy of power.

Assertiveness training has been touted as a way of learning how to be more direct in interpersonal influence. Such training supports direct, honest, non-aggressive expression of one's desires in social interactions. Trainees are given practice in saying "no" firmly, and are taught techniques for making requests, lodging complaints, and stating opinions clearly and unwaveringly. Such training gives the individual both motivation and methods for being more direct as an influencer. It may also provide an expanded vision of the possibilities in relationships with other people. It is not, however, a panacea. Effective influence depends not only on the influencer's behavior, but also on the context of that behavior.

Unfortunately, although there seems to be much to gain by using direct instead of indirect power, its use by women and members of other low-status groups is often clouded by a "catch-22." Low-status people who try openly to exert power are often misinterpreted, or they are characterized as "uppity" and are therefore easily disregarded and disliked. For example, a woman who uses nonverbal cues associated with power may be seen as communicating sexual availability rather than power. And rare is the outspoken feminist who has not experienced rejection and careless dismissal of her opinions when making a direct attempt to influence an unreceptive audience.

For a person in a relatively low-status position, such as a secretary in a large office or a teller in a bank, open influence attempts are more difficult and risky than they are for people in high-status positions in the same contexts. Women often occupy such low-status positions at work— where the self-image benefits of being direct are balanced by the economic disadvantages of being fired or overlooked for promotion. Thus, for women, the use of more direct influence methods is not a simple solution to overcoming a sense of powerlessness. While women may benefit from developing more direct influence styles, they should also continue to be sensitive to the context in which they try to exercise their influence. As many women and members of other low-status groups are aware, there are a multitude of problems in trying to exert direct influence from a position of relative powerlessness. It is for this reason that feminists and other activist groups emphasize the necessity of changing the structure of organizations rather than merely seeking individual solutions to the problem of powerlessness.

Another type of behavior that builds a sense of power is the development of special competencies and strengths. Some have suggested that this may hold especially true in the realm of *physical* strength; that a sense of physical weakness or vulnerability contributes to a more general sense of powerlessness. If the latter notion is correct, women, who have historically been labeled the "weaker sex" and have been discouraged from developing their physical capacities for strength, speed, and endurance, have much to gain by rejecting this old definition. Kathryn Lance (1978) is one of many who has argued that, by building physical strength, women can derive the psychological benefits of increased security, a lessening of physical fear and the sense of being a potential victim, and a general increase in confidence and sense of control. In many respects, one's physical capacities provide one's most basic sense of power; it makes little sense to ignore the potential contribution of those capacities to feelings of power or powerlessness. Of course, as some researchers have found, even a superb athlete can attribute success in competition to external factors (McHugh, Duquin, & Frieze, 1977). But for those women who are able to build their strength and stamina to lift heavier weights or run increased distances, it becomes difficult to attribute these new-found capabilities to anything but the internal cause of increased strength brought about by their own determined efforts.

FREEDOM AND PERSONAL RESPONSIBILITY

The Importance of Choice

Implicit in any definition of power is that it includes a certain freedom to act and to decide how to act. Powerlessness implies a situation in which one has no choices, but is acted upon by external forces. We characterize learned helplessness as the feeling of a person who is convinced that she or he can make no impact on a situation. The helpless feelings may stem from a sense that regardless of the actions one takes, one can make no difference to what happens. There are times, however, when one's very freedom to *choose* a particular action—whether or not it appears likely to make a difference—is threatened by some external force. For example, a person may be offered a job but may be urged strongly by a spouse not to take it, as in the case of a homemaker who wants to return to paid work but whose husband objects. Here, the initial reaction may not be helplessness (unless the woman has learned through long experience that her husband is immovable once he makes up his mind), but rather *reactance*.

Reactance theory (Brehm, 1966) argues that people are motivated to protect their behavioral freedom if it is threatened. People may react against a threat to their perceived freedom to choose a particular behavior in several ways: by trying to reassert or regain the threatened freedom, by anger and hostility toward the person or institution threatening the freedom, and/or by wanting and valuing the threatened choice more than they did before the threat. The theory explains why perceived rights and freedoms are taken for granted until it appears they may be taken away. For example, hundreds of thousands of Americans marched on Washington in April of 1989 in an unprecedented show of public support for women's legal right to choose abortion because that right appeared to be strongly threatened by an upcoming court case. For reactance to occur, the person must believe that she or he has the freedom or right to choose the threatened alternative. If the homemaker in the first example has always felt that accepting paid employment is not her right but only a privilege that can be granted or not by her husband, she will probably experience helplessness rather than reactance in the face of her husband's objections. If a woman has always felt that she has no moral right to terminate a pregnancy, however unwanted, she will not feel reactance at the prospect of losing her legal right to do so.

Since reactance is often a response to an attempt at social influence, examining it is important to the question of power. When someone tries to influence another, what method of influence is likely to produce the most reactance (i.e., the most digging in of heels) and hence the least influence? To what extent does compliance with an influence attempt relate to feelings of power and powerlessness? Everyone knows from experience that different styles of influence, different ways of using power to get the same thing, produce different reactions in the person toward whom the influence is directed. From the perspective of the would-be influencer, the worst reaction to an influence attempt is that the target person becomes offended or suspicious and therefore more stubbornly resistant to influence.

Social psychologists Judith Rodin and Irving Janis (1979) suggest that in some circumstances the person who is the target of expert and coercive power use may experience feelings of lessening personal control. This person may feel a threat to freedom of action and may be motivated to regain control by disregarding or flouting the instructions or advice of the influencer. According to Rodin and Janis, such a reaction may be the reason why large numbers of patients do not follow the advice of their physicians. Furthermore, these researchers note, when people comply in response to the exertion of expert, coercive, or reward power, they tend to attribute their compliance to external reasons. They are less likely, in these circumstances, to see themselves as having personal responsibility for or control over their actions. Thus, these methods of influence seem to encourage a sense of powerlessness in the target person in some situations.

Referent Power

The insights of Rodin and Janis apply to relationships other than that of doctor-patient. In particular, teachers searching for ways to encourage students to take responsibility for their own learning, and professors struggling to define a feminist pedagogy that de-emphasizes the power of professor over student and focuses on the empowerment of the student might wish to pay close attention to the styles of influence they rely on. Are there ways of influencing people that do not leave those people feeling a loss of freedom, control, and personal responsibility? Social psychologists have demonstrated that if the external incentive used to convince people to perform a behavior is very small, the convinced people are likely to see themselves as having internal, or their own, not someone else's, reasons for their actions. From a cynical perspective, such findings imply that if one gives people the illusion that they have choices—that they are not being bossed, coerced, or bribed—while at the same time channeling them in subtle and careful ways toward a particular decision or behavior, one can influence them without producing a sense of either reactance or helplessness (e.g., saying "Do it the way you want," while subtly making one option particularly unappealing). This method involves an indirect or manipulative style of power use. On the other hand, the influencer can be direct but noncoercive, giving the other person a real rather than an illusory choice (e.g., saying "I don't advise doing it that way, but I will support whatever decision you make"). In this case, the influencer's success rate may be lower, but the person to whom influence is directed does not feel diminished in freedom, control, or responsibility, regardless of the outcome.

Rodin and Janis suggest that the use of referent power, which is based on seeing the power holder as likeable and admirable, is unlikely to threaten feelings of internal control. If I do something that you ask of me because I like and respect you, then I see myself as acting because of my internal feelings rather than any external limits. Although you have influenced me, I do not see myself as being controlled; I see myself as choosing to do something for someone whom I like and admire. Of course, if you have tried to induce my feelings of liking and admiration specifically to have this power over me, the process becomes, in its own way, a manipulation.

What does all this mean with respect to female-male power relationships? For one thing, it helps explain the perpetuation and effects of the gender differences in influence styles that occur in some situations. In certain relationship situations, because of power differences and/or differences in habits of interacting with others, women rely more heavily on indirect, personal strategies of influence; men are more likely to be direct and concrete. It is as if women unconsciously try to avoid provoking reactance in the other person when exercising influence, while men make no such effort. This analysis is oversimplified, yet it does give some insight into why members of two groups who differ in access to resources may differ in power strategies. The individual who has access to many resources with which to back up demands can afford to be direct enough to arouse anger, hostility, or other reactions. The person who has little or no access to concrete resources with which to bargain and threaten must be more cautious.

If a female-male relationship follows the stereotypical pattern in which the woman wields power indirectly and personally, while the man is more direct and concrete, the two parties will tend to attribute their compliance to very different causes. When she complies, in response to direct pressure, the woman will attribute it to external influence from him, and she will feel little sense of personal control or responsibility for her decision. But when the man complies, in response to less obvious, indirect pressure, he may do so in the belief that his behavior is not compliance at all but the product of his own decision. Thus, he (in contrast to her) maintains a sense of control and responsibility, and the power difference between them is reinforced. In any relationship based on equal power, neither party would have to be circumspect about influence attempts for fear of provoking the other into some feared behavior; each person would comply about equally often; each would be open about and responsible for her or his arguments for doing things one way or another.

Power Not at Someone Else's Expense

There are relationships in which the parties, almost by definition, start out with unequal power: parent-child, employer-employee, for example. In such relationships, must one always feel powerful at the expense of another's powerlessness? Surely not. Feelings of power can be connected with accomplishments that have nothing to do with influencing others: exceeding some self-defined standard of achievement, creating a magnificent work of art. But even the feelings of power connected with the successful exertion of influence need not reflect an increase in the powerful-powerless gap between the influencer and the influenced. A teacher, for example, may feel powerful in the realization that he or she has contributed to the empowerment of students. Writers and lecturers may feel powerful in the knowledge that they have opened new possibilities for strength in the minds of an audience. Yes, such individuals have exerted influence on others, but that influence is liberating rather than constricting, enabling rather than disabling. It is possible to exert influence on another without robbing that person of her or his sense of personal control—by safeguarding the individual's perception that she or he has not lost the freedom of choice, or, indeed, by expanding the range of choices.

Personal Empowerment

Much of the discussion in this chapter points to the idea that feeling powerful is not limited to feelings of control over other people. Indeed, power may be felt chiefly *for* the self, and only secondarily, or not at all, may imply control over others. Power for the self—a sense of one's capacities and potential effectiveness—is often called *empowerment*, or personal power. Feminist theorists have provided much of the exploration of this aspect of power.

Delineating a new perspective on the psychology of women, Jean Baker Miller (1977) noted more than a decade ago that the traditional concept of power, which implies a winner-loser situation, should be broadened. In the traditional framework, which still colors most thinking about power, power of another person is always seen as dangerous, and the quest for power means a struggle between individuals or groups for control over the other. In this competition, any increase in power for one of the parties automatically leads to a decrease in power for the other. Miller suggests that an equally and perhaps more important type of power is the capacity to develop one's abilities. This kind of power implies a lack of constraints by and dependence on others, but not domination of them. Miller argues that when an individual becomes more powerful in this way, the result is ultimately beneficial to others too, because it lessens the individual's need to restrict others through domination or dependence.

In terms of "feeling powerful," Miller writes of ways in which we label feelings as weak or powerful. She argues that many so-called feminine weaknesses should be "re-seen" as actual or potential strengths. For example, in Western society, men have been taught to deny and women to cultivate the feelings of vulnerability and weakness that are an inevitable part of the human experience. Miller suggests that although this pattern contributes to the label of women as the weaker sex, that women can tolerate feelings of vulnerability is actually a strength. Psychological growth, she notes, may depend on one's reaction to the feelings of vulnerability that one encounters throughout one's life. If an individual flees from or denies such feelings, rather than working productively with them, she or he loses possibilities for growth. Women, then, can learn to look on the stereotypically feminine qualities of openness to and understanding of weakness as a strength rather than accepting the dominant culture's denigration of such qualities. According to Miller's work, feelings of personal power involve a sense of being able to grow and to develop one's abilities, while at the same time not regarding every feeling of weakness as a threat or defeat.

Miller was one of the first theorists to explore in detail the notion that being or feeling powerful did not necessarily imply following the traditional masculine model of competition and control. For both women and men, power could take other forms, and a disinclination toward dominance or a recognition of one's own feelings of vulnerability and uncertainty need not imply weakness. Other writers have also contributed to this perspective on power. Adrienne Rich (1976) wrote of a type of power that involves self-expression rather than domination. She labeled as *powerfulness* "the expressive energy of an ego which . . . was licensed to direct itself outward upon the world" (p. 55). Feeling powerful in this sense implies feeling the ability and freedom to direct one's expressive energy outward in some creative effort rather than being forced to suppress it. Similarly, Mary Daly (1973) wrote of a "power of being," which involves a radical recognition, enhancement and development of the self. More recently, Carol Gilligan (1982) has argued that the feminine tendency to be concerned about and sensitive to relationships—which has often been portrayed in our culture as a weakness—is a valuable source of moral insight and courage. In a similar vein, Mary Field Belenky and her colleagues (1986) have suggested that the preference for "connected knowing" represents a powerful source of understanding and discernment. But the educational system is dominated by masculine "separate knowing" perspectives that often deter women from studying academic subjects deemed abstract and impersonal.

All of these theorists have contributed to the *re-valuing* of qualities associated with femininity. In their writing, feminine qualities traditionally viewed as weaknesses and liabilities have been identified as possible sources of strength, and limitations in the traditional (masculine) images of power, strength, and competence have been exposed.

The process of re-valuing qualities traditionally associated with femininity provides new roadmaps to empowerment for women. Gradually, it is becoming clear that there is more than one route to acquiring a sense of powerfulness, that women need not necessarily emulate men (or the style that has become identified with masculinity) in the way they develop strength, competence, and confidence. A source of empowerment for women is the realization that negative labels often attached to feminine qualities do not reflect any indisputable truth. They simply mirror a long-time cultural infatuation with the idea that what is masculine is good.

It is understandable that many women have embraced these realizations with fervor, building on them by singing the praises of female-male differences and claiming the superiority of female virtues. This path is a seductive one: After years of feeling inferior and trying to change, the liberating and energizing effects of understanding that many of one's customarily belittled habits of thought, reflexes, and patterns of behavior can be sources of strength rather than weakness can be as overwhelming as a religious conversion experience. Freed from the heavy burden of inferiority, some women may rise and float fearlessly over the battlefield on which they had formerly felt compelled to hold the line against proponents of the common wisdom that women and men are different. Gleefully abandoning their former position that the sexes are more similar than different, feminist women may rush to claim an alternative stance: "Yes, women and men *are* different—and women are better."

But where have we heard this before? We have heard it in the echoes of old arguments disallowing women access to the vote, to education, to birth control information: "Women are too good, too pure, to be exposed to such things." We have heard it in protective labor legislation for women—legislation protecting us from heavy, dirty, dangerous jobs that simultaneously protected us from a decent paycheck. We have heard it in the tired and tiresome observation that "boys will be boys . . . but girls must be good." Do women really want to find themselves in the same indefensible position that antifeminists have held for years, defending the existence of differences for which the evidence is, at best, equivocal? Stuck in the binary thinking that feminists have criticized for so long? Heady though the lure of female superiority might be, the road in that direction is filled with potholes. Rather than take that path, cautious women might do well simply to revel in the empowerment that comes with the realization that there is no magical correctness at all about the masculine way of doing things, that feminine approaches to getting things done are not in any way second-rate, and that men can learn as much or more that is useful from the feminine style as women can from the masculine one.

CONCLUSION: WOMEN AND MEN FEELING POWERFUL

Despite the popular idea that women and men have very different approaches to feeling powerful, some research suggests that power is actually thought of in fairly similar ways by the two sexes. When asked to explain what power meant to them, university women and men alike included themes of influence over others, achievement, and self-worth in their definitions (Lips, 1985). However, certain specific types of experiences were more linked to feelings of power for men than for women:

having material possessions, being physically strong, and participation in sports. In a population in which physical strength and sports participation were encouraged as much for females as for males, some of these gender differences might well disappear.

While females and males may differ little in the way they feel powerful, there are many indications that they tend to differ in how powerful they feel. As we have seen in this chapter, feeling powerful can involve many factors: the sense of personal control over one's outcomes, the feeling of freedom of choice in one's behavior, the tendency to see oneself as competent and effective by taking credit for one's accomplishments, and the sense of capacity to develop and implement one's abilities. It is apparent that in many of these areas the experience of women differs from that of men in North America. Women more than men have been encouraged to feel a sense of external control over their lives and, perhaps as a result, less readily take credit for their personal successes. Men tend to use power strategies that enhance their vision of their own effectiveness; women are more likely to use indirect strategies, which result in less sense of power.

Women influenced by men in direct, concrete ways may find it difficult to maintain a sense of freedom, control, and responsibility about their behavior in relation to these men. Men influenced by women in ways that are indirect, covert, and personal, on the other hand, maintain (accurately or not) a belief that they are making their own decisions. Even in the area of personal power, or empowerment, women have not seemed as free as men to explore and develop the sense of their own abilities.

On the face of it, this picture leaves little hope for the vision of women as powerful human beings or women and men as equal partners in the human race. Yet, despite obstacles, there are and have been countless examples of women with a sense of their own power great enough to attempt difficult, demanding, even dangerous tasks: Elizabeth Knowlton, the first woman to climb to 20,000 feet in the Himalayas in the 1930s (the men on the expedition refused to let her go higher); Irene Opdyke, using her traditionally feminine position as a domestic worker to spy on the Nazis in Poland during the Second World War; Teresa Edwards, leading her basketball team through a grueling series of challenges to an Olympic gold medal in 1988; the list could go on and on. And many would argue that this is an exciting time in history to be a woman in Western society. Women, through a re-visioning of culture, are discovering a new sense of their own power and value. They are moving into new career areas, exercising their relatively new freedom to decide what kinds of sexual relationships they want, when and whether to marry or to have children, and winning some political victories. Some men, too, are finding a new sense of empowerment in the lessened financial and emotional dependence of women on them. Yet, in many respects, the power differences between women and men remain entrenched. The hierarchical structure of the male-female power relationship is strongly resistant to change.

As we will see in the next chapter, the complex of habits and expectations that maintain this hierarchy of dominance is so extensive and deeply rooted that often even people who wish to destroy it may find themselves maintaining it through their behavior.

CHAPTER SIX

Dominance: The Structure of Power

W hen I tell a stranger that I am writing about gender and power, a frequent response from anyone uncomfortable with feminist questioning of the status quo is a query about the natural dominance of males over females. Would I not agree, the individual asks innocently, that there is ample evidence from the animal world that males are meant to dominate females? Do not male baboons defend the troop? Do not stallions prevail over mares?

I can fire back my own examples in such discussions: Does not the lioness do all the hunting? Does not the female spotted hyena dominate the male? Does not the male seahorse carry its young to term? However, citing animal examples to prove that a particular behavior pattern is natural or unnatural for humans is much like quoting scripture to prove that a particular behavior is moral or immoral—if one looks hard enough one can find support for almost anything. This is true even if we restrict ourselves to our closest relatives, the primates: A focus on baboons or orangutans leads to the conclusion that male dominance is natural, but a focus on the social lemurs leads equally persuasively to the conclusion that female dominance is natural (Hrdy, 1981). The point that gets lost in this hail of examples is that dominance in human beings and other species is so complex and multilayered, so reflective of the conditions under which the organisms live, that examples from other species have a limited usefulness. They can tell us something about the signals of dominance and submission, the environmental conditions that are likely to elicit high levels of dominance behavior, and the situations that are likely to cause stable dominance hierarchies to shift. They cannot tell us whether male dominance over females is natural among humans.

Why does the issue of human male dominance so often get tangled up with discussions of other animals? Perhaps because most of the early behavioral research on dominance was done with non-human animals. Perhaps also because, under the general label of power, dominance is the only area in which the emphasis on sex as an important variable has a long history in behavioral science. The backlog of studies appearing to show male dominance in other species has made it popular for apologists of human male dominance to adopt a simplistic version of the evolutionary perspective. From this precarious sociobiological base, they assert that because male baboons dominate female baboons, it is natural and right for human males to dominate human females. As we will see in this chapter, not only are such generalizations to humans from other animal species risky, but the very definitions of dominance that have been used in the past are too limiting to encompass the whole meaning of this concept.

DEFINING DOMINANCE

In the context of individual relationships, dominance has tradition-ally been defined as the imposition of one's will on someone else. Regardless of the influence strategies used, the individual who exerts the most influence when two people interact is characterized as the dominant party. In some situations, dominance derives merely from influential behavior; however, usually it is also a matter of *rank, position, and relative status.* For example, a person of high status can often dominate or exert influence over a lower-status person through mere presence without making any overt behavioral attempt to do so. Thus, the study of dominance is con-cerned mainly with the structure of power—the stable, asymmetrical re-lationships that maintain the dominance of one person or group over another.

In its concern with the structure of power, the study of dominance transcends the level of individual will or individual agency. It encompasses the notion of a system of power that, once in place, maintains itself almost without the conscious participation of the members of that system. Gender power relations form one such system of power—a system in which males and females are assumed to be in a hierarchical relationship, with males in the dominant position.

Psychological and Ethological Research on Dominance

The now common term, pecking order, as well as the notion of dominance hierarchies, comes from a classic study in which strange hens were placed together in an enclosure. The hens fought among themselves by pecking each other until a linear hierarchy was established and the hens could be clearly ranked in terms of their ability to peck others (Schjelderup-Ebbe, 1922). Out of this research came a notion of dominance that assumes that animals organize themselves socially according to their ability to intimidate or physically defeat others. Later researchers have broadened the concept to include priority of access to resources, whether or not it is achieved through physical intimidation (Fedigan, 1982).

Researchers have tried to measure dominance by devising situations in which one individual must defer to another. In animal observation studies, a dominant animal is one whose threats result in withdrawal by other animals, who wins out in conflicts over resources, toward whom submissive gestures are made, and who is typically followed by other members of the group. In studies of animal dominance, two animals are paired in confrontation over a reward such as food, and the animal who forces the other to give way is called the dominant one. In studies of humans, dominance is measured by the emergence or election of an individual to a leadership position, the number of contributions to a joint decision made by each individual in a pair, the number of challenges to his or her opinion that a person can sustain in an argument, the number of times one person interrupts the other, and other behavioral indications that one person is exerting more influence than the other on the inter-action and its outcomes. Psychologists have also studied the tendency toward dominance by measuring *attempts* at influence in various situa-tions: attempts to control peers, number of orders or suggestions given, and speaking intensity.

Research has established that more or less stable dominance hierarchies play a role in the power relationships of various species, including humans. A dominance hierarchy is an implicitly agreed-upon social arrangement in which certain individuals—perhaps the largest, the strongest, the smartest, the luckiest, the most persistent—have acquired a status that demands deference from other individuals. In some cases, such hierarchies hold across situations; in others, they are in effect only under particular conditions. In all cases, the hierarchies, while reasonably stable as long as conditions are stable, are *mutable*, changing in response to a high-status member's loss of power (for example, the physical or mental deteriora-tion of that highest-ranking individual), or an increase in strength by lower-status members. When a stable hierarchy exists in a group, knowl-edge of the relative positions of two individuals in the hierarchy enables an observer to predict, with reasonable but not perfect accuracy, which one will win out in a conflict. The presence of a dominance hierarchy provides a structural solution to the problem of who gives way to whom:

The individual lower in the hierarchy is expected to defer to the more dominant individual. Among non-human primates, this may mean that the dominant animal gets first crack at any disputed source of food. Among humans, it may mean that the person most highly placed in an organization is given the floor when there is competition for speaking time.

The human and non-human situations are far from identical; for one thing, rank and status in human groups are less likely than in non-human groups to be significantly determined by physical size and strength. However, a dominance hierarchy serves a similar function in both species: As long as the hierarchy is stable, it reduces the need for conflict. Perhaps it is not surprising, given the conflict-reduction function of stable hierarchies, that people often shy away from rocking the boat, from challenging stable power arrangements that exist in a society, an organization, a family, or even a friendship group. The conflict, the unpleasantness, the disruption of smooth interactions that accompany a challenge to an existing hierarchy are often viewed as a price too high to pay for change.

Studies of Dominance Among Non-Human Animals

The existence of stable dominance hierarchies was first inferred from the study of non-human animals. Early studies led researchers to conclude that dominance hierarchies were an important aspect of social organization in most animal species and that individual rankings in such hierarchies held across a wide variety of situations. The generality and simplicity of these early conclusions have since been questioned. Critics have noted that the emphasis on dominance hierarchies derives mainly from studies of animals confined in spaces much smaller than their natural range (Archer, 1971). Such a situation is likely to produce an emphasis on competition and dominance that may not reflect accurately the behavior of animals in their natural habitat. Moreover, in natural habitats, many different biological and ecological factors—from the plentifulness of the food supply to the amount of energy investment required of each parent to produce and rear an offspring—affect the kinds of behavior and social organization characteristic of a particular group of a particular species at a particular place and time. Non-human primates, now probably the best -studied mammals, are diverse in their patterns of behavior. So species-specific are these patterns that respected primatologist Jane Lancaster (1984) is able to say confidently that "it is virtually impossible to generalize about what male primates do or how female primates act" (p. 3).

The assumption that males tend to dominate females in most animal species, and that females are not concerned with dominance, has also been criticized as simplistic. In some species, male and female animals tend to form separate dominance hierarchies and to confine much of their social interaction to members of their own hierarchy. A considerable body of research on various primate species now shows that females, within their own groups, show just as much concern with dominance as do males (Fedigan, 1982). When a dispute between a female and male does occur, the male often wins because he is larger and stronger than the female. Smaller and weaker animals are generally dominated by larger, stronger ones—which gives the males in most species an advantage. However, observers have noted many instances in which females successfully challenged male dominance behavior. Among patas monkeys, the smaller female can successfully threaten the male, particularly when she is protecting an infant (Hall & Mayer, 1967). Among macaque monkeys, some females dominate some males, and a female occasionally dominates a whole troop (Washburn, Jay, & Lancaster, 1965). Older females in this species sometimes determine whether a new male will be accepted into the group (Lancaster, 1976).

The presence of dominance hierarchies, while creating a framework for social relations, is not always a guarantee that a lower-ranked individual will defer to a higher-ranked one. Lancaster reports that among some monkey species, such as vervet, langurs, patas, and zeladas, it is quite common for adult females to form coalitions against dominant males who try to monopolize a special food source or frighten an infant. She notes that even the lowest-ranking females will chase a male who has made one of their infants scream.

> A typical sequence might begin with a female screaming and soliciting aid by giving rapid glances back and forth between the adult male and the females whose support she sought. The coalition would then attack, running and usually screaming, at the male. The male would turn and flee. He would run as fast as he could until he reached the nearest tree or rock. He would then run up it and turn to face his chasers who threatened from below. After a minute or so of exchanging threats, the females would then move off, perhaps going back to the food or infant which was the cause of the problem. After that the male might be free to join them, but now on their terms and not on his. (Lancaster, 1976, p. 35)

Although these coalitions and attacks do not seem to affect the rank of the male in question or enhance the positions of the individual female members, they do seem to affect the male's behavior. Lancaster reports that males become more cautious about frightening infants. She describes several instances when, after an infant vervet monkey had screamed, all nearby adult males, apparently anticipating a female attack, immediately left the area. Although the rank-ordering of the hierarchy itself is unchanged, the potential for dominant behavior by the males in these groups is somewhat tempered by the female coalitions. The dominance hierarchies of females and males in some species of monkeys are apparently intertwined with each other. In some species, it is sufficient to know the individual's mother and birth order to know its rank in the group hierarchy (Hrdy, 1981). In Indian and Japanese macaques, dominance relations among young monkeys are entirely determined by the relative ranks of their mothers. As Lancaster (1976) explains, this may occur because mothers respond to threats to their offspring in ways that reflect their own rank in the group. If the threat comes from a lower-ranking animal, the mother will respond aggressively; if it comes from a higher-ranking animal, she may flee with her infant or make placating gestures. The young monkey learns, through a model, to respond to other monkeys in the group according to their status, while the other group members learn which infants have powerful mothers to defend them. Gradually, the young monkey acquires a position in the dominance hierarchy based on its potential to behave aggressively and/ or to enlist help in behaving aggressively; and the learning of a social position is apparently part of this process.

DOMINANCE AMONG HUMAN MALES AND FEMALES

For humans, unlike other animals, aggression and dominance are not as closely correlated. There are many ways for one person to exert influence over another without relying on actual physical force. As discussed in Chapter Four, one person can exert a great deal of influence over another by behaving in ways that appear helpless and submissive. It is when dominance is narrowly defined in terms of aggression that most similarities between human and non-human dominance hierarchies appear.

Studies in several cultures have investigated dominance hierarchies in four- to ten-year-old children (Omark & Edelman, 1975; Edelman & Omark, 1973). When children in these studies were asked to rate one another in terms of toughness, there was a great deal of agreement about the toughness hierarchies of both boys and girls. Boys were rated as tougher than girls, and within each sex the hierarchies were reasonably stable (although less so for girls). The children were paired, each child given a crayon of a different color, and were set to work drawing a picture together. Dominance was gauged according to which child's color was predominant in the main outline and the available space of the picture. According to this measure, boys dominated girls in mixed-sex pairs at every grade except kindergarten. In same-sex pairs, however, toughness ratings were not strongly related to dominance; the relationship between toughness and dominance in the drawing task was statistically significant in only two grades out of five. Thus, the toughness ranking, which might be considered a ranking in the dominance hierarchy, did not seem to endow a child with the pervasive capacity to dominate others.

Clearly, obtaining a dominance ranking for children in a group does not necessarily provide a complete picture of the social organization of that group. For one thing, even the meaning of the dominance ranking itself is uncertain; dominance rankings obtained from teachers, peers, and children themselves do not always agree (Silverman, 1984). Furthermore, while the social organization of same-sex groups of children has been found to be quite stable, that stability is a function not only of dominance, but also of affiliation (Jones, 1984). Finally, there is some evidence that dominance ranking plays a stronger role in the social organization of groups of male than of female children (Jones, 1984).

Other research suggests that toughness or aggressiveness is only one aspect of dominance in human groups. Characteristics of children described by other children as influential include politeness and pleasantness as well as toughness (Gold, 1958). Among adolescents, leadership in both female and male groups is related to a variety of qualities such as popularity, attractiveness, athletic skills, and social interests (Marks, 1957). Furthermore, dominance in any one aspect of a relationship does not always imply dominance in all aspects of a relationship.

Some studies of adults suggest that men are often more obviously concerned with dominance than are women, and that much of men's dominance behavior is directed toward one another. On paper-and-pencil measures of dispositional dominance (the tendency to want to dominate others), males tend to outscore females (Hoyenga & Hoyenga, 1979). A study of small-group interaction by Aries (1976) showed that all-male groups established more stable dominance hierarchies than did all-female groups. Similarly, among adolescents, female groups have been found to be less structured and to show less evidence of linear dominance hierarchies than male groups (Paikoff & Savin-Williams, 1983). Later research by Aries (1982) demonstrated that whether in same-sex or mixed-sex groups, males' behavior was characterized more strongly by task- and control-oriented behavior (giving opinions, suggestions, and information), while females' behavior showed a stronger emphasis on reacting (agreeing and disagreeing) to the statements of others.

It is possible, then, that men are more concerned with dominance than women are. However, it is equally possible that, as Sarah Hrdy (1981) suggests, women's concern with dominance is no less intense than is men's, but that it is expressed in more subtle ways—ways that have not been measured by researchers. One need only spend a few days at a professional meeting where women predominate, or casually observe the inner workings of women's organizations, to suspect that the notion that women are not concerned with dominance is pure myth.

Dominance According to Social Custom

When it comes to male–female interactions, the demands of the situation appear to take precedence over the personality dispositions of the individuals involved—social rules are such that men lead and women follow. For example, when males are paired with females to do a task, they take dominant roles—and the females let them do so.

Megargee (1969) paired subjects who had scored high and low on a questionnaire measure of dispositional dominance, and asked each pair to work together in a situation that demanded that one of them be the leader and one the follower. Among same-sex pairs, the high dominance person was most likely to become the leader. Similarly, when a high-dominant male was paired with a low-dominant female, the male usually emerged as the leader. However, when a high-dominant woman was paired with a low-dominant man, the gender power relations system apparently took precedence over personality disposition: The man still became the leader 80% of the time. Although under the other conditions it was usually the person emerging as leader who made the decision to lead, in this high-dominant woman low-dominant man condition it was often the woman who decided that the man should lead. Would such findings, obtained 20 years ago when the impact of the feminist movement was only beginning still occur today? Apparently, the answer is yes. The Megargee study has been replicated recently by other researchers (Carbonell, 1984; Nyquist & Spence, 1986), with very similar results.

A similar triumph of social expectations over personality dispositions occurs when women and men interact in small groups. Elizabeth Aries and her colleagues (1983) found that within all-female and all-male groups, individuals' scores on a personality measure of dominance predicted how much dominance behavior they would exhibit in their groups (Aries, Gold, & Weigel, 1983). However, when women and men were placed in mixed-sex groups, the relation between individuals' personality measures of dominance and their behavior was small. The researchers speculated that "the presence of group members of the opposite sex invoked sex role expectations that inhibited the manifestation of dominance-oriented behaviors consistent with the subjects' behavioral tendencies" (p. 784). Both the women and the men reacted to the mixed-sex situation by guiding their behavior more by the situation than by their personality tendencies. Clearly, there are very strong social expectations associated with the dominance aspect of male–female relations. These expectations can and do outweigh the impact of individual tendencies. Even when the leadership of a dyad (two individuals) is determined by the researcher rather than allowed to emerge, female leaders are perceived, by both their subordinates and themselves, to be less dominant than male leaders—with female leaders paired with male subordinates rating themselves as least dominant, and romantically unattached female leaders interacting with males rating themselves least dominant of all. The authors of this study argue that the female leaders are affected by a role conflict between the contradictory roles of dominant leader and subordinate female (Snodgrass & Rosenthal, 1984).

Studies of dominance often focus on the ability to prevail in the face of opposing opinions. Such an ability is based not just on stubbornness and a loud voice (although the importance of such qualities in certain situations should not be underestimated), but on the parties' perceptions of their status or rank. Thus, position in an implicit dominance structure influences a person's (or group's) ability to take charge, to persuade, to resist challenge. This understood dominance structure is shaped by social expectations: In the absence of other personal information, a person's sex and race are used, along with the norms of the situation, by others in determining her or his status and expected performance (Berger, Wagner, & Zelditch, 1985). Where maleness is associated with higher status, as in much of North American white middle-class society, a man has an automatic advantage over a woman in an influence-related situation: He gets more respect and deference from others than she does even before he starts to talk. He may lose that initial status advantage by demonstrating ignorance or social ineptness, but as long as he can maintain a moderately competent, articulate image, his advantage is safe. It is not surprising that studies show a male advantage over females in holding the floor in group discussions (Lockheed & Hall, 1976); withstanding challenges to their opinions (Adams & Landers, 1978); and a variety of other measures of influence in small, task-oriented groups (Lockheed, 1985).

The impact of automatic initial status differences associated with sex can be reduced by providing females with a source of increased status, such as recognized expertise. When group members have high task-related performance expectations of an individual, that individual has the opportunity to be more influential. In a now much-cited study, Lockheed and Hall (1976) provided females with task experience in order to build expectations of competence before putting them into mixed-sex groups to work on a task. The strategy had a dramatic effect: Males in the task groups were four to seven times more likely than the females to emerge as leaders *unless* the females in the group had developed competence on the task ahead of time. In groups where the female participants had been given, through experience, task-specific expectations of competence, female ranking improved markedly: Females were more active than in the other groups, and a female was ranked either first or second in leadership-related behavior in all these groups. The latter study does not stand alone. In an analysis of 29 studies of gender differences in social influence in mixed-sex groups, Lockheed (1985) found task-related performance expectations were related positively to an individual's influence in the group. To offset the power disadvantage experienced by females because of their automatic low status, women had to be made to appear more competent than men in order to attain the same level of influence. These studies suggest a kernel of truth to the feminist proverb that "A woman has to do twice as well as a man to be considered half as good."

Biological and Evolutionary Roots of Male Dominance

If men are more concerned with dominance than women (and remember that this gender difference has not been established in any conclusive way), could it be that there are evolutionary reasons for this? Could the often-observed tendency of men to dominate women have an evolutionary basis? These questions, however innocent they may seem, arise in a political context in which many people advocate changes in the gender power relations system. The answers are more likely to be used as weapons by the various sides than they are to be weighed dispassionately to throw new and interesting light on human behavior. It is appropriately cautious from a scientific, or a political, point of view to say that the questions cannot be answered with certainty. However, given the frequency with which evolutionary arguments are cited, it is useful to have some grasp of the available evidence.

Have men evolved to be more concerned than women with dominance? As already noted, early studies of non-human primates suggested that dominance hierarchies appeared more pronounced and stable among male than female animals. It was concluded that dominance was an overriding concern among males, while nurturance was the overriding concern among females. Projecting these conclusions to humans lent support to both sides in the debates about women's proper role. For proponents of male dominance as natural and right, the research findings led conveniently, although not with seamless logic, to the conclusion that man's proper place is out in the world competing with other men for status and other rewards; woman's proper place is at home with the children. For proponents of greater equality between women and men, the conclusion that males were naturally more concerned with dominance led equally easily (and equally dubiously) to the notion that women, by nature uncompetitive and nurturant, were morally better suited than men to run things.

Unfortunately for both sides, new primate field studies have undercut the notion that males are more concerned with dominance and status than are females (Hrdy, 1981; Fedigan, 1982; Lancaster, 1984). Rather, in many species, females appear to form stable, linear dominance hierarchies and to be as obsessed with status as are males—although competition may take different forms for females and males (e.g. Whitten, 1984). For non-human primates, the nature of the usefulness of dominance for the animals' presumed biological goal of reproductive success may differ for males and females: High rank may give males more access to females and thus more opportunities to reproduce; but high rank may give females more access to energy resources necessary to bear and rear young. From an evolutionary standpoint, a concern with dominance would appear to be as beneficial for females as for males. These findings make it hard to argue that if human males are more concerned than females are with dominance, this greater concern is a natural outgrowth of evolutionary pressures.

Does human male dominance of females have an evolutionary basis? In many species, the females appear to defer to the males most of the time. However, as noted at the beginning of this chapter, in some species female dominance of males is the norm. Clearly, there is no law of nature that says for a species to survive and prosper, male organisms will be dominant over female organisms. Rather, dominance relations between the sexes appear to be shaped by environmental conditions and by the way organisms have adapted to them. Across the generations, the conditions under which a species or sub-group lives help to determine what behaviors are most useful to that species' or group's survival. Although a variety of evolutionary responses may be appropriate to a particular set of environmental conditions, over the generations a set of characteristics that works for survival under those conditions is selected for. In other words, the species evolves in a particular direction because individuals with certain characteristics are more likely to survive to breeding age to mate and reproduce successfully than are individuals without those characteristics.

Proponents of sexual selection theories contend that different selection pressures operate on male and female members of many species, ensuring that different qualities promote reproductive success among males than among females. For example, dominance might promote reproductive success among males, giving dominant males more simultaneous access than non-dominant males to many fertile females. Since females are by nature more limited in number of procreations they can be involved in simultaneously, it would not help their reproductive success to, for example, control a harem of males. Some theorists argue that male dominance over females is more likely to be adaptive, in evolutionary terms, than is female dominance over males.

While the above argument may capture some of the truth in certain species, it ignores a number of complexities—including the variation in conditions that makes certain adaptations useful under some conditions but not others. The case is made on the notion that the male's investment in reproduction consists of nothing more than depositing his sperm in the right place (or in as many right places as possible) at the right time. In many species, however, the male's investment must be considerably greater than this if his progeny are to survive; his reproductive success may be equivalent to that of his mate. He must stay around to help feed and protect his young, for if he does not they will perish before they mature. In such species, mating pairs tend toward monogamy; there is less pressure for competition and dominance among males; and dominance is rarely an issue between mates (Hrdy, 1981). There is little evolutionary basis for male dominance in such species.

Even looking beyond the monogamous species, one can identify qualifications and contradictions to the "male dominance is adaptive" hypothesis. For instance, some primate species that have a short breeding season during the year do not select for male dominance because for most of the year there is nothing for the males to compete over. Such species, which include squirrel monkeys and talapoin monkeys, have small bodies and high metabolic rates. The small bodies are apparently an adaptation to the scarcity of the food supply. For these monkeys, it seems to be adaptive for males to conserve their energy for most of the year rather than squander it in wasteful displays of dominance and competition. Outside of breeding season, males in these species will sometimes defer to females.

The examples described briefly here show that a number of factors may affect whether dominance confers an evolutionary advantage on males. But the argument is still more complex. For one thing, all of the above considerations have emphasized male behavior and choices, ignoring the possibility that females are more than passive resources to be fought over, but are actively involved in choosing their mates. There is now plenty of evidence that female choice plays a role in primate mating—and that female preference does not always run to the dominant or most aggressive male (Fedigan, 1982). In laboratory studies, female macaques and rhesus monkeys have been found to prefer males who are not aggressive toward them. Once female choice is added to the equation, the notion that dominance in males is always adaptive appears unlikely—

although its adaptiveness in certain species is not ruled out. One final caution remains: Dominance, per se, is not really an individual trait, but a relational one. An individual's dominance rank is not completely stable, but changes over time, when she or he experiences victories or defeats, or when she or he changes groups. Qualities such as size, strength, and aggressiveness may be inherited, but dominance itself is not passed on genetically (Fedigan, 1982). Thus, it may be incorrect to speak of dominance itself as a trait that is or is not adaptive.

Given the complexities involved in determining whether male dominance over females is adaptive in various species, what can we conclude about the evolutionary basis for male dominance over females among humans? Very little. For one thing, evolutionary theorists do not even agree which species of non-human primate provides the best model for the way humans have evolved (Fedigan, 1982). Is it the baboons, whose hierarchical organization and male dominance appear to be echoed in some human cultures? The geladas, who seem to have had to adapt to an environment and diet similar to those of the early hominids? The chimpanzees, who, according to much evidence, are the species most closely related to us? Scientists disagree and are unlikely ever to know for sure. Furthermore, there are many gaps in our knowledge about how these primate species themselves evolved—and even about how they live now. Humans, alas, cannot turn to the data about primates for a comforting certainty about what human social organization, and the relationship between females and males, is supposed to be like.

Social Roots of Male Dominance

One thing that the study of non-human primates does reveal is that different conditions support different dominance relations between females and males. If we move away from the evolutionary perspective and look simply at the more immediate impact of social arrangements, it may be possible to identify some of the ways in which male dominance over females is supported by social and environmental conditions.

Various theorists have argued that male dominance in a particular society is supported by variables such as frequent warfare (Divale & Harris, 1976); a reliance for food on the hunting of large game (Tiger & Fox, 1971); male control over subsistence resources or the means of production (Blumberg, 1984); social structures emphasizing patrilineal descent (tracing descent through the father) and patrilocal residence (located or centered around the residence of the husband's tribe or family) (Coontz & Henderson, 1986; Ross, 1986); social complexity (Leacock, 1986; Ross, 1986); cultural prestige systems and symbolism that emphasize notions of "great men" and masculine creator myths

(Sanday, 1981); and a sexual division of labor that leaves child rearing almost exclusively in the hands of the mother (Chodorow, 1978; Dinnerstein, 1976; Stockard & Johnson, 1979). It is possible, even likely, that many of these variables are interrelated and reinforce one another in circular chains of cause and effect. Thus, we are not in a position to unearth a single cause of male dominance. We can, nevertheless, identify some of the variables that support and maintain it.

Male dominance and the lack of male "mothering."   A number of theorists have argued that male dominance over females comes from assigning the task of mothering exclusively to females (Chodorow, 1978; Dinnerstein, 1976; Stockard & Johnson, 1979). These writers reason that an important step in reducing men's tendency to dominate women is to have childcare divided equally between men and women.

How might the early relationship between parent and child be related to male dominance over females in adulthood? One possibility is that children raised by both parents grow up with less need to act out strongly differentiated gender scripts that include male dominance over females. Another is that when both male and female adults are intimately involved in child rearing, there is less tendency for them to emphasize their own or their children's gender differences. Still another is that male sharing of the work of childcare frees women to take on a greater share of other work, increasing their access to authority and decreasing the social tendency toward male dominance.

Proponents of the shared childcare hypothesis have generally emphasized the first of the above possibilities. Relying heavily on psychoanalytic theory, they have highlighted two themes that may underlie, in boys raised exclusively by mothers, the development of an especially strong need to dominate females: the unconscious fear and envy that children of both sexes are said to feel toward the mother because of her power over them, and the alleged special problems encountered by boys in establishing a secure sense of their own gender identity when their father plays little role in their socialization.

The first of these themes has a long history in psychoanalytic theory. Analysts such as Melanie Klein, Karen Horney, and Ernest Jones all argued that males feel unconscious anxiety, envy, and inferiority regarding women—stemming from the boy's early fear of rejection by the mother or his fear and envy of her procreative powers. Horney, in fact, asserted that many of men's achievement strivings are unconsciously motivated by a desire to compensate for their inability to bear and suckle children. Dorothy Dinnerstein's more contemporary analysis suggests that both males and females reared exclusively by mothers grow up with unconscious feelings of threat from female power. She argues that society allows men to hold the power outside the mother-child relationship precisely because the power held by the mother over the infant is so all-encompassing and threatening. As the infant grows into an adult, he or she flees from the overwhelming power of the mother, and thus finds it easier to accept male rather than female authority. Dinnerstein further suggests, because of these early experiences, that men are especially fearful of becoming overly dependent on women. If men were to join women in caring for infants, the overwhelming power of the caretaker would be shared; children reared by both parents would have no reason to develop a special fear of female power; and one of the basic motives for maintaining a social structure of male dominance would disappear.

A similar conclusion is reached via a different route by those who emphasize the second theme: A heavily maternal system of child rearing causes gender identity problems for the male child. Psychoanalysts have argued that males have a more tenuous gender identity compared to females because their first close relationship is with their mother— someone with whose sex and gender they cannot identify. Social learning theorists concur with this notion. They say that the female child has an appropriate gender model with whom to identify (the mother); but the male child has little access to an appropriate gender model (the father). The male is therefore forced to construct a male gender identity and role largely from the prescriptions and prohibitions of the mother and other (usually female) adults. Boys growing up in almost exclusively female care are often ridiculed or punished if they act feminine. Furthermore, boys are expected, often without much positive guidance, to separate themselves clearly from dependence on their mother as they reach adolescence. Without guidance as to what being masculine means, boys in this situation may form a masculine identity based largely on an avoidance of feminine behavior and a denigration of femininity and of women.

Stockard and Johnson argue that:

> . . . societal arrangements which actually give prestige and authority to males provide the most effective and concrete support for masculine identity. The system of male dominance allows men to demonstrate concretely that they are not only different from but "better than" women. Furthermore, defining masculinity as superior, giving the highest prestige to the things males do (very much a part of male dominance), is a way of inducing men to give up "femininity" and take on a masculine identity. The greater rewards and power of masculinity then act as an inducement to men to break with femininity. (p. 209)

Evidence regarding the social origins of male dominance. The above analyses show how the absence of significant childcare by fathers might contribute to a social structure in which male dominance is institutionalized. Other possible mechanisms exist as well: Where men do not have to care for children they may be less likely to develop the abilities required for a non-dominance-oriented, cooperative society; where men do not have to care for children, women have little time to do anything else. But is there, in fact, evidence that the involvement of fathers in early childcare has any impact on the degree to which men are expected and allowed to dominate women? Scott Coltrane (1988), through an analysis of data on a cross-cultural sample of 90 nonindustrial societies, has provided just such evidence.

Coltrane divided the societies in his sample into those in which father-child relations could be characterized as either distant or close. This closeness measure reflected a combination of paternal proximity, caretaking, affection, and nurturance measures. He compared the societies with distant and close father-child relationships to see how they differed on a number of variables, including a measure of women's status: the amount of female participation in decision making. What he found was that societies with close father-child relationships also tended to exhibit high female participation in public decision making; while societies with distant father-child relationships tended to have low female participation in public decision making. In effect, his investigation demonstrated that the father-child relationship does seem to be strongly linked to female status.

Additional variables, however, tended to affect the relationship between father-child closeness and female public power: the degree to which the society was patrilineal or patrilocal; and the degree to which its economy rested on a developed resource base. Societies with a male-oriented social structure (patrilineal and/or patrilocal) and which were based on developed resources such as agriculture or trade rather than on subsistence economies were less likely to promote high public status for females even when father-child relationships were close. Coltrane also found that the frequency of external warfare was significantly and negatively associated with the exercise of female public authority.

Coltrane's data provided no support for the notion that a society's reliance on hunting was linked to low female status, nor was there any evidence that the sharing of childcare among (usually female) nonparents had any relationship to female status. Another hypothesis for which Coltrane did *not* find any support, no matter how he looked at his data, was that women would have higher public status in societies in which they controlled the means of production. Whether or not women made strong contributions to the economic subsistence of their society apparently made no difference to their status. This finding is surprising to many who feel that control over production is crucial to societal power. But, as Coltrane suggests, it appears that control over the distribution of resources, rather than over their production, is the crucial aspect of power relations between the sexes.

At first, it may seem surprising that control over the production of resources does not guarantee a strong voice in control over their distribution. However, particular political and economic structures and cultural ideologies that emphasize male dominance can affect the degree to which a woman keeps control of the resources she produces. In North America, with its veneer of sexual equality, it is not unheard of for a wife to hand over her paycheck to her husband on a routine basis. In societies where the ideology gives unequivocally higher prestige to males, it is common for the women to do the bulk of the productive labor while the men control what they produce. An interesting and dramatic example of this practice can be found among the residents of Cheju, a small island off the coast of South Korea. This island is the home of the legendary *henyo* divers—all women—who support their community by diving deep into the frigid South China Sea for sea urchin, octopus, and abalone. These women perform highly skilled, dangerous work. They have been so admired for their prowess that on old Chinese and Japanese maps, Cheju was known as the "Isle of Women." The women are the primary contributors to their society's subsistence, but they have practically no control over their income. They defer to husbands, sons, and other male relatives on financial decisions, and they are obliged to contribute 10% to 20% of their income to support patrilineal ancestor rituals. Although the men do none of the diving (the women have been heard to speculate that the men are lazy, or intolerant of cold water, or not as tough as the women), they hold virtually all of the public authority (Schoenberger, 1989). A cultural ideology of male dominance holds this system in place despite the women's role as primary contributors to the subsistence of the group.

SIGNALS OF DOMINANCE AND SUBMISSION

Maintaining the Gender Power Relations System

A power structure is not simply a given once it has been established; it is maintained through the actions of the people involved. Those on the top end of the structure behave in dominant ways; those on the bottom defer to those on the top; the environment is arranged to reinforce the power difference. Often these patterns of dominant and deferent behavior are so routine that they are unnoticed by the members of either group. A well-entrenched power hierarchy is maintained so smoothly that the deferent and dominant behavior seems simply normal; and it is this very behavior that helps to keep the hierarchy in place. The way people allocate and use space, their facial expressions, gestures, touch, and body position, the way they regulate their language and conversation, all are indicators of power relationships and props that maintain those relationships.

Control over space   Simple observation tells us that the higher status people in organizations have the larger offices, that parents control more space in the home than do children, and that the most privileged members of society tend to control access to the most desirable territory, whether it be beach-front lots or the best seats at the theatre. In terms of purely personal space, rigid, straight body positions that occupy less space are said to communicate fearfulness and low status (Mehrabian, 1972). Both formal and informal rules designate the distances that must be maintained between people of unequal status (Hall, 1966).

Males and females tend to differ in their control over and use of space, and the male–female differences parallel those expected for high-low status and dominance-deference. For example, mothers are less likely than fathers to have a special room in the family home, or a special chair reserved for them. In the work world, women's space is often more public and crowded than that of men (Frieze & Ramsey, 1976). This control over space is institutionalized early in life. In the schoolyard, boys frequently take the bulk of the space for team sports in which girls are not welcome; girls are restricted to the edges of the yard (Mahony, 1983). The pattern continues on college campuses, where large amounts of recreational space are often devoted to billiard tables and video games; these spaces quickly become male preserves.

It has been found repeatedly that females yield space more easily than males. Women move out of the way more frequently and earlier than men when being approached on the sidewalk (Silveira, 1972). Also, in situation after situation, women tend to choose postures and body positions that take up a minimum of space, while male positions are often characterized by a spreading out of legs or arms (Frieze & Ramsey, 1976; Henley, 1977). Any woman who has been unlucky enough to be assigned the middle seat between two men on a long airplane trip has probably discovered for herself that "women contract and men expand."

Facial expression   The face may be a major channel for the display of power and authority. We tend to connect stern or impassive expressions, unwavering stares, and clenched jaws with dominance, but, as Nancy Henley (1977) notes, smiling sometimes indicates deference:

> . . . smiling is a human facial expression also associated with subordinate status. The unctuous Uriah Heep, the shuffling Uncle Tom, anyone seeking to ingratiate is depicted with a perpetual grin. The "nervous" smile, like the nervous laugh, conveys tension more than pleasure, and in many people has had to be held so long and so often that it has become a habit and an etched facial expression. Though little research has been done on smiling, it is understood as a gesture offered upwards in the status hierarchy; indeed, a powerful and successful person may be said to be surrounded by a thousand suns! (p. 171)

Many writers have suggested that women smile more than men, and that women are more facially expressive than men. Not only do they smile more, they also cry more. Such expressiveness may make them more vulnerable than men, who control their expressions and thus hide their emotions (Henley, 1977). In mixed-sex group discussions, women smile more than men do when taking their speaking turn, and their smiles seem to undermine their ability to hold the floor in the discussion: Women are more likely to be interrupted when smiling (Kennedy & Camden, 1983).

The eyes are thought to be especially important in dominance. According to Henley, two aspects of eye contact are used to define hierarchical position. In the first instance, staring is used to assert dominance, while averting the gaze is a gesture of submission. Men tend to stare more than women; women are more likely to drop their eyes than men. In the second instance, a secure dominant position is reinforced and maintained by visually ignoring the other person (such as looking away while the other speaks), but a subordinate person must engage in considerable eye contact as a feature of attentive listening. Here again, in male-female interactions, the characteristically dominant behavior is more often found in males and the subordinate one in females.

Touch   Although we tend to think of touch as something that communicates affection, it conveys dominance in many situations as well. When touch is reciprocal, or mutual, it communicates affection; but when it is nonreciprocal, it communicates power, status, and dominance (Henley, 1977). Although the president of a company may slap the back or put a hand on the shoulder of a new employee, it is clearly inappropriate for the employee to initiate such behaviors toward the company president. They signal a degree of familiarity that is a violation of the president's status, and, by implication, authority.

Observational studies support Henley's argument. The initiation of nonreciprocal touch is associated with higher status variables: being male, senior, or of higher socioeconomic status (Goffman, 1967; Henley, 1973; Heslin & Boss, 1980). Furthermore, touch is interpreted as conveying dominance and status. In one study, observers watched slides of cross-sex and same-sex nonreciprocal touch and no-touch interactions. They rated the touchers significantly higher than the recipients of touch on status/dominance, instrumentality/assertiveness, and warmth/expressiveness (Major & Heslin, 1982). In fact, the recipients of touch in this study were rated lower than were the no-touch controls. In other words, "the act of touching *enhanced* the perceived status, warmth, and assertiveness of the toucher relative to persons not touching while it *diminished* that of the recipient relative to those not touching" (p. 158). These findings—seen in the light of observations that men are more likely to initiate and women to receive touch—imply that touch, like use of space and facial expression, acts as a mechanism to maintain the structure of male dominance.

Who talks? Who listens?   The way we talk to, about, and with one another reflects much about dominance and status in our relationships. When a businessman tells his colleague "I'll have my girl send that over to you," rather than "I'll have Ms. Smith send that over to you," he is conveying information about the low status of his secretary, who is less likely to be a "girl" than a 30-year-old woman and who is certainly not "his." The implied insult becomes clear if we imagine a reverse situation: a businesswoman telling a colleague "I'll have my boy send that over," when referring to her 30-year-old male secretary.

Not only what we say, but our degree of success in getting it said signals and maintains status and dominance. Research indicates that status is related to the ability to control a conversation. For example, adults interrupt children frequently (Sacks, 1972), and the department chair is the person least frequently interrupted during department meetings (Eakins & Eakins, 1976).

Gender power relations are reflected in patterns of conversational control. Men talk more than women do in a mixed group, often because they interrupt women or jump in to answer questions that were not addressed to them. Women have a difficult time getting and keeping the floor in such a group, or even in a mixed-sex dyad. Don Zimmerman and Candace West (1975) recorded conversations in public places on a university campus and analyzed them for the occurrence of interruptions, overlaps (one speaker starting to speak before the other has completely finished), and silences. Their findings showed striking differences between same-sex and cross-sex conversations. Although in same-sex conversations, the overlaps and interruptions were distributed fairly evenly between speakers, in cross-sex conversations virtually all the interruptions (98%) and overlaps (100%) were by male speakers. In contrast to the talk patterns of the same-sex pairs, interruption seemed to be normal rather than exceptions for female-male pairs. Notably, none of the women in these conversations ever protested about being interrupted. The researchers found that in cross-sex conversations, women more often fell silent than men, and that these silences occurred most frequently after an interruption or after a delayed minimal response by the male (for example, a long pause followed by a disinterested "mmhmm").

It appears that tactics used by males in cross-sex conversations tend to discourage females and subdue their efforts at conversational control. Fishman (cited in Parlee, 1979) analyzed more than 50 hours of spontaneous conversations between the members of three couples. He found that 96% of the topics introduced by the men succeeded (resulted in a conversation in which they were discussed), but only 36% of those introduced by the females did so. Men frequently did not respond or responded minimally to topics raised by women; women almost always responded to those raised by men.

Even when they hold positions that have higher status than their male interaction partners, women do not seem to gain the advantage of conversational control. Their sex seems to undermine their high status position and make them vulnerable to interruption. In a detailed analysis of actual videotaped interactions between physicians and their patients, Candace West (1984) showed that the power relationship between physicians and patients is asymmetrical: Physicians are far more likely to interrupt their patients than vice versa. However, this pattern breaks down when the doctor is a woman. In the latter case, patients, especially male patients, interrupt at least as much or more than the physicians do, and the interruptions appear to subvert the physicians' authority.

Environmental Symbols of Dominance

Power structures are often built into the environment, usually through the degree of accessibility to individuals the environment allows. The higher an individual's status, the less accessible she or he is. For example, dominance can be conveyed by barricading an individual behind a desk (the larger the better) or by placing a number of secretaries or assistants between him or her and the public.

Clothing, the environment closest to our skin, also indicates and reinforces status—partly through the mechanism of accessibility, through what it signals about economic status, and through the restrictions it imposes on behavior. Clothing styles may well reinforce power differences between women and men. Women's clothing tends to restrict their actions more than men's does (it is difficult to run, or even walk, in high-heeled shoes) and helps to channel their movements into feminine patterns. Years ago, *The Radical Therapist* published a series of exercises for men that illustrate the way in which clothing may affect women's behavior. For example:

> Bend down to pick up an object from the floor. Each time you bend remember to bend your knees so that your rear end doesn't stick up, and place one hand on your shirtfront to hold it to your chest. This exercise simulates the experience of a woman in a short, low-necked dress bending over.[1]

---

[1]*Willamette Bridge* (Liberation News Service), 1971.

A woman's clothing, often designed to be more revealing than that of a man, makes her more vulnerable and less powerful, since status is related to difficulty of access—even visual access. In a vicious circle, clothing that is very feminine seems to convey low status simply because of its association with the cultural stereotype of femininity, a stereotype that emphasizes ineffectiveness and emotionality rather than competence and power.

CONCLUSION: SEX AS A "MASTER STATUS"

What becomes clear in the research reviewed in this chapter is that dominance, far from being simply an individual personality trait, can be said to be the institutionalization of the control of one group or person over another. The tendency to dominate comes not just from individual disposition (although individuals do differ to some extent on their desire to dominate others) but from the way the social environment is arranged to make that domination easy or difficult.

In much, perhaps all, of our society, sex and gender are important dimensions of the status structure that shapes dominance-related interactions. Being female or male (sex) affects an individual's status in the eyes of others; socialization into feminine or masculine roles (gender) affects the way an individual approaches power relationships. We have seen that individual tendencies toward dominance predict behavior well in same-sex groups or dyads, but lose their predictive power when the sexes are mixed. Similarly, we have seen that high-status position predicts dominant behavior—unless the holder of the high-status position is female and the holder of the low-status one is male. The link between sex and status is so pervasive that sex may be called a "master status" (Hughes, 1945)—an aspect of status that can alter or outweigh other, more specific ones. The ways in which the two sexes come to differ in status are complex and still a matter of research and debate.

In the chapters that follow, the focus is on the ways that institutionalized female–male status differences are translated into power differences in specific areas of social life. As we shall see, the expectation of male dominance has a pervasive influence on personal life in areas ranging from sexuality to politics.

CHAPTER SEVEN

Power, Sexuality, and Reproduction

N owhere is the power relationship between women and men alternately so stark and so obscured as in the realm of sexuality. The language of sex is filled with images of male dominance and female submission—as is much of the language of romance. Pornography celebrates men's control of, even violence against, their sexual partners; love songs sometimes celebrate men's *and* women's willingness to give up power- and ego-related goals in favor of an important relationship. On the one hand, our culture leads us to expect men's dominance of women, even in the closest of heterosexual love relationships; on the other hand, such a relationship may be the one realm where a man and woman find the personal motivation to transcend the cultural messages about male dominance.

The links between power and sexuality can be examined from a variety of perspectives: the interaction between sexuality and status, sexuality as a power resource, the sexuality-reproduction link as a source of power and vulnerability, sexuality as an expression and instrument of male dominance, and sexuality as a positive source of empowerment. In much of Western society, all of these perspectives can be viewed within the framework of a pervasive cultural notion: the double standard.

Many years ago, Nina Colwill and I co-authored a chapter on "Power and Sexuality" for my book *Women, Men and the Psychology of Power* (1981), now out of print. I was grateful for her collaboration then, and I am grateful for it again now as I mine that chapter for its ideas.

To most of us, the term double standard automatically implies sexuality. It conjures up images of man as sexual aggressor and pursuer sowing his wild oats; woman as sexually restrained and passive, a gatekeeper, or even as a virginal (or almost virginal) prize to be won by the man. As the images suggest, the double standard has implications for more than just sexual behavior; it is wholly related to power and control.

One of the assumptions that maintains the double standard is that sexual activity is more important for men than for women. Men's supposed greater need for sexual release lends legitimacy to their role as sexual aggressors. Armed with the power of legitimacy, men adopt a role where they initiate and direct sexual activity—even if they feel unsure of themselves or of the direction in which they want the relationship to go. Women, likewise armed with legitimacy by the double standard, adopt a role in which they limit and restrict sexual activity. Men and women often want heterosexual relationships on their own terms, but they find themselves working at cross purposes to control these relationships. An impartial observer from another planet would probably conclude that the human race had unwittingly played a huge joke on itself by setting up such different standards for women and men.

Both women and men use power in sexual encounters. The stereotypical male heterosexual role of initiator, leader, expert—even conqueror—presents a more powerful image than does the stereotypical female heterosexual role of gatekeeper or sexual prize. The reciprocal roles require that the male decides, acts, pushes, insists while the female simply waits, fends off, and (only when the time is right) gives in. Indeed, the very language that is used to describe men's sexual performance—centering on the term potency—implies that power is what it is all about. However, like any role, this one of sexual aggressor/expert can be a trap. When men become trapped in their image of sexual leader, women sometimes cooperate in maintaining that image, a charade that is reminiscent of the fable "The Emperor's New Clothes." In the fable, no one dares tell the emperor, parading naked down the street, that his new suit of clothes is so invisible as to be nonexistent. In the sexual context, women are sometimes hard-pressed to bring themselves to let men know that the male cloak of sexual expertise is similarly invisible.

Men themselves are caught in a role that allows no revelation of ignorance or uncertainty; they often discover sexual information only by chance. Both research and personal accounts indicate that men find it more difficult than women do to seek sexual information from others (London, 1974; Singer, 1976). The man's refusal to seek information and the woman's refusal to challenge his role as expert often combine to keep heterosexual couples from the kind of open discussion that would improve the sexual interaction for both parties. Women sometimes even fake orgasm, providing their male partner with false feedback about what gives them sexual pleasure (Hite, 1976). In these situations, both members of the couple maintain power and limit vulnerability with respect to the other person by withholding information about themselves. In traditional fashion, men play expert while women play helpless; the combined effect of both strategies is to avoid taking personal responsibility for the sexual relationship.

Women and men are restricted by the norm that men initiate and direct sexual activity, but changes in the norm produce discomfort. For a large proportion of men, control of the partner plays an important role in sexuality; male sexual fantasies frequently center on autonomy, mastery, and physical prowess (Person, 1986). Some men are ambivalent about sexually active women and have difficulty accepting sexual invitations from them (Komarovsky, 1976). Years ago, women were warned that by taking sexual initiative and asserting their own needs and preferences they would create an increase in impotence among men (Ginsburg, Frosch, & Shapiro, 1972). Must a change in the sexual power relationship have such dire consequences for men? Alan Gross (1978) argued that whatever men suffered from the change, it should be blamed neither on the feminist movement nor on individual women; rather, ". . . it seems more appropriate generally to attribute 'new' male impotence to restrictive socialization and sex typing which has made it difficult for men to relinquish control, to accept and enjoy less structured and more egalitarian sexual relationships" (p. 100).

Even beyond an ideology of female–male equality, compelling reasons exist for changing the sexual power relationship between women and men. With the current risk of sexually transmitted diseases such as AIDS, the traditionally masculine posture of sexual expertise and sexual aggression and the traditionally feminine posture of allowing the man to make sexual decisions can be dangerous beyond threats to the success of a relationship: The costs of ignorance or lack of assertiveness can be life-threatening. There are indications even on college campuses that many students are not particularly well-informed about practicing "safe sex": They are unaware of the importance to themselves and their partners of using condoms during intercourse or of the risk associated with indiscriminate sexual behavior (McDermott, Hawkins, Moore, & Cittadino, 1987). Furthermore, among many men, the use of a condom is apparently viewed as threatening to their image as macho sexual aggressors. Strangely, given women's stereotypical role as passive in the sexual process (but perhaps not so strangely, given their assigned role as gatekeeper), the pressure is on them to make sure that men wear condoms. Women are asked in magazine advertisements, "Would you buy a condom for this man?" or they are told by attractive female models that "Sex is important, but I'm not willing to die for it." The apparent objective is to get women to take the responsibility of buying condoms and insisting that their male partner wear them during intercourse. This is a heavy burden to place on women alone, especially given their stereotypic image as nonexperts in the sexual realm. Furthermore, just as one might expect from the double standard, a woman who is prepared to offer a condom to a new sex partner risks being thought of as loose (Monagle, 1989). One irate female reader of *Ms.* magazine wrote, "How much more must we do? . . . it is a woman's duty to get it up, to keep it up, and now to spend her hard-earned money to dress it up. *Enough is enough!* I say if a man is too cheap and irresponsible to supply his own condom we should respond to him as Nancy Reagan suggests we respond to drugs—*Just say no!*"[1]

The difficulties that women sometimes encounter when saying no are a stark reminder in a society that emphasizes male sexual dominance that any implied threat to that dominance may be interpreted by the man as an insult and strongly resisted. When a woman asks a man to wear a condom she risks an accusation that either she is cheating on him or she does not trust him—and, in a violent relationship, he may respond with violence (Halpern, 1989). Resistance to the use of condoms is widespread among heterosexual males, particularly in ethnic groups with strong traditions of male sexual leadership. A report by the Women and AIDS Resource Network (WARN) states flatly that ". . . females who are powerless in a male-dominated society are just as powerless in a male-dominated bedroom. If a man does not want to wear a condom, he won't. With the coming of AIDS, the age-old battle of the sexes is literally becoming a life-and-death struggle for women" (quoted in Halpern, 1989).

SEXUALITY AS AN INTERPERSONAL POWER RESOURCE

Since sexuality is bound up with strong desires and vulnerabilities, there are many ways in which it can be used as a power resource—a source of power that one person can use to influence another. Sexual favors can be used as rewards, withdrawn as punishments, or exchanged for money. Sexual information can be used as the basis of blackmail. Knowledge about sexuality can be used, in some situations, as a source of "expert" power.

[1]Nancy Datres, letter to *Ms.* magazine, June 1989, p. 8 (Vol. 17, Number 12).

Sexual Attraction and Sexual Activity

A person who is sexually attractive to another—whether that attraction is heterosexual or homosexual—holds a powerful resource that can be distributed as a reward or withheld as a punishment. As with other kinds of resources, the more the target individual wants what the power holder has, the more she or he will be willing to do to get it. The resource is a highly personal one when someone who is strongly drawn sexually to another person is willing to make sacrifices for the privilege of being with that person, even though other opportunities for sexual relationships exist. In such a situation, the attracting individual can be very powerful in the relationship, particularly if she or he is not as strongly pulled toward the other person. Stereotypically, popular literature tends to picture this scenario with a woman as the irresistible seductress and a man as the helpless victim of her charms. However, observation tells us that women have no monopoly on seduction and men are not the only ones who can be hopelessly beguiled by the wiles of another.

In a situation where one person not only is attracted to another, but also sees no other opportunities for sexual relationships, sexual availability as a power resource can be a mixture of the personal and the real. In this case, both the personal sexual attraction and the more general desire for sexual activity render the sexually attracted person susceptible to the power of the other. Examples of this situation are seen in monogamous relationships where one partner tries to control or punish the other by holding out sexually. Again, stemming from the double standard-based assumption of greater male than female need for sexual release, the stereotypic power user in the heterosexual case is female: a wife ordering her long-suffering husband to sleep on the couch. However, while some women may find that the threat of cutting off their husbands is one of their few sources of power, a great many wives complain that they themselves do not get to have sex with their husbands as often as they would like (Levin & Levin, 1975). Women's magazines attract many readers with articles such as "Is there sex after marriage?"

Prostitution

The most concrete use of sexual availability as a power resource occurs in situations where impersonal sexual activity is exchanged for money. Power is easily measured by the amount the client is willing to pay and is strongly influenced by the amount of competition. When this exchange occurs between heterosexuals, it is almost invariably the woman who sells her sexual availability and the man who pays. On a smaller scale, some men sell their sexual companionship to women; however, the circumstances tend to differ. Male gigolos, as they are called, are almost never picked up on the street by women looking for quick, uncomplicated sex; but many female prostitutes make their living on the street in just this way. Once again, the differences between female and male patterns have sometimes been attributed squarely to the notion that men need sex more than women do. It is extremely likely, although, that the structure of society is a strong contributing cause.

In a society that expects male dominance, men are more likely than women to have both the money to pay for sex and the freedom to go out and look for it, and more women are likely to turn to prostitution because they need the money. The social approval of male dominance probably also ensures that more men than women will have the sense of superiority and detachment that makes the buying of sex comfortable. Furthermore, men have less to fear from female violence than women do from male violence. Women working as prostitutes use their sexual availability as a power resource, but they are rarely in a truly powerful position with respect to their male clients. Still more rarely are they in a powerful position with respect to society, since their failure to conform to the double standard is used as a weapon against them. They are harassed by police, frequently jailed, and often regarded with contempt, even by the very people who pay for their services. Many women working in prostitution see their sexual availability as their only power resource; they are often more desperate for money than their clients are for sex. That desperation can lead prostitutes to take big chances; for instance, there are now many reports that male clients are offering to pay prostitutes extra money if they will agree not to require a condom (Halpern, 1989). When a woman gives in to her client's pressure on this, she places herself, her other sex partners, the man, and his other sex partners at risk of infection from AIDS and other sexually transmitted diseases. A person who can be pressured to balance her own, and others', health and safety against the promise of an extra fifty dollars cannot take much comfort from the notion of sexuality as a power resource.

Who Uses Sexual Availability as a Power Resource?

In reviewing the above examples, one cannot help but be struck with the impression that it is women rather than men who are usually seen as using sexual availability as a power resource. This impression agrees with findings, discussed in Chapter Four, that the use of sexual- and relationship-oriented bases of power is viewed as characteristic of women (Johnson, 1976). In general, men are not seen as exploiting this particular source of power. Why not? The stereotype derives partly from mistaken notions about female and male sexuality. The double standard reflects a long-standing belief that men want and need sexual release more than women do. Deriving from this belief is a cultural myth of a woman, aloof and unmoved, shamelessly manipulating the men blinded by their sexual desire for her. Many women probably wish life were that simple. Women have strong sexual drives and desires too, and there is no reason why they should have a monopoly on the use of sexuality as a power resource. One probable reason for the stereotype of female sexual power is that for many women sexuality is the major or only power resource available.

In relating to women, men can often use physical strength, wealth, or position as power resources. Women are less likely than men to control such resources; they are often physically weaker than men, though not dramatically so, and they control less of the wealth and hold fewer positions of authority than men do. Thus, women may well be more dependent than men on power resources such as sexuality and attractiveness—though they may not like to admit to themselves that they are exchanging such resources for other rewards. In the case of young, attractive, single women, a dependence on sexuality is not easily seen as a disadvantage. Indeed, such women may feel very powerful in relating to the men who court their favor, even if they depend on those men for financial resources. It is often uncomfortable for women in this position to realize that the financial obligation implies some loss of control over their sexual choices. Also, with rare exceptions, women's sexuality-based power fades somewhat as a woman ages and falls victim to the societal insistence that beautiful means young. As a man ages his power resources of income, status, and expertise may well be growing—even if his physical prowess is not. Clearly, a total long-term reliance on sexuality or any other single power resource disadvantages a person compared to those with more diverse resources.

Sexual Blackmail

Danny, a young man struggling with the knowledge that he had contracted AIDS, wrote in his diary that he did not know how to share this information with his family, who had no idea he was gay. "First, I'll tell them I have AIDS," he speculated. "Then, when they get used to that, I'll tell them the worst part."[2]

Why would someone think his family would be more upset to find out that he was gay than that he was dying of AIDS? Probably because he was well aware of, and had suffered from, the intensity of negative reaction that homosexuality arouses among many people. But homosexuality,

---

[2]This story was reported on the KVOA local news, in Tucson, Arizona, June 7, 1989.

while perhaps the most dramatic revelation is far from the only aspect of sexual behavior that can cause strong disapproval if revealed. Information about sexuality in our culture is loaded information—information that, released, can have strong consequences for the way a person is viewed, accepted, loved, or rejected. In a culture that places strong sanctions on certain types of sexual behavior, sexual information about someone can be a powerful weapon. The person who publicly jokes about a spouse's lack of sexual interest or performance can inflict considerable hurt. The person who boasts far and wide about sexual conquests can cause injury to the partners' reputations. The individual who discloses the homosexuality, adultery, promiscuity, or other socially disapproved aspect of another's sexual behavior can cause serious problems for that person. People are therefore often hesitant about sharing sexual information about themselves with others. Anyone who has this type of knowledge about us has a potential source of power that increases according to our desire to keep the information private.

Information about sexual behavior can be used as a source of power over either men or women. However, our double standard of sexual expectations and morality renders specific types of sexual information more harmful to males and others more harmful to females. Even though some data suggest that the female and male sides of the double standard are no longer as far apart as they once were (Hendrick, Hendrick, Slapion-Foote, & Foote, 1985), there is still much evidence that women and men are not punished in the same way for violating various sexual norms. Female prostitutes suffer far more legal retribution than their male clients. Rape victims sometimes experience as much social rejection as rapists. And it has often been documented that women pay a higher price than men for sexual indiscretion in the workplace (Colwill & Lips, 1988). A woman is particularly vulnerable to certain types of sexual blackmail because she is thought to be tarnished by too much sexual activity. Joined with this attitude is the notion that any woman who would allow herself to be tainted in this way is either a fool or very weak. The woman who breaks with the conventional sexual morality of the day is seen in a doubly negative light. Even though a man may be severely publicly sanctioned for promiscuous sexual behavior, particularly if he holds a respectable political office or some other position that requires his morality to be above reproach, he may simultaneously be the object of private admiration among other men for his exploits.

If women are more easily victimized by information that they are too active sexually, men can be more damaged by information that they are not doing enough (impotence, virginity, or the inability to "score") or that they are doing it with the wrong people (homosexuality). The revelation of a person's homosexuality can be damaging whether that individual is male or female, but the evidence suggests that homophobia is stronger in relation to male than to female sexuality (Herek, 1988; Morin & Garfinkle, 1978). Homophobia—the irrational fear and abhorrence of homosexuality—is prevalent enough to make it not only awkward, but literally dangerous for individuals to reveal their homosexuality. Furthermore, the accusation of homosexuality against a man is considered more serious than almost any other insult. Witness the way members of Congress, as a group notoriously shameless at delivering the most outrageous of insults and thick-skinned at receiving them, became outraged and embarrassed in 1989 when the staff of the Republican National Committee tried to smear the new Speaker of the House with a veiled reference to homosexuality. These men spoke of the insults "finally going too far," "crossing a line," and the President himself declared that he was "disgusted" with the offending memo. This from individuals who gleefully hurl charges of "lying," "cheating," and even "womanizing" across the floor at one another without flinching.

Particularly for males, the social disapproval of homosexuality serves to maintain the rigidity of sexual roles and also of gender roles. Any display of "feminine" behavior by a man is likely to arouse the suspicion that he is homosexual (Deaux & Lewis, 1984). A man's reputation may suffer at the disclosure not just of homosexual interest or activities, but even of any preference or behavior that might be considered effeminate.

Whatever the effect on individuals, the general effect of attaching so much power to sexual information is to pressure people to adhere to sexual norms and to keep sexual information secret. As a society, we pay a high price for this pressure in sexual rigidity, confusion, resentment, despair, and cynicism. Many individuals can ill afford to use sexual information as a power source for fear of equally damaging retribution, but a few others can ride to fame and fortune on it: the prostitute who tells the story of her relationship with an eminent politician; the servant who exposes his or her famous employer's sexual peccadillos. This type of sexual power will never be obsolete as long as strong social sanctions against particular expressions of sexuality exist.

CHILDBEARING: WOMAN'S POWER OR WOMAN'S VULNERABILITY?

We cannot consider the power resources associated with sexuality without including one crucial one: the ability to bear children. In some contexts, women's ability to become pregnant and to bear a child has been and is a source of tremendous power. In the years before the male contribution to conception was understood, childbearing women were believed to hold the power to bring forth life and were viewed with awe in some societies (Davis, 1971). Later, when the connection between intercourse and pregnancy was recognized, the pendulum swung in the opposite direction: Men's sperm provided the substance and form of life, and women were seen as mere vessels for the carrying of the fetus to term.

Now that the biological contributions of both women and men to conception are understood, women's power to bear children is no longer considered magic, but pregnancy does confer some legitimate power on women. For example, pregnancy provides a legitimate excuse for some women to be treated with special consideration. In many couples, the woman gains temporary interpersonal power through pregnancy, even if it is only to have her mate pull on her winter boots or lift the heaviest packages.

Yet pregnancy also represents a loss of power and an increase in vulnerability for many women. Many battered wives trace the first instance of violence against them by their husbands to some time during their first pregnancy. In many circumstances, employed women find it difficult to hold on to their jobs when they become pregnant, even when there are maternity leave provisions. As well, pregnant women are increasingly vulnerable to interference by authorities of the state. There is a growing tendency to charge pregnant women with child abuse if they drink or take drugs during pregnancy. Although the issues are complicated, the legal and personal implications of this latter tendency are alarming: Supplanting women's autonomy with fetal rights could lead to pregnant women's being charged with abusing the fetus whenever they do anything that runs counter to orthodox medical opinion.

We are not at that extreme now, yet it is clear from the bitterness of the debates over abortion and fetus-abuse issues that when a woman becomes pregnant she forfeits some of her autonomy—not just, in the physical sense, to the developing fetus, but also, in the social and legal sense, to the state. Furthermore, with the advent of surrogate mothering, recent years have seen some return to the notion of women as mere vessels for the carrying of a fetus to term. The woman who contracts for money to carry a pregnancy to term for a couple who want a child is often seen as having no rights whatsoever to the baby when it is born, even if she is the biological mother. The relationship between such a woman and her baby is considered of negligible importance, and the mothering service she sells is seen, although perhaps not with such negative overtones, as somewhat like prostitution.

Within a couple, impregnation requires at least minimal cooperation from two people, except in cases of rape. If a man wishes to have a child, he must have the cooperation of a woman, and vice versa. Such cooperation becomes a potential source of interpersonal power in the relationship:

Either party can threaten to withhold it. The balance of power can, however, be disrupted by force, trickery, or technology. A man can rape his wife (or any other woman) in an attempt to impregnate her. A woman whose husband or lover does not want her to become pregnant can have intercourse with others or can quietly stop using contraception without informing him. A woman who wants a child but not a husband can seek out a man, seduce him, and have him father her child without ever telling him, or she can be very direct in recruiting him for his sperm. The shock to traditional male–female power assumptions of such a strategy can be great, even if the woman does tell the prospective father what she is planning to do. Men are used to believing they are doing the sexual hunting; the traditional sexual power relationship has given them little practice at being recruited explicitly for their potential reproductive contribution.

Even greater is the shock to a man who, believing he has seduced a woman, discovers later that he has been deliberately and unknowingly used to father a child—and that his presence in the relationship is no longer required. Simone de Beauvoir (1952) once said that even when a woman set out deliberately to seduce a man and succeeded, "the victory is still ambiguous; the fact is that in common opinion it is still the man who conquers, who *has* the woman" (p. 649). The tenacity of the double standard still renders that argument true, except, perhaps, in the latter case. It is a strange state of affairs when a woman can win only by tricking and using the man. However, the double standard, the aura of conquest that pervades sexuality in our culture, seems to make such an outcome inevitable for the most part, if not in all individual cases.

Developments in New Reproductive Technology

Artificial insemination, in vitro fertilization, fetal monitoring, embryo transplants, and surrogate motherhood have still further muddied the traditional female-male power relationship with respect to reproduction. In some respects, and for some people, these technologies expand choices and increase personal control over the very personal issue of childbearing. Single women and lesbian couples can choose to have a child through artificial insemination. In vitro fertilization sometimes makes it possible for a couple previously unable to conceive to have a child that is biologically their own. Fetal monitoring sometimes saves the life or health of a developing fetus, making it possible for women to carry high-risk pregnancies to term.

However, the new technologies also raise troubling questions, particularly about women's autonomy and control over their bodies and their reproductive choices. Pregnancy, which historically has been a very personal experience, is now increasingly subject to technological in-tervention. The joy of being able to get help with conception or with a high-risk pregnancy is balanced by the other implication of the availabil-ity of high-tech intervention: the spectre of being forced to accept medical interference at the behest of a doctor or a judge. The potential increase in freedom of choice that comes from the new possibilities inherent in embryo transplants and surrogate motherhood is tainted by a social structure that often emphasizes the priority of men's needs over women's needs, the assumption that money ought to be able to buy even the work of actual childbearing, and the ownership of children by their parents.

Whose Choice?

For many women, the problem lies not in finding someone to cooperate in having a child, but rather in avoiding pregnancy. The effect of years of male dominance of church and state institutions is felt in laws and rules that forbid women control over their own reproductive processes—despite that it is women to whom the work of child rearing has customarily been assigned. For years, man-made legal and religious laws curtailing contraception, abortion, sex education, and affirming a husband's right to intercourse with his wife whether or not she consents have undercut women's power and forced women to bear unwanted children. Until well into this century, spreading information about birth control was illegal in North America. Even women who had been warned by their physicians that another pregnancy could well be fatal were not provided with information on how to prevent another pregnancy. Instead, they were simply warned, married or single, not to have sex. Not only unplanned conception, but also death in childbirth or from self-induced abortion, was a real and significant risk for any sexually active woman.

Contraception is now legal in North America, and its availability represents a crucial increase in power for women. A woman who chooses to be sexually active need not accept the whole package of marriage and children if her own values do not dictate that she do so. However, reluctance to provide sex education for adolescents and the difficulty in many jurisdictions of obtaining legal abortions still conspire to restrict women's reproductive freedom. Women's access to legal abortion is increasingly restricted in the United States and Canada, a development that saddles women once again with the major responsibility for the reproductive consequences of sexual activity. And women are very much aware of those consequences. Women are more likely than men to report that fear of pregnancy interferes with the free expression of their sexu-ality (Rubenstein, 1983).

Yes, childbearing can be a source of power for women, but only under certain conditions. If women are not allowed control over childbearing, it becomes a source of vulnerability rather than power.

SOCIAL EXPRESSIONS OF MALE SEXUAL DOMINANCE

Much of our social environment reflects and reinforces the idea that males exert leadership, control, and dominance in the sexual realm. The message that part of being a man is the sexual dominance of women, whereas part of being a woman is sexual surrender to a man, is pervasive in private language and public media. Indeed, the message is so strong that it contributes to the ultimate in male sexual dominance: rape.

The Language of Sexuality

The words colloquially used to describe male genitals are active, powerful words: prick, pecker, tool; the words used to describe female genitals—cunt, pussy—are static and passive. In addition, there are derogatory terms—nymphomaniac, slut—for a woman who desires and engages in a lot of sexual activity, but there are no comparably insulting terms to describe men. What is the male equivalent of a slut? Perhaps stud comes closest, but the implications of the two terms are very different. In some contexts, a man might take the label stud as a compliment; there is no context where a woman would be flattered to be called a slut.

The language of sexual intercourse has changed somewhat in recent years, perhaps reflecting a shift in sexual mores. Whereas it used to be said that men "laid," "screwed," or "fucked" women—never the reverse—these words are now used sometimes to describe the activities of women. Regardless of whose activities they describe, it is striking that the words are so aggressive in tone. They seem to reflect *only* the power dimension of sexuality—a clue, perhaps, to just how important a dimension that is.

Swearing is another use of language that is charged with power, perhaps because it is so often used in anger. Many profane words are sexual and anti-female in nature. The use of dirty language helps to keep women in their place, both figuratively and physically, by reminding them of their lower status and by providing reasons to bar them from places where their delicate ears might be offended. Women may well suspect that it is not profanity per se from which they are being protected, but from the knowledge of how men speak of women. Profanity serves two functions in maintaining the gender power relations system: keeping women in their place and keeping women out of places.

One of the ways in which sexual language is used to exert power is through jokes. As with profanity, aggressive power is a strong theme in sexual jokes, most often in the form of antifemale humor (Puner, 1974). Women take less pleasure than men do in aggressive humor. However, this finding is difficult to interpret because aggressive humor tends to be antifemale, and women, not surprisingly, prefer antimale humor (Priest & Wilhelm, 1974). The feminist movement has been the spawning ground for aggressive antimale humor; witness the T-shirt slogans "Adam was a rough draft" and "A woman without a man is like a fish without a bicycle."

The Power of Pornography

Erotica—films, pictures, or literature that is meant to arouse sexual feelings—has been a dimension of the human sexual experience in many cultures for thousands of years. In cultures where male dominance is an important part of the sexual mystique, erotica is often the sexualization of male dominance and female submission. When this happens, erotica takes the form that feminists have labeled pornography: erotica that implies violence against or domination of one person by another. Such dominance and violence have become relatively common in softcore pornography (Malamuth & Spinner, 1980) and are frequently important themes in X-rated videocassettes that make pornographic movies available for take-out (Cowan, Lee, Levy, & Snyder, 1988).

Political battles over pornography have intensified as its availability and general visibility has increased. On one side are people concerned about censorship of freedom of speech. On the other are people who argue that pornography is really hate literature directed against women and thus exempt from concerns about free speech. Although it is difficult to know how the problem of pornography can be solved, there are good reasons to be concerned about it. First, since much of it reflects the eroticization of male dominance and female submission (to the extremes, for example, of showing naked women being chained, beaten, and even killed for the sexual gratification of a male partner), it reinforces a vision of sexuality that degrades women and provides support for the belief that "sex in our society is construed as a dirty, low and violent act involving domination of a male over a female" (Herman, 1979, p. 59). It does not necessarily require a feminist perspective to question whether this power-and-domination vision of sexuality is indeed the one that society should promote.

A second reason for concern about pornography is its possible influence on people's reaction to and participation in sexual coercion and assault in the real world. It seems reasonable to suspect that by reinforcing fantasies of sexual degradation and violence, pornography might increase the likelihood of rape and other forms of sexual assault. Feminist writers have argued for years that pornography reinforces the fantasy that every woman secretly wants to be raped, or at least possessed and dominated sexually, and that no real woman cares if she gets kicked around a bit in the process (Brownmiller, 1975; Clark & Lewis, 1977). Recent research shows that exposure to pornography does reinforce such myths and may indeed increase the likelihood that viewers will engage in sexual coercion and rape.

Studies have now shown that exposure to violent pornography is linked to men's increased acceptance of interpersonal violence against women (Demare, 1985; Malamuth & Check, 1981); more frequent violent sexual fantasies (Malamuth, 1981a); and a greater willingness to aggress against women in a laboratory setting (Donnerstein & Barrett, 1978; Malamuth, 1984). Exposure to depictions of sexual violence apparently also has a desensitizing effect. Subjects exposed to sexually violent films over several days have been shown to perceive the films as less violent, offensive, and degrading to women by the last day, and later to rate the victim in a videotaped rape trial as less injured than did subjects who did not see the films (Linz, Donnerstein, & Penrod, 1984). There is also evidence from the self-reports of male university students that the use of sexually violent pornography is associated with the self-reported likelihood of raping and using sexual force against a woman (Demare, Briere, & Lips, 1988).

While none of these findings prove that exposure to pornography directly increases the likelihood that male viewers will commit rape, they do strongly suggest that pornography is one important factor contributing to a constellation of rape-supportive attitudes. Whether or not pornography can be unequivocally indicted as a direct cause of rape, it is clear that it promotes negative attitudes toward women. The research is far beyond the point where pornography can be labeled harmless.

Sexual Violence

In many instances, sexual approaches take on the character of attacks. Such instances range from street harassment, in which a woman passerby is taunted with catcalls and sexual innuendos; to sexual intimidation at work, in which a supervisor implies more or less explicitly that a worker's job is not secure if she complains about unwelcome touches, improper comments, or pressure for dates; to the use of physical force in rape or other forms of sexual assault. Women are far more likely than men to be the victims of the various forms of sexual violence, and men are far more likely than women to be the perpetrators of such violence (Herman, 1981; Russell, 1984; Tangri, Burt, & Johnson, 1982).

Even the most extreme form of sexual violence, rape, is not a rare crime but a relatively common one: Careful survey research in the United States suggests that 14 of every 1000 women may be victimized in this way in a given year (Koss, 1989). Koss and her colleagues report that 28% of college women have experienced rape or attempted rape (Koss et al., 1987). The gender imbalance, and the very existence of sexual coercion, has frequently been attributed to natural male–female differences (men's allegedly stronger sexual needs), but it seems more likely that the pattern is simply a reflection of power differences between men and women and the ideology of male sexual dominance.

Feminist writers have long argued that rape is a crime, not of passion, but of power (Brownmiller, 1975; Greer, 1977), and that men who rape women are simply drawing the notion of male sexual dominance to its logical conclusion (Russell, 1975). This argument is bolstered by evidence from a variety of quarters. For instance, the history of rape is intimately bound up with the notion of women as the property of men (Brownmiller, 1975). Rape was a crime, not against the woman, but against the man who owned her. In some societies, a man was compensated for the rape of his wife or daughter by a financial payment—or the opportunity to rape the rapist's woman. In Anglo-Saxon law, payment extracted from a rapist was determined by the worth of his victim, which was in turn determined by the financial worth of her husband, brothers, or father. Present rape laws make no mention of the victim's worth, but it is a well-documented fact that a rape charge is much more likely to be brought, and more likely to stick, if the victim is of high socioeconomic status and can establish herself as a virgin or a monogamous wife (Clark & Lewis, 1977). If the victim is shown to be sexually active or promiscuous before the rape, there is a tendency to consider the rape as less serious—or perhaps not a rape at all.

In some societies, rape has also been used as an explicit method for controlling women and/or for punishing them when they failed to conform to social rules (Sanday, 1981). Among the Mundurucu, a woman who contrived to see the sacred trumpets, which she was forbidden to do, was penalized by gang rape. Similarly, an infrequently reported practice among the Cheyenne was for a husband frustrated with his wife's strong-willed or adulterous behavior to invite unmarried men from his military society to a feast at which they would take turns raping his wife. While rape is not formalized as a punishment for women in our society, it is often depicted in just this way in pornography. Evidence suggests that it is used this way in at least one version of rape: marital rape. Marital rape is often part of the battering and humiliation that violent husbands inflict on their wives (Frieze, 1983).

Another argument for viewing rape as a crime of power rather than passion comes from an analysis of male–male rape, commonly reported in prisons (Lockwood, 1980). The men who engage in this behavior do not define themselves as homosexual. In the prison situation, it is very clear that the rape of one man by another is not an expression of sexual desire, but rather an example of the use of sex to humiliate and control another person. Susan Brownmiller (1975), who analyzed this phenomenon in terms of status, contends that the selection of rape victims in prison is not a random process; rather, the youngest and most feminine-appearing men are victimized because they are the least powerful. She argues that cell-block status is determined by a prisoner's ability to maintain the toughness and aggressiveness associated with traditional masculinity, and that rape occurs only downward in the status hierarchy. Male–male rape in prison appears to be a violent power strategy that serves to maintain the status hierarchy and mirrors sexual coercion in the outside world.

More support for the notion that patterns of sexual coercion spring from the acceptability of male sexual dominance come from questionnaire studies of attitudes toward rape. A significant proportion of male college students indicates on confidential questionnaires that there is at least some possibility that they would rape a woman if they could be sure of not being caught. Across studies, the average number of college males reporting this is approximately 35% (Malamuth, 1981b); although in different samples it has been as high as nearly 60% (Briere & Malamuth, 1983) and as low as 17% (Demare, Briere, & Lips, 1988). Furthermore, there is some reluctance, at least among young people, to condemn rape under all circumstances or even to define forced sex as rape. When a broad spectrum of Los Angeles teenagers were questioned as to whether it was "all right" for "a guy to hold a girl down and force her to have sexual intercourse" under each of nine specific conditions, only 21% of the sample said that it was not "all right" in any of the conditions (Zellman & Goodchilds, 1983). It appears that rape is not viewed as a completely abhorrent behavior, but rather that there is a certain amount of acceptability attached to it under certain circumstances—at least as long as it happens to someone else. Again, these findings suggest that sexual force springs in part from an ideology that accepts male sexual dominance.

The Myth of the Willing Victim

One widely accepted rape myth is that all women secretly want to be raped, or at least that women enjoy being sexually overpowered. This myth is reinforced in hard- and soft-core pornography where the woman is often portrayed as initially resisting the man's advances but then being carried away by her sexual desire after he forces her to continue. A common defense of apprehended rapists is "she enjoyed it," and many rapists try to extract expressions of enjoyment from their victims (Gager & Schurr, 1976).

College students have been found to estimate that 32% of women would enjoy being raped if they could be sure that no one would know about it. However, when the same group was asked for their own projected reactions to rape, only 2% of the women reported any likelihood at all that they would enjoy being raped (Malamuth, Haber, & Feshbach, 1980). Apparently, the myth of the willing victim is easier to accept for others than for oneself.

Some women report sexual fantasies of being overpowered and sexually dominated (Hariton & Singer, 1974), but there is no evidence that they enjoy the reality of sexual assault. Given the way women have traditionally been told, through the double standard, that they must be responsible for acting as gatekeepers and holding back men's sexual advances, it is not surprising if women sometimes fantasize about being swept away and sexually aroused against their better judgment. In a way, what the double standard has said to women for years is that the only time they are allowed to relax their vigilance and enjoy sex is when they can't help it. The focus of these fantasies may be more on the removal of sexual responsibility than on physical violence. It seems likely that the sexual fantasies of both women and men would be different in a society that had no double standard and no emphasis on male sexual dominance.

There is another side to the question of women as victims, however. The socialization of females to be weak, passive, fearful, and to rely on men for protection is, in many respects, the socialization of females to be powerless, to be vulnerable victims (Russell, 1975). Vulnerable does not mean willing, but it does mean that someone may be too frightened, or too unskilled, to fight back when attacked.

Research on the avoidance of rape suggests that women who do not fit exactly into the traditional feminine image are more successful at avoiding attempted rape (Bart, 1980). Bart found that background differences involving women's autonomy, competence, and self-reliance were related to the ability to avoid rape. Women who were larger and stronger, had never married, had participated regularly in sports, or had training in first aid, self-defense, or assertiveness were more likely than their counterparts to be able to get away from a would-be rapist without being raped. Moreover, in the actual attack situation, women who used the most ways to avoid rape were the most successful; the likelihood of being raped increased when the woman relied on only one strategy to avoid it. The feminine influence strategy of pleading with the rapist was used by 33% of the women who were eventually raped and by only 22% of those who avoided it. The women who avoided rape reported that they had used the strategy of reasoning with the rapist as a way to buy time while they prepared to use another strategy—running, screaming, or physical force. These data suggest that women should not assume they are powerless in the face of an attack; rather, they should be prepared to use many methods of defense. Overreliance on the stereotypically feminine modes of influence, such as tearful pleading, may be a big mistake. Women are not helpless or powerless; they must assume the burden of their own safety. No one has a greater interest in protecting a woman than she does herself, and no other guardian is so constantly available.

Personal Power, Sexuality, and Responsibility

Running through the discussion of power and sexuality is the theme that both women and men are taught, each in their own way, to exert power without acknowledging responsibility. A man may sexually coerce or harass a woman and evade responsibility by claiming that he was overwhelmed by his own sexual needs, that she asked for it by her dress or demeanor, or that she really wanted it despite her protestations. Men are taught by the double standard to try to evade responsibility for sexuality. Women are taught a good deal about the negative or avoidance aspect of sexual responsibility, but they are given very little encouragement to take positive responsibility in seeing that their own needs and feelings are met in a sexual relationship. They are cautioned against looking too sexy, staying out too late, hitchhiking alone, accompanying a man to his apartment, or frequenting certain areas of town. The sum total of these cautions teaches a woman not how to be sexually powerful, but only how to accept and cope with powerlessness by being very, very careful.

The restrictions women are expected to accept in the name of caution about sexual assault are impractical for most of us. If women are being attacked in downtown parking garages or in shopping mall parking lots in the middle of the day, it is not helpful to say, as some law enforcement officials have, that women should not go to such places alone. Women must act, as individuals and collectively, to make themselves less vulnerable and to make their social environment less dangerous. As former Israeli prime minister Golda Meier once suggested, it is perhaps time to accept the notion that if anyone is going to have freedom of movement restricted by the threat of sexual assault, it should be the potential assaulters rather than the potential victims. In this regard, Mexico City has set an interesting precedent: During rush hours, when women are likely to be sexually harassed on crowded subway trains, there are some trains reserved just for women and children. Women may ride on the same trains as the men, but if they do not want to, they have a choice. This is not an ideal solution; it would be preferable to find a way of stopping sexual harassment so that everyone could ride on the same train without worrying. Nonetheless, it is one way in which a society has taken responsibility for ensuring that women's freedom of movement is not impaired by their vulnerability to harassment.

A stripping away of the double standard and of the ideology of male sexual dominance would pave the way for the acceptance of other forms of responsibility as well: responsibility in sexual relationships. With the current power relationships in place, women have to be cautious about any show of sexual interest and any initiation of sexual activity. Under the rule of the double standard, a woman who indicates even a minimal level of sexual interest and encouragement to a man may later be charged with leading him on if she tries to limit the sexual relationship. Such cautions and restrictions encourage women to see themselves as objects, even in a desired sexual encounter, rather than taking responsibility for sexuality on their own terms. As well, the double standard inhibits honest communication about sexuality in relationships. It is not easy for a woman schooled in the gatekeeper role mandated by the double standard to show her partner what gives her sexual pleasure or to insist that her sexual needs be taken seriously. For a man trained in the sex-as-conquest approach, it is not easy to abandon a macho stance in favor of the sensitivity required for real give-and-take in a sexual relationship. Yet, these are the kinds of changes that help sexuality to become a source of empowerment rather than a drain on personal power.

Under an ideology of gender equality, both women and men can potentially integrate sexuality and power in a more positive way than that prescribed by the double standard. Sex makes people feel good—under the right conditions—and the positive experience of sexuality is one that includes, besides physical pleasure, a sense of empowerment and enhanced self-worth. But feelings of energy and personal power are more likely to be generated by sexual activity when one does not feel objectified, victimized, or humiliated by that activity; and a sense of personal worth is more likely to be generated from a sexual relationship in which one feels appreciated, respected, and valued. It is difficult for women to find such feelings for themselves in sexual relationships characterized by male dominance; in the long run, after the thrill of the initial conquest fades, it is difficult for men too.

Some women, despairing of changing the built-in male dominance in heterosexual relationships, have opted with relief and joy for celibacy. Some women and men struggle to build lesbian or gay relationships that do not echo the power problems that societal endorsement of male dominance creates for heterosexual relationships. Some women and men are committed to developing heterosexual relationships in which equality is the watchword. Yet every sexual relationship, even same-sex ones, exists in a power context in a society that accepts the eroticization of dominance and submission.

If individual women and men want to move away from the sexual scenario in which men push and women resist, women wait and men pay, they can do so with conscious effort. Certainly, some women and men have been able to form sexual relationships with each other that are empowering instead of limiting. Yet, even when determinedly celibate or comfortably ensconced in what may feel like the best of all possible relationships, no one is completely sheltered from a wider social world in which violence is a turn-on, where sexuality is still viewed as an expression of male dominance, and nice girls are thought of as those who avoid rather than pursue sexual activity. In such a world, rape and sexual harassment will continue at epidemic rates, young male AIDS sufferers will continue to wonder whether their parents will feel worse about the fact that they are dying or the fact that they are gay, and relationship after relationship will founder on the shoals of misunderstanding and frustration. To change all this requires individuals to examine their own beliefs about sexuality, about dominance and submission, about pornography and rape. It requires that sex education of the young does not perpetuate established patterns of the double standard, of male dominance and female subservience. It requires teaching young people that women and men have sexual needs and desires and that both have the responsibility to balance these needs and desires against those of others. None of this is as simple as it may sound; we have seen repeatedly in this chapter just how emotionally charged is the topic of sexuality. But many would argue that it would be well worth the struggle to see the double standard dissolve into a single standard for humane people.

CONCLUSION: SEXUALITY, DOMINANCE, AND THE DOUBLE STANDARD

Sexuality and power are linked in a variety of ways. For women and men, the linkage is mediated by the double standard, which decrees that men are the sexual experts, leaders, teachers, and aggressors; women are the followers, the objects of men's desires, and the gatekeepers. Stereotypically, men's power is directed at obtaining more sexual gratification, whereas women's is directed at setting limits on sexual engagement. Various aspects of sexuality can, however, be used by both men and women as power resources. Sexual attractiveness, sexual information about another person, and childbearing can all be used by one person to gain leverage over another.

Men's dominance over women is a recurrent theme in our culture's notions about sexuality. This theme, which is an aspect of the double standard, is reflected in pornography and is acted out most destructively in the sexual harassment and sexual coercion of women by men.

Sexuality involves personal power, or empowerment, as well as the power of one person or group over another. The power to achieve one's own sexual pleasure and to communicate one's desires and feelings to a partner form an important source of positive sensations and emotions and may contribute to an individual's self-esteem. As women and men take responsibility for sexuality in a positive sense, they may find that an increase in this sense of personal power reduces the need for power over their partners.

In the next chapter, we examine the ways in which the male dominance/female submission script for heterosexual relationships shapes the patterns of power in families.

CHAPTER EIGHT

Power in
the Family

For almost everyone, life's initial adventures in wielding and reacting to interpersonal power occur in the family. The first power struggle is between parent and child—with the child gradually gaining ground and the parent, filled with mixed feelings, yielding it. The struggle is joined each time the child refuses to bow to parental authority—when a five-year-old defies her mother's instructions to go outside to play, when a ten-year-old refuses to help his father with the dishes.

The subtext of the parent-child power struggle is a series of lessons taught, wittingly or unwittingly, to the child by the parent (and vice versa), and those lessons are about power—about getting other human beings to cooperate, to meet one's needs, to accede to one's requests. As most parents know to their occasional chagrin, children learn quickly, and sometimes it is the unintended lessons that they learn the fastest of all. So children learn about power not just from what their parents try to teach them but also from observing their parents' interactions with them, with each other, and with other persons inside and outside the family. They learn, through trial and error and through example, which power strategies work, which ones are acceptable, and what they can get away with. They learn about the rules for family and other relationships, and about cultural values concerning power, effectiveness, and influence.

I am indebted to Lillian Esses, who authored a chapter on power in the family for my earlier book on the psychology of power. Although she did not contribute directly to the writing of this chapter, it reflects some of her ideas.

Since it provides the first context for learning about power, and since it institutionalizes in many ways male-female power relationships, the family system cries out for examination by anyone seeking an understanding of gender and power.

Among the maxims about power that children learn as they survive the growing up process are three that will especially concern us in this chapter: The first is that power comes from implicit or explicit bargaining; the second is that sometimes legitimate power and authority are assigned according to basically irrational cultural rules; the third is that under some circumstances "might is right."

In the first instance, children learn that it is easier to gain cooperation from parents and others if they have something to offer in return. Parents are at pains to teach children that the family runs most smoothly when everyone contributes something; and children quickly absorb the lesson that, for instance, a request is more easily granted if it is preceded by the dutiful and uncomplaining completion of an assigned chore than if it conflicts with the completion of that chore. Furthermore, while a child may not analyze the exchanges that go on in maintaining power relationships between parents and/or among other family members, these exchanges do not pass completely unnoticed. Even the unspoken understandings about resources and reciprocal contributions to the relationship that exist between the parents may have a strong impact on the child.

The second early lesson about power is that the culture, as mediated by the family, has some seemingly arbitrary rules about the distribution of formal power and authority. Children learn that certain people are considered more important than others: perhaps, for example, that fathers are more important than mothers; that adults are more important than children; that boys are more important than girls; that rich people are more important than poor people; that professional people are more important than working-class people. When there is a conflict, the interests or the authority of the "important" groups take precedence over those of the "lesser" groups. Such observations teach the child the cultural norms that grant more legitimacy to the exercise of power by some groups than by others and socialize the child into ways that power is institutionalized in the culture.

A third, and pivotal, power lesson learned by the child is the extent to which force works, the extent to which might is right. Coercion of the weak by the strong is experienced as extremely effective by a child, who, being small and weak relative to parents, other adults and older siblings, may be particularly vulnerable to such coercion. Yet, depending on the family environment, the child may learn very early that certain factors curb the use of sheer physical force as a source of power: Parents may inhibit the use of physical force out of concern for the child's well-being, out of a sense of fairness, or even out of fear of the disapproval of observers. When such reassurance is missing, the potential victims of force live with constant anxiety. Research on abused children shows that such children are more attentive to their mothers than their mothers are to them—a reversal of the pattern found in non-abusive mother-child relationships (McCloskey, 1989).

The family is not only a system in which a group of people live out power relationships but also a context which sets the stage for future power relationships by transmitting shared understandings about power from one generation to the next. In examining the processes of family power and the content of the shared understandings about power that are transmitted, we come face to face once again with one seemingly fundamental rule about the relationship between gender and power: Apparent gender differences in behavior are often power differences. The distribution of resources and accepted norms of society often give men more sources of family power than women. Where this is the case, women behave in more powerless ways than men do, but such behavior has little to do with femininity and masculinity and much to do with the options available to the two sexes.

SOURCES OF POWER IN THE FAMILY

On July 14, 1976, the women of Belgium celebrated the obliteration of the last vestiges of male dominance in their country's marriage legislation. The legislation took away the husband's role as head of the house and replaced it with an ideal of shared power between spouses. No longer was it legal for a husband to make such decisions as selling the family home without the wife's consent. No longer could a husband legally demand that a wife turn over all or part of her income to him. The new legislation enshrined the principles of equal autonomy (the possibility of acting without the other spouse's agreement in such areas as the pursuit of job or one's own income) and equal solidarity (the obligation to act with the other spouse's agreement in areas crucial to the family welfare, such as the selling of family property). Under the new Belgian law, wife and husband were for the first time granted equal power in the marriage relationship (Gysels & Vogels, 1982).

Belgium is not the first or the only country that has moved to legislate equality in the marriage relationship. France, the Netherlands, and West Germany also have legislation designed to promote equality of power between spouses. Sweden has an unusually long history of trying to guarantee such equality; their Marriage Code of 1920 established that each spouse owned his or her own property during marriage; managed and could freely dispose of that property; was responsible for his or her own debts (Saldeen, 1987–88); and the economic partnership of spouses could be dissolved without dissolving the marriage. The Soviet Union also has a decades-long legal tradition of official equality between spouses, first enshrined in the Family Law Code of 1919 (Glass & Stollee, 1987). Policy and practice are sometimes a vast distance apart, however, as contemporary studies of families in the latter two countries show (O'Kelly & Carney, 1986).

Given the difficulty of forcing social change through legislation, why is there so much concern with laws to "make" spouses equal? Perhaps it is because the old laws enshrine an ideal of extreme spousal inequality that is now distasteful to many. Assumptions about the naturalness of male authority have been unquestioned for so long in so many societies that they have literally been built in to laws about families. Thus, the assumptions of male dominance that have colored sexual relationships have tended to become solidified when those sexual relationships are formalized in the framework of marriage. The marriage laws of a number of countries, such as the United States, still reflect, not equality between spouses, but rather such inequalities as restrictions on the wife's surname and place of residence, the imposition on the husband of the financial support of the family, and a concept of property ownership favorable to the husband (Weitzman, 1985).

Today's legalized inequalities are not, however, as severe as they have been in times past. In legal terms, men have often owned their wives and children and have had almost complete rights of authority over them. In many jurisdictions, until the last 20 years, a married women could not own property, had no control over her own income (if she were allowed to earn any), and could be divorced for refusing to follow her husband to live in whatever section of the world he might choose. The law has even given men the right of physical punishment over their wives; for example, a 19th-century law, kept on the books in some states until recent decades, gave a husband the right to beat his wife as long as the stick he used was "no thicker than his thumb" (Walker, 1979).

The legal changes that have pushed the marriage relationship in the direction of equality over the last two decades not only force changes in the balance of marital power, they also reflect changes in that balance that have gradually occurred. Researchers who study families note that the traditional nuclear family with a male head and breadwinner and a female fulltime helpmate and homemaker has become more myth than reality in recent years. With the weakening of that tradition and the rise of a multitude of different family forms, power in the family belongs less automatically to the husband. Rather, power in any particular family is based on the resources the family members bring to the relationship, on the division of labor within the family, and on the laws, customs, and expectations of the culture in which the family exists. As will soon become obvious, however, these three factors are not independent of one another.

Resources and Family Power

In marriage, the spouses develop a more or less stable system of resource exchange. They divide up the tasks; they build implicit agreements that "If you will take care of this, I will take care of that." Yet most of us do not like to be reminded of the exchange that goes on in a couple relationship. We would prefer to focus on feelings, not exchange; on love, not power. When marriages do not work, we speak of love problems rather than power problems (Haavind, 1984).

Even less do most of us like to be reminded that marriage, embedded in a system of social inequality between women and men, institutionalizes that inequality by regulating the ways that power and love are distributed between the marriage partners. This does not mean that all love is an illusion or that it is hopeless to achieve equality in any spousal relationship. What it does mean is that we must make the implicit, or unspoken, contractual aspects of marriage explicit, or clear, before we can hope to achieve marital relationships that do not automatically privilege the husband (Haavind, 1984). In the following sections, some aspects of the implicit exchanges of marriage are explored.

The Division of Labor and Control Over Economic Resources

In the North America of the 1950s, certain aspects of the division of labor in the family were clear: the man was expected to be the breadwinner, the source of economic support for the family; the woman was supposed to care for the children, look after the home, and be a source of moral and emotional support for her husband. To label a man a "poor provider" or a woman an "unfit mother" was to offer a devastating insult.

The traditional division of labor described above is hardly traditional at all, but a fairly recent invention. Until the middle of the 19th century, American women were active in business and professional pursuits, and rural families shared many of the family tasks. It was only with the industrial revolution and the transition from a subsistence to a market economy that the good provider role became a male specialty (Bernard, 1981). The division of labor into a male good provider and a female good mother role required that the husband deal extensively with the outside world while the wife focus more narrowly on the domestic realm—a task specialization that, if rigidly followed, would result in the honing of different skills and the acquisition of control over different resources for the two individuals involved. Sociologists even argued that the interpersonal roles "naturally-adopted" by and appropriate for wives and husbands were complementary: The wife took on the expressive (socio-emotional, nurturing) role; the husband emphasized the instrumental (task-oriented) role (Parsons & Bales, 1955).

The task versus emotional role specialization paints a stereotypic picture that has probably rarely been echoed in real life. Even in the most role-specialized of nuclear families, men may spend a lot of time at home and may provide nurturance and emotional support for their wives and children; women's home management and child rearing responsibilities frequently require them to take on instrumental, organizational tasks. The role of traditional wife does not limit the woman to her home, but often, in fact, requires her to interact actively and assertively with the outside world in the form of school systems, doctors, neighborhood associations, and the like.

Perhaps a more useful distinction to draw between the roles of women and men in the traditional Western family is that men's access to economic resources is directly controlled by forces outside the family, whereas women's access to economic resources is subject not only to those external forces but also to her husband's mediation of those forces. In other words, the husband in the traditional family earns income through employment; the wife in such a family must depend on income flowing through to her from her husband's employment. Regardless of how much each spouse is task- or emotional-oriented, or how much each is focused on the public sphere of organizations and politics or the private sphere of the home, the crucial difference is that the economic resources are more directly controlled by the spouse who earns an income—in the traditional case, by the man.

The control of economic resources is a critical factor in the distribution of power in a family. The woman who follows the pattern of giving up her own source of income and becoming financially dependent on her husband is placed in a position where she must consult him about decisions she would formerly have made by herself. Similarly, the children in a family find they have little power to make their own decisions as long as they depend on parents to finance them. Numerous studies of American families show that the greater the economic resources (income, occupational status, education) brought by a husband to a marriage, the greater his decision-making power within the marriage; and that as the comparative economic resources of the marital partners become more equal, so does the spouses' power with respect to each other (Blood & Wolfe, 1960; Blumstein & Schwartz, 1983; Centers, Raven, & Rodrigues, 1971; Fox, 1973; Safilios-Rothschild, 1976).

Researchers have also demonstrated that when the wife's financial dependence on the husband is increased by the presence of children, her powerlessness is similarly increased (Morris & Sison, 1974); and conversely, when a husband becomes unemployed and loses his access to economic resources, he may simultaneously lose some marital decision-making power (Komarovsky, 1935).

Yet, the simple fact of employment is not sufficient to guarantee a wife equal power with her husband. Research on dual-earner families shows that the one reliable difference between the family power positions of employed and nonemployed women lies in the area of financial decision-making: Employed wives report a greater role in financial decisions than do nonemployed wives (Blood, 1963; Bahr, 1974). But, being employed does not guarantee that a woman will be able to turn over half of the household work to her husband. The division of labor, even in families in which the wives are doctors, professors, lawyers, or other professionals, with the professed ideology of the couple as egalitarian, is strangely traditional. Although research shows that employed women spend less time doing housework than do nonemployed wives, women still do most of the housework (79%, according to Berardo, Shehan, & Leslie, 1987). Husbands show little variation in the amount of time they devote to housework, regardless of the employment or career status of their wives. Financial resources do influence marital power, but clearly there is more going on here than simple, rational economics.

One thing that is increasingly clear about the division of labor and the distribution of economic resources within families is that it is in a state of flux. Changing relations between the sexes have eroded assumptions about women's natural domesticity and men's natural authority. Whereas, earlier in this century, North American women felt they should be able to depend on their male partners for a lifetime of economic security, many women now either cannot or choose not to count on men this heavily. The reasons for this change are at least fourfold, according to Kathleen Gerson (1986).

First, heterosexual partnerships have simply become less stable, and thus, less dependable. Divorce and separation rates have risen markedly in recent years, as have the rates of cohabitation without marriage and permanent singlehood. Women are somewhat less likely to marry than they were before, and when they do marry, they can be less certain than previous generations that the marriage is for life. They must, therefore, be concerned with their own economic support.

A second reason for women's decreasing dependence on men is the increasing perception that two paychecks are required to support a family. The necessity for women to work to help support the family has provided them with justification for seeking employment. An employed woman not only has increased leverage in negotiating with her husband but also the possibility of escape from the relationship if it becomes too unhappy or oppressive.

Third, women, while still discriminated against and paid less well than men, are less vulnerable to blatant discrimination in the workplace than they used to be and so can depend more on their jobs for economic support. Women can no longer be dismissed from most jobs because they get married, divorced, or pregnant. Indeed, some employers have begun to make previously unheard-of concessions to female workers: The American military accommodates pregnant servicewomen; the Central Intelligence Agency has a daycare center for the children of its personnel. True, the average woman still makes less than seventy cents to the average man's dollar, and women are a long way from taking over the corporate boardrooms of North America, but their position in the workforce is far from being as precarious as it once was.

Fourth, the massive movement of women into the workforce has tended to undermine the notion that the male–single-earner family is the only workable or justifiable family form. In fact, with that form now being outnumbered by a combination of other alternatives such as single-parent and dual-earner families, the argument that the woman-at-home/man-at-work arrangement is the only natural or morally defensible one has lost much of its former power. Employed mothers are moving out from under clouds of accusation and guilt and into a climate where their decision to work for pay is seen as legitimate. This change, in combination with those previously listed, works to free women from economic dependence on men and provide them with new sources of power. On the other hand, the changes inevitably create new sources of insecurity and vulnerability by weakening traditional protections for women.

The female-male couple relationship is not the only family relationship whose power is influenced by control over economic resources. A key factor that interacts with economic resources is lifespan. When children are young, they are almost completely dependent on their parents. Often, as parents age, they become in turn dependent on their children. Economic resources play an important role in shaping the power reversal experienced in families where elderly parents become dependent on their adult children for assistance. With age, the interpersonal, physical, and financial resources of a parent may decline until the child becomes more powerful than the parent. In such situations, elders sometimes use economics—the direct or implied promise of an inheritance—to maintain some control in the relationship. If the elder is destitute, or has given over most financial resources to the offspring, she or he can be left with little bargaining power. However, even in this situation, the creative use of "implied" economic resources can go a long way. Barusch (1988) offers the following example:

Guamanians tell of a poor, old man whose children were not very respectful. One day when they had been especially rude the old man went to a friend's house and borrowed a large box which he proceeded to lock and drag back to his home. When he saw his children he explained that he had asked his friend to take care of his treasure, but now that he was growing old and feeble he wanted it near him where he could watch it. From that day on his children took exemplary care of him anticipating the time when the treasure would be left to them. (p. 50)

Love and Family Bonds as Power Resources

Economic resources are not the only ones exchanged for power in family relationships. In fact, studies of married couples suggest that the source of power most commonly attributed by partners to each other is referent power: the power to exert influence based on a desire for familial identification. Both male and female members of couples report that their most likely reason for doing something their mates asked was that they felt they "were both part of the same family and wanted to think alike on things like this" (DeJarnett & Raven, 1981, p. 56). This pattern holds for both European-American and African-American middle- and lower-class couples (Raven, Centers, & Rodrigues, 1975; DeJarnett & Raven, 1981).

Even when they control few economic resources, North American wives may gain leverage in the marital balance of power by controlling emotional resources that are highly valued and needed by husbands (Safilios-Rothschild, 1976). Wives who see their husbands as more in love than they themselves are also see themselves as holding more decision-making power; when partners perceive themselves as equally in love, marital power tends to be shared equally (Safilios-Rothschild, 1969).

In families with more than two members, power also comes from the building of alliances and coalitions. Such coalitions often involve mothers and children. Cultures that place little importance on love between spouses are not devoid of the use of love as a power resource within the family. In kinship networks that go beyond the nuclear family, power based on emotional and affectional bonds between generations is often a major factor shaping the interactions.

In Chapter Seven, it was noted that having children reduces a woman's power relative to her husband, but the following example shows that the opposite pattern sometimes holds true. Investigators of the contemporary Yugoslav family report that mothers assume an influential and authoritative role in the lives of their adult children despite the formal organization of Yugoslav culture as male-dominated and patriarchal (Simic, 1983). The mothers' power stems from their early close relationships with their children—relationships that are maintained through a social structure that emphasizes multigenerational families, places no positive value on children's leaving the nest, and views close emotional ties between spouses with uneasiness. Yugoslav tradition does not encourage a wife and husband to become strong emotional allies early in their marriage; it emphasizes instead the relationship of each to their children and to extended family members. This attitude is typified by the following comments, reported by Simic (1983). One middle-aged male, commenting on the death of a friend's wife, observed that "a man can always find household help, but he has only one mother" (p. 75). Another, a Yugoslav visitor to the United States who was impressed by laundromats, exclaimed, "In America you don't need a wife, just a pocketful of quarters!" (p. 74).

Apparently, the role of wife does not confer much power in the Yugoslav family—but married women do gain power by becoming mothers, and that power is based on the emotional bonds they develop with their children, particularly their sons. Since love between the spouses is not emphasized in the marriage relationship, a married woman attaches herself to her children. Her son, who is her husband's heir and her mother-in-law's pride and joy, becomes the wife's protection and weapon in her battle against the dominance of these two family members. A son is carefully taught how much his mother loves him and the extent to which she has suffered and sacrificed for him. He is thus bound tightly to her through affection and obligation and, as an adult, feels called on to defend her in any conflict, even a conflict with his wife. The maternal image is one of devotion and sacrifice, creating in children the sense of a debt that can never be paid.

> The power of this maternal image is rooted in a moral superiority derived from self-abnegation and suffering phrased in a mother's devotion to the well-being of her children at the expense of other forms of self-realization. In this way "maternal sacrifice" provides the keystone for the support of a structure of guilt on the part of children, especially sons, assuring the perpetuation of a mother's influence and power throughout her lifetime. (Simic, 1983, p. 81)
> . . . the mother's capacity for mobilizing the support of all her children against anyone who opposes her is a sort of "calling in the chips." (Halley, 1980, p. 131)

Clearly, although women exert direct control of few economic and public status resources in Yugoslav culture, they exert a great deal of informal power based on affectual resources. While a man's role calls on him to act out dominance and extravagant masculinity by carousing and brawling in public bars and cafes, he must behave decorously in his mother's home, and he may mourn the death of his mother for years.

VIOLENCE AND POWER IN THE FAMILY

The least common reason given by couples for compliance to a partner's request is coercion—the belief that the partner will respond to noncompliance with punishment (Raven, Centers, & Rodrigues, 1975; DeJarnett & Raven, 1981). Moreover, couples who attribute coercive power to the partners show the lowest levels of marital satisfaction. Nonetheless, the capacity for violence is apparently a common source of power in family relationships. Newspapers present a daily catalogue of child abuse, wife battering, abuse of the elderly, and marital rape, often with details so grisly that the accounts are almost unbearable to read. Clearly, family members are sometimes kept in line by brute force—or the threat of that force.

The use of violent coercive power in the family is not rare: Estimates of the incidence of husband-wife violence in the United States range from 25% to 60% (Pagelow, 1984). These rates may reflect the degree to which violence is accepted as a demonstration of power in American culture. As well, they may be the outcome of socializing males from boyhood to expect an unrealistic degree of power and control in their relationships. As Denzin (1984) remarks, a "society which promotes the ownership of firearms, women and children; which makes homes men's castles; and which sanctions societal and interpersonal violence in the forms of wars, athletic contests, and mass media fiction (and news) should not be surprised to find violence in its homes" (p. 487). Indeed, family violence is less common in societies where tolerance for aggression in general is low, and where men do not expect to be the lords of their homes (O'Kelly & Carney, 1986).

Violence and the threat of violence certainly produce an atmosphere of fear and compliance among family members who feel trapped as victims. The fear is typified in the following statement from an abused wife: "He always terrified me. Each time he made me more scared. I just sat like a mouse, just sat quietly" (Dobash & Dobash, 1979, p. 138). Yet, for some abusers, no amount of meek compliance seems to be enough, and they go through increasingly brutal and bizarre rituals of cruelty toward their supposedly loved victims. Russell (1982) reports the following case in which a husband subjected his wife to hours of terror while claiming all the while that he loved her:

> He allegedly held her captive from 2:00 A.M. to 6:00 A.M., disrobed her, then raped and choked her and finally dangled her nude over a bridge in Abington, all the time professing his love for her. . . . "I'd drop you if I didn't love you," Mrs. Ludwig says he told her. (p. 373)

The power involved in such abuse is more than the forcing of another to behave in a certain way. There is little or nothing that the victim can do or say under such circumstances that will satisfy the abuser, and many victims are baffled as to how they can behave in order to placate their abuser. As Denzin (1984) suggests, it may be that what the abuser is trying to gain through the violence (self-esteem, self-control, control over the other person) is simply not attainable through violence. The violence may even have the opposite effects of what the violent person intends: It may shake his self-esteem instead of boosting it and remind him that his self-control leaves much to be desired. Perhaps most importantly, the violence may cause the other person to retreat inwardly from him, leaving him less in control of her heart and mind than ever before, even though she may be outwardly compliant. The abuser and the victim can thus both become trapped in a cycle of violence as he escalates his attempts at control, and control becomes ever more elusive.

Violence as a form of control is available especially to family members who exceed other members in the resources of physical strength and size. It is used by parents against children, husbands against wives, and adults against those who are older and more frail. This is not to say that wives do not strike husbands, that young children do not kick or bite parents. However, in a family that is characterized by violence, it is the weaker, more vulnerable members who live in fear. Both men and women may behave violently toward their partners, but it is men who inflict the most serious harm (Straus, Gelles, & Steinmetz, 1980). Moreover, women who report violent acts against their husbands are usually being treated violently by their husbands; they are fighting back. On the other hand, men who report being physically or psychologically abusive toward their wives are often not the recipients of similar abuse from their wives (Mason & Blankenship, 1987).

It is sometimes argued that the difficulty women often have in leaving an abusive relationship reflects a feminine tendency toward masochism, a satisfaction in being hurt. Women who have been in this situation report they do not stay because they enjoy being hurt but because of a combination of the effects of the abuse on their self-confidence and a perceived absence of other alternatives. What the abused woman faces is the necessity to make a very frightening change in her life in the absence of most of the supports and much of the power needed for making such a change.

First of all, the abused woman has often lost many of her inner resources—any feeling of powerfulness, any sense of real competence and effectiveness. This loss occurs through the process of abuse in which she finds herself unable to stop or control her husband's violence no matter what she does. She learns very quickly to feel helpless. Moreover, the physical violence is often accompanied by verbal abuse, where the woman is told repeatedly and savagely that she is stupid, ugly, useless, and so on.

In the face of such attacks, it is difficult for the woman to maintain a sense of self-worth.

A second difficulty is the lack of external resources: The woman who wants to leave an abusive marriage often has no money, few ways of protecting herself from retaliation by her husband, no family or friends to help her, and no accessible shelter for battered women (Frieze, 1986). It seems clear that the difficulty women face in leaving an abusive relationship is rooted in power, not in femininity.

Family power relationships exist, not in a social vacuum, but in a context of laws and social norms that encourage, or at least tolerate, certain kinds of behavior. As long as this context is such that male dominance of the family is approved and violence as a way of enforcing that dominance is tolerated, family violence, particularly wife abuse, will continue.

Culture, Norms, and Family Power

Patriarchal vs. egalitarian norms and family decision making   A cultural ideology that says males should be dominant provides men with legitimacy in their attempts to exert influence in the family. In other words, a culturally endorsed ideology of male dominance gives men a perceived right to exert power over women. Such patriarchal ideology is stronger in some cultures than in others. The evidence is mixed as to whether the presence of this ideology enhances the actual or only the apparent family power of men relative to women. We know, after all, that it is easier to be open and direct about an influence attempt if it is believed to be accepted by society; this openness does not necessarily render the influence more effective.

Research shows that variables such as education, social class, and cultural background are related to couples' adherence to patriarchal ideology. A study of Ghanaian couples showed that those who were less educated reported a stronger ideology of male dominance (Feldman, 1967). Studies of Puerto Rican families reveal a strong cultural tradition of male dominance and female submissiveness (Comas-Diaz, 1988). Research on African-American couples shows greater endorsement for the notion of male dominance among lower-class than among middle-class women—and greater endorsement of this notion by males than by females (DeJarnett & Raven, 1981). What research fails to show with complete consistency, however, is the connection between couples' acceptance of patriarchal ideology and the presence of a husband-dominated decision-making pattern. In the just-cited study of African-American couples, for instance, there was a slight negative correlation between male dominance ideology and the attribution of power to husbands in the household.

The endorsement of patriarchal ideology within a culture enhances the public exercise of power by males. In Puerto Rican culture, the concept of *machismo*, meaning maleness or virility, stipulates male superiority and authority, sexual freedom regardless of marital status, and physical dominance over women. Women are supposed to embrace the concept of *marianismo*, based on the cult of the Virgin Mary, to develop the ability to endure all the suffering inflicted by men's macho behavior, including accepting and adjusting to a husband's extramarital relations (Comas-Diaz, 1988). Within European-American culture, the endorsement of male dominance is less dramatic, but the evidence suggests that it is there. Studies show that couples characterized as wife-dominant are less happy than husband-dominant or egalitarian couples—perhaps because these couples feel they are out of step with the way things are supposed to be (Gray-Little & Burks, 1983). Jessie Bernard (1972), writing about marriage in North America, noted couples often conspired to hide the wife's power, again, most likely in conformity to the notion that the man is supposed to be the boss.

Controversy has raged in the field of anthropology in recent years over the question of whether women are as powerless as they appear in many cultures. Studies of families in rural Mexico illustrate both the importance of male dominance ideology *and* the divergence from that ideology that occurs in actual home life. The machismo ideal in Mexican villages provides that the man is granted authority by nature and is the unchallenged head of the house, whereas the woman is obedient, submissive, and sacrificing to the wishes and demands of her husband. A woman asserting independence is seen as unfeminine by both women and men (Stevens, 1973). In practice, however, couples tend to report that household decisions, purchases, investments, and child rearing require joint decision and agreement. Thus, power is divided more evenly in these couples than the machismo ideal would suggest. However, male dominance ideology is not ignored: Husbands and wives almost always assert that the husband has the last word (Wiest, 1983).

In a similar vein, Friedl (1967) reports that Greek village women wield considerable power in the household because of the land they contribute as a dowry, but they acknowledge the formal authority of their husbands. Cronin (1977) shows that in Sicilian families the frequent deviations from the ideal that men are supposed to direct all activities and make all decisions within the home are carried out in secret. Rogers (1975), speaking of life in a French village, notes, "Women buy their power by granting men authority and respect, assuming that if they allow men to believe that male dominance actually exists, men will not notice that women are actually wielding a considerable amount of power" (p. 748).

In the privacy of the family, or in certain specialized arenas, women may find strong, covert sources of power. Some Puerto Rican women use *espiritismo*, the belief that spirits communicate and intervene in human life, as a coping mechanism and source of power. In becoming *espiritistas*, or healers and communicators with the spirits, these *puertorriqueñas* obtain power from supernatural sources and are thus transformed from powerless members of the family to the most powerful ones. However, their power comes through passivity, through acting as a vehicle for the power of the spirits, and thus does not change the oppression of women that is perpetuated through cultural beliefs.

Resources in cultural context: the interaction of norms and resources
As discussed earlier, a resource theory of power claims that a spouse's power in the family is based on resources such as his or her economic holdings or status in the larger community. According to this perspective, the greater the socioeconomic status of a husband, the greater should be his power relative to his wife. This theory has received a great deal of research support, but it tends to treat the distribution of power in marriage as a private, interpersonal phenomenon, unrelated to the cultural context in which the family is situated. In particular, it neglects the limitations on women's power that stem from social norms and practices that work against gender equality. The importance of cultural context is highlighted by contradictory findings in cross-cultural studies of family power. Some studies in Greece and Yugoslavia have shown that the greater the husbands' socioeconomic resources, the less his power within the family. Responding to such apparent contradictions, Rodman (1972) proposed that resources must be evaluated in a cultural context. In other words, the reason for the contradiction is that the relevance and meaning of the husband's (and presumably the wife's) social and economic attributes (education, occupation, income, etc.) depend on cultural norms.

Rodman, whose theory is still controversial, classified four societies at different levels of economic development to illustrate the argument. At one end are patriarchal societies with a low level of economic development, such as India. In such societies the strength, prevalence, and inflexibility of patriarchal norms make the husband's socioeconomic resources virtually irrelevant to his power in the family; his power comes from simply being the senior male in a family that exists in a male-dominated society.

In somewhat more industrialized societies, the norms emphasizing male authority are replaced to some extent, in the upper classes, with egalitarian norms favoring partnership and sharing between spouses. Rodman calls such societies, of which Greece is an example, modified patriarchal societies. In these societies, social class is related to egalitarian attitudes and values. The higher a man's socioeconomic status, the lower his decision-making power relative to his wife tends to be. In this group of societies, then, upper-class men do not have patriarchal norms to legitimate their authority in the family and are thus likely to have less power relative to their wives than do lower-class men, whose authority in the family *is* augmented by patriarchal norms.

As economic development reaches still higher levels, societies become what Rodman has labeled transitional egalitarian (the United States is an example). Egalitarian norms tend to replace patriarchal norms at all levels of society. Here, individuals can modify their worth and status through economic achievements, and those achievements become sources of bargaining power in the marriage relationship. In this type of society, a man's socioeconomic status acts as a power resource in the couple: The greater his socioeconomic resources, the greater his influence on decision making.

At the highest levels of economic development, Rodman argues, are egalitarian societies such as Sweden. In these societies, egalitarian norms are so strongly held and pervasive that socioeconomic status is irrelevant to marital decision making: Egalitarianism is favored regardless of the socioeconomic resources held by the two spouses. These societies represent the opposite extreme from the patriarchal societies in which male dominance is favored regardless of socioeconomic resources.

While Rodman's typology is not universally endorsed by social scientists and may not be exhaustive of the possibilities for interactions between norms and resources (for instance, there are nonindustrialized societies in which egalitarianism is the norm), it does provide one possible way of understanding cultural differences in the correlates of family power. One test of the model on two generations of Puerto Rican families living in New York City supports the expectations provided by the model (Cooney, Rogler, Hurrell, & Ortiz, 1982). This study compared the link between socioeconomic variables and the marital power relationship for the parent and child generations of intergenerational families. The parent generation, in their mid-fifties at the time of the study, had been born and raised in Puerto Rico and settled in the United States as young adults in their mid-twenties. The child generation, in their late twenties, had been born and raised in the United States. Comparisons showed that the parent generation adhered more closely to the modified patriarchal norms traditional in Puerto Rican culture, whereas the child generation was closer to the transitional egalitarian norm pattern characteristic of mainstream American culture. Thus, Rodman's model would predict that husbands' socioeconomic status would be inversely related to marital decision-making power in the parent generation and positively related to marital decision-making power in the child generation.

The findings support those predictions. They also show that, in both generations, the wife's education is positively related to both her power relative to her husband and a pattern of shared decision making. Interestingly, in both generations of couples, shared decision making was common: One-half of the decisions asked about by the researchers were reported by the couples as shared. This pattern is in notable contrast to the image of the male-dominated family described in the ideal of machismo/marianismo. Once again, the quiet reality is somewhat at odds with the proclaimed image of female-male relations.

Family Centrality and Power

The old saying, "The hand that rocks the cradle rules the world," suggests that men have traditionally held power in connection with their position as head of the family; and that women derive power from their role as the family's heart. This epigram, and others like it, has often been invoked in thinly disguised attempts to pressure women to stay in the home and maintain primary responsibility for childcare. It is usually greeted by feminists with cynicism. Yet, a careful examination of family power cannot fail to include a consideration of the way that a wife/mother's traditionally central position in family communication relates to her power in the family.

An example of female centrality and family power can be found in a study of families living in small Portuguese villages (Hollos & Leis, 1985). Female power in such families is of particular interest because rural Portuguese culture, like many other Mediterranean cultures, has been described as one in which most of the formal power is ascribed to men and in which women "buy" covert power only by being deferent and respectful to men. Family interactions were studied through the medium of a marbles game that required family members (wife, husband, and child) to work together to create designs on a board using colored marbles. It might be expected that, especially under the watchful gaze of an anthropologist, the Portuguese wives would be quiet and deferent in such a situation. Quite the opposite turned out to be the case. Women emerged as the most actively interacting family members: talking more, asking more questions, giving more directions, and making more comments than other family members. Furthermore, the women turned out to be not just the most talkative and directive but also the most influential members of the family. Mothers made more design suggestions than did fathers or children, and their suggestions were the ones most often accepted and executed. Mothers were especially interactive with their children; in fact, the researchers observed that, compared with the mother–child pairs, the fathers often appeared peripheral.

Perhaps the power of the mother in this situation is a function of the particular task used to measure it. Is expert power perhaps attributed to women in the area of design, color, aesthetics? Still, the outcome is intriguing; it shows that mothers can be openly powerful in at least one type of family situation. In this unlikely cultural setting, in which women are markedly deferential to their husbands in the outside world, the inner world of the family reveals the possibility of a significant amount of female power. Within the family, even when in the presence of relative strangers, women were seen to play openly a central and directive role. They were not indirect, manipulative, covert, or apologetic in exerting power in front of their husbands; there was no question here of "letting him think he's in charge."

Some have discounted the domestic power exerted by women as irrelevant to the real power of the marketplace. Of what use is power in the family if it cannot be translated easily into power in the formal institutions that actually control society? This question has a definite sting to it in when considered in the context of North American or northern European culture, where the private sphere of home and family is accorded less importance than the public sphere of business and politics and where power does not carry over particularly well from the private to the public sphere. Cultures differ widely, however, in the centrality and importance attached to the domestic sphere. In the Portuguese rural culture described earlier, like other Mediterranean cultures, the family is apparently the most important social grouping in society; it is the major unit of production, consumption, and social interaction. For a woman to hold the most central and influential position in the family unit in such a culture is arguably to hold the most important role in society. The catch is that that role may still not be the most visible nor the most widely acknowledged as powerful.

The taking on of a central, relationship-oriented role can be a source of power for women within the confines of the immediate family circle and also in the larger family of the community. This process can be seen in the use by Puerto Rican women of the concept of *hembrismo*, meaning, literally, femaleness (Comas-Diaz, 1988). Hembrismo has roots in pre-Columbian times when the original Puerto Ricans, the Taino Indians, lived as a matriarchal society and embraced an earth mother concept that gave women considerable power. It is used now to connote the self-affirmation and survival ability of the Puerto Rican woman and her central role in the development of the Puerto Rican community. Whereas marianismo, discussed earlier, entails submissive, passive self-sacrifice, hembrismo "entails a sociopolitical commitment involving action-oriented behaviors aimed at accomplishing 'what is needed' for the benefit of the family and/or the community" (Comas-Diaz, 1988, p. 24). The concept provides women with a culturally meaningful framework for leadership-oriented behavior, despite the strong conflicting pressure toward subordination that is prescribed for Puerto Rican women in their various family roles.

It appears that even in the relative absence of public ideological supports, the central role that women in some cultures occupy in the family and in the community confers on them a significant amount of power. Women are often the ones who maintain lines of communication among family or community members, who hold relationships together, who gather information about the needs and wants of others in the family or community system. They thus may have the power to bring people together—a process that is often the first step in making change or achieving a goal. Once that first step has been accomplished, however, norms of patriarchal authority may take over, and the women's power goes unrecognized. Furthermore, even in cultures where women's family power is recognized as significant, family power does not necessarily translate easily into power outside that sphere.

The communal relationship skills that women are forced to develop in this role—sensitivity, compromise, emotional expressivity—do, in a sense, give women the last, if not the best, laugh. These skills seem to provide women with a staying power that helps them adapt to personal and social change, smoothing the process of aging and facilitating the survival of their communities (Rabin, 1986). The importance of these survival skills is not to be denied, but they are not as dramatic as the bursts of achievement that come from individual, agentic (influence-related) power, or as well-rewarded and applauded as accomplishments that reach beyond the family or immediate community. Women often out-survive men, but, many would argue, this is not enough compensation for the powerlessness they experience in the public sphere.

CONCLUSION: PARADOXES OF FAMILY POWER

At first glance, gender power relationships in the family seem straightforward. Patriarchal norms give husbands more power than wives, to a greater or lesser extent depending on the society. The effect of these norms is augmented by a distribution of resources which ensures that the average man will have more money and status in the public sphere than the average woman. The male advantage is further reinforced by the tendency for men to be bigger and stronger than women, making them more able to use physical coercion or intimidation against their spouses and children. All this is true on the surface, but a deeper examination of family power shows that despite the many factors operating to tilt the family power relationship in favor of men, paradoxes abound.

The real distribution of power within the family does not always match cultural ideologies of male dominance, although the wife and husband may both conspire to make it appear that way. Wives who make virtually all the decisions in their households may steadfastly maintain that their husbands run the show. Husbands who appear tyrannical to the outside world may not be in private. In short, the evidence is clear that couples' attempts to live up to an ideology of male dominance in public are not always consistent with their power-related behavior in private.

Similarly, public assertions of adherence to an ideology of female–male equality are not always matched by private behavior. Couples who take pride in their egalitarianism are found to be far from equal in their sharing of household labor and childcare. Perhaps most dramatically, couples who display an untroubled, united front to the world are sometimes disguising private patterns of terrifying violence and intimidation.

Perhaps the lack of fit between public and private realities of family power should not be surprising. After all, marriage and family are topics invested with strong emotions and important cultural norms. It is perfectly normal for people to try to act as if their marriage fits cultural prescriptions—this pattern is consistent with years of research by social psychologists showing that people often try to present a socially acceptable face even when it is at odds with their private feelings or behavior. What puzzles gender researchers is not so much the inconsistency between publicly maintained norms and private family realities, but rather the strong persistence of patriarchal norms under conditions where they appear to have little or no basis in practice.

If women in a society have a power advantage anywhere with respect to men, it is likely to be within the family. This is because the exchange currency of the family is not just money, education, legitimate authority, or status, but also emotional resources such as love, support, attention, guilt, personal information, and trust. The cultural assignment of the relationship sphere to women, particularly relationships with children, can give them a central position with respect to family communication, the formation of alliances and coalitions, and family identification and loyalty—all linked to family power. It is no wonder that some women feel ambivalent about putting their energies into the public sphere of the workplace where these traditional sources of female power may count for less than they do in the family. In fact, women who transfer a major component of their efforts from the family to the workplace must give up some of their relationship-based family power, becoming less available for confidences from their children or for supportive interactions with their spouse. Career women, who must make the largest commitments to the employment sphere, also make the most sacrifices in the family sphere, frequently deciding to have no children at all.

Employed women clearly gain power by acquiring an income and job-related status, yet they cannot escape the realization that they have lost some power (less obvious family power) as well. This knowledge is a source of particular ambivalence to women who face the most severe discrimination and powerlessness in the workplace. Is it worth it? Many women clearly think so, judging by the large-scale movement of women into the workforce in recent years. The power that comes with income and work-related status is more tangible than family power, and women are increasingly opting for it. There are media rumblings about disillusioned women abandoning the workplace for the home. Yet, the continuing rise in women's employment appears certain.

As described in the following chapter, with this comes a rapidly shifting set of new issues concerning gender and power in the workplace.

CHAPTER NINE

Power in
the Workplace

The date is International Women's Day, 1989; the place, Moscow. A Soviet woman, Tatyana Geoshvili, is asked by a curious Western journalist whether sexual equality has been achieved in the Soviet Union. "Equal with men?" She laughs. "Yes, the law says we must be. And we also have to be equal with horses to get the strength."

In a country that has paid lip service to female-male equality for the last 70 years, women still work harder, at lower-level jobs, and receive less pay than men. Women represent more than half of the national work force, but only 2.5% of them hold managerial jobs. In agriculture, which employs many Soviet citizens, women tend to be field hands, whereas men are tractor drivers, mechanics, and collective farm managers. Most Soviet women hold full-time jobs *and* do most of the housework. As one disgruntled woman wrote in response to a magazine article about sexuality, "What kind of sex can a run-down 30-year-old woman think of? Off to work in the morning, eight hours at work. . . . Shopping during the lunch break. After work, another two hours in queues. Then comes a second shift at home, cooking, washing, doing dishes, looking after the child. . . . What kind of sex can I have on my mind, dear men? Naturally, my husband sulks but sees no need to help me" (Sallot, 1989, pp. A1, A9).

The themes that characterize the plight of Soviet women with respect to work—poor pay, segregation into low-level jobs, the double day—are not so different from those that haunt North American women. In the United States, women predominate in six of the eight lowest-paying jobs, comprising about 97% of practical nurses, 97% of seamstresses and stitchers, 87% of childcare workers, 85% of hairdressers, 84% of nurses' aides, and 83% of health-care workers. On the other hand, the well-paying jobs of stock and bond sales agents, managers and administrators, and wholesale and manufacturing sales representatives have been less than 20% female during the past decade (Kleiman, 1989). Women make up 73% of the work force at Canadian banks, but only 2.4% of senior managers and 17.7% of middle managers (Top banker lauds affirmative action, 1988). In both countries, women make less than 70% of what men make. Old habits die hard: It appears that it takes more than the official endorsement of an ideology of sexual equality to balance women's power with men's in the workplace.

In the workplace, it can be argued that equality of power between two groups implies that both groups have equal access to the full range of available jobs, to advancement and influence within these jobs, and to respectful interpersonal treatment as they work at these jobs. If women and men had equal work-related power, we would expect that they would have equal access to employment; would not be clustered into jobs in such a way that one group was disproportionately represented in low-paying, low-status jobs; would be equally likely to be promoted into influential positions; would be paid equal average salaries; and would have equal likelihood of being treated with consideration and respect by other people in the workplace. None of these conditions holds true for women and men in North America, or in most other parts of the world.

ACCESS TO (GOOD) EMPLOYMENT

There is little argument that women confront more barriers than men do in their pursuit of good, gainful employment. These barriers come in the form of gender stereotypes regarding abilities, social attitudes about the proper place of women, ingroup exclusionary attitudes and practices on the part of men, and structural difficulties concerned with balancing child rearing with employment and with personal safety. All of these factors limit women's impact on and in the workplace, despite the increasing numbers of employed women.

Gender Stereotypes and Discrimination

Traditional stereotypes work against gender equality in the work-place because they help to promote the idea that women and men are suited for different kinds of work—and that the jobs for which women are best suited are the least powerful, lowest-paying ones. Perhaps the aspects of the stereotypes that create the most barriers to women's entry into powerful positions are those that involve the incompatibility of femininity with competence, leadership ability, toughness, and mathematical and technical abilities.

Competence   In the absence of any other information but sex, women are considered less competent than men in a wide range of areas. When there is no actual track record to evaluate, raters tend to infer a lower level of ability in females than in males (Nieva & Gutek, 1981). Furthermore, when women succeed, that success is less likely to be attributed to their ability and more likely to be attributed to luck, effort, or other nonability factors than is similar success by men (Deaux & Emswiller, 1974; Etaugh & Brown, 1975). These patterns suggest that women are less likely than men to be given a chance to prove their competence in a new area, and that even when women do succeed, their success is likely to be discounted as irrelevant to their abilities.

Many anecdotes illustrate this tendency to discount women's competence. A recent newspaper story tells of a Canadian judge who charged a female defense lawyer with contempt of court for allegedly "using her charm" on a jury (Judge says lawyer used female wiles, 1988). The judge charged that the lawyer had won her case, not through competent legal maneuvers, but through using her eyes to establish a "personal rapport" with the jury. (The newspaper report itself compounds the stereotype by describing the lawyer as "a slender, dark-haired woman"—a description that would surely be considered irrelevant in story about a male lawyer.)

The masculine image of the leader   For many people, the image of a powerful person is inescapably male—and research suggests that the image of "leader" is similarly masculine (Lord, Foti, & Phillips, 1982). In 1965, a *Harvard Business Review* survey of 2000 business executives found that 31% of the male respondents described women as "temperamentally unfit for management." The ideal manager was perceived as masculine in character: competitive, aggressive, dominant, firm, vigorous, and rational. Against this standard, women were perceived as inadequate (Bowman, Wortney, & Greyser, 1965). More recent studies fit with these observations. A national survey of 884 male managers showed that every difference they perceived between male and female employees was seen as unfavorable to women aspiring to higher-level positions (Rosen & Jerdee, 1978). Harlan & Weiss (1982) found that both male and female managers held stereotypic attitudes toward women, viewing them as lacking in career commitment.

The masculine images of power and leadership place managerial women in a double bind, forcing a role conflict between femininity and leadership. When a female manager "displays the culturally defined traits of a woman, she is rejected as an unacceptable manager. If she acts according to the male defined role of a leader, she is condemned as being unfeminine" (Putnam & Heinen, 1976, p. 48).

Recently, there have been stirrings in the business world suggesting that the old image of the leader is no longer workable, that the new style of leader is someone who possesses many stereotypically feminine abilities. Experts argue that for firms to survive in the global economy they will need to de-emphasize hierarchy and emphasize instead power-sharing, teamwork, partnership, and building lifelong relationships with customers (Peters, 1989). So perhaps masculine competitiveness is out and feminine relationship-building is on its way in, in the corporate world. If so, it is too early to see many encouraging effects for women—who are still largely locked out of the boardrooms of America and other countries as well. A look around the world reveals that stereotypes can vary, but the distribution of power remains the same. In the relationship-oriented world of Japanese business, virtually all the power is in the hands of men: Of the 16.2 million women who work outside the home, only 48,600 hold administrative positions (Chira, 1988).

Toughness   Part of the feminine stereotype is weakness and frailty—although this stereotype has often been overlooked when it was inconvenient. The Soviet women who work as fieldhands while their male counterparts operate heavy tractors might be bemused by the idea that they were frail; the African-American women who were literally worked to death under slavery certainly did not benefit by any notion that women were delicate. Yet the doctrine that women are not tough enough, physically and emotionally, to do certain work has effectively barred them from a variety of jobs. The most obvious current example is the set of barriers to women's advancement in military careers.

In just over a decade, the percentage of women in the United States armed forces has almost doubled. Today, women make up 10.7% of the military forces. More women—224,000 of them—serve in the United States armed forces than in any other military forces in the world (Moore, 1989a). These women are not relegated to desk jobs: They fly aerial tankers to refuel fighter planes in midair, work in ship engine rooms, crew Coast Guard ships, pilot Navy fighter planes, and command anti-aircraft missile equipment. Many of them have joined the military in response to promises of educational and career opportunities, and out of a sense of patriotism and social responsibility.

In joining the military, they join an institution that offers equal pay for equal rank and work, but their careers are often brought to a halt by an insurmountable barrier: The 41-year-old law barring women from combat positions. Since combat is what the military is all about, it is difficult for women to make significant advances in the military if they are barred from positions that might involve combat—a full half of all military positions. For instance, the first woman to command a Navy flight squadron, Cmdr. Rosemary Mariner, notes that without a tour of duty on an aircraft carrier, without the opportunity to build up the flight hours and experience at sea that are a prerequisite for many top Navy jobs, women cannot compete for high-level positions: "You cannot get there from here. . . . You cannot, theoretically, reach the top of this profession because you cannot participate in its fundamental business. In the Navy, the world revolves around going to sea" (Navy women find obstacles on way to top, 1988, p. 14A).

The combat exclusion law is an emotional and politically sensitive issue. It appears that few Americans want to think of women as people who are tough enough to withstand the rigors of combat—or perhaps the more difficult notion to confront is that, in fact, most *men* are not tough enough for combat. Is anyone, female or male, really suited for the job of administering, or being exposed to, deadly force? Yet, the cold hard facts are that in the world of high-technology war machinery, there is no neat line between combat and non-combat positions. Front lines and rear units may be less than a 30-second jet flight apart, and missiles can hit targets on the other side of the world. In or out of combat positions, in or out of the military, women's lives are at risk in the event of armed conflict. Yet the combat exclusion law, based in part on American society's refusal to accept the idea of combat-style toughness in women, bars women from advancement in the military.

In some countries, such as Canada, Belgium, the Netherlands, Denmark, and Norway, women are allowed into combat positions. The commander of one Canadian forces training camp wryly titled his first report on the change "The Sky Isn't Falling" (Moore, 1989c, p. A18). Women have not flocked to such positions, but those who have, have met with a reasonable degree of success. Canadian women have successfully trained for artillery and tank crew positions, but only one of the 60 women recruited for the infantry has been able to pass the physically demanding training course. A small number of Norwegian women now serve as submarine crew members. Despite the initial misgivings of some male officers, the female recruits have not been any more reluctant than the males to get dirty, to work hard, and to accept physical challenges. Rather, they have been determined, stubborn, and courageous in their attempts to meet the training standards. Whereas the infantry experience shows, at least at present, that few women may have the physical strength to serve in this particular branch, it has become very clear that for every other combat-related job, women are tough enough.

Race and gender stereotypes   Gender stereotypes are not uniform across racial groups, so not only gender stereotypes, but the interaction of these stereotypes with racial stereotypes, has affected the reception accorded to female and male workers in various jobs. African-American women, unlike their European-American counterparts, have not been stereotyped as weak, or delicate, or regarded as people in need of protection. Indeed, the history of slavery shows that African-American women were treated as beasts of burden and as breeders of more slaves in an era when European-American women were aspiring to an image of fragile gentility (Fox & Hesse-Biber, 1984). Furthermore, African-American women have tended to have less choice than European-American women about whether or not to join the work force while their children are young; the vulnerable economic position of African-American men has made it more difficult for them to support their families. These facts have contributed to a "strong Black woman" stereotype that belies the effects of the double burden of racial and sexual discrimination that these women face. Truly, African-American women have not traditionally been allowed the luxury of being frail and helpless. They are employed more continuously and for more years than are European-American women. However, they are still more likely than European-American women to be employed in service and blue-collar positions, and they participate in a markedly narrower range of professions than do African-American men (Fox & Hesse-Biber, 1984; Wallace, 1980).

Attitudes Toward "Woman's Place in Man's World"

Although the traditional dictum that "a woman's place is in the home" has been gleefully converted by politically savvy feminists to "a woman's place is in the House," the attitude persists among some people that women have little right to paid employment under certain conditions (when their children are young, or when they are "stealing" jobs from men), or in certain jobs (the police force, the military, politics, the priesthood). Such attitudes seem to spring not only from stereotypic views of what women and men are like, but from a desire to protect a particular version of the social order. This version is one in which the division of roles is clear: Women can count on men to support their families, and men can be undisturbed by women's presence in various male situations.

The "woman's" place emotional response can be seen in the arguments that letting women into certain jobs will wreak havoc with the normal order: the military men who predicted that allowing women onto armed forces bases would undermine morale, cause an epidemic of romances, and force the military to do everything differently; the businessmen who resent the possibility that they will have to be careful what they say if there are women in the boardroom; the women who feel that the traditional feminine role of housewife will lose respect if women are allowed into men's jobs. Who agrees with the woman's place argument? A 1978 survey showed that only one third of the Americans sampled disagreed with a statement that "women's place is in the home" (Yankelovich, Skelly, & White, 1980). In 1982, only 38% of Canadian census respondents approved of employment for women with young children (Mikalachki & Mikalachki, 1985). However, recent years have seen so many changes in women's labor force participation that new norms are beginning to form. Only about one fifth of United States families were supported on only the husband's income in 1987 (Blau & Winkler, 1989), and sexual equity in the workplace is now favored by most North Americans (Tougas & Veilleux, 1989). Yet it requires only a few emotional proponents of the women's place argument to make life difficult for employed women.

One obvious effect of the woman's place argument is to bar women from certain employment situations. A less obvious one is that women's employment is not considered as legitimate or important as that of men. Yet, women work for the same reasons as men do: out of financial necessity, for personal identity, for status, for a sense of accomplishment (Fox & Hesse-Biber, 1984). So pervasive is the myth that employment is a peripheral concern for women that while volumes of research have addressed the problems created for men by unemployment, very little focus has been given to the parallel situation for women. For both sexes, however, job loss and unemployment is a demoralizing, disempowering, stressful experience (Schlozman, 1979). For men, part of the negative effect of unemployment has traditionally come from the expectation that a man should be the provider for his family. Many women are now providers for families, and they, like men, feel a strong sense of failure when they cannot fulfill this role.

One study of the effects of long-term unemployment among a group of Latina (mostly Mexican) women laid off when a large California cannery shut down shows how unemployment led to a host of difficulties (Romero, Castro, & Cervantes, 1988). The majority of these women experienced economic, occupational, and family stressors after their job loss. They had difficulty buying basic necessities, could not afford to buy presents for their families, found their resources insufficient to provide for their children, found they lacked the skills to find another job, experienced worsened relations with husbands and children, missed their former co-workers, and simply felt sad when remembering their old job. The researchers noted that, while unemployment was a major financial setback for these women, "their jobs represented more than a means of collecting a paycheck. Their jobs provided them with a social network in which friends, co-workers, and job responsibilities contributed to their total sense of well-being. Thus upon job termination, the psychological attachment they felt toward their jobs contributed to greater distress and feelings of loss" (p. 294).

Occupational Segregation

Women and men tend to enter the labor force in different kinds of occupations. Women are more likely than men to become elementary school teachers, nurses, secretaries, social workers; men are more likely than women to become administrators, doctors, lawyers, professors. The feminine occupations generally have less power, prestige, and pay than the masculine ones (Dexter, 1985) and serve less well as springboards to bigger and better positions. Nonetheless, women are disproportionately encouraged to follow the educational and training paths that lead to low-prestige, feminine occupations; and men are more likely to be pushed to acquire the type of training typically associated with higher salaries and more prestigious occupations.

Even within relatively high-power careers, women tend to cluster in specialties that are typed as feminine—specialties that may be associated with relatively less influence and prestige. For example, in university administration, it may be easier to find female deans of student affairs than to find female academic vice-presidents. Women are moving increasingly into traditionally male-typed occupations: The number of women receiving degrees in such fields rose by 88.6% between 1970 and 1980. However, no such trend is apparent for specialties within occupations (Blau & Ferber, 1985).

Some writers have suggested that occupational segregation is partly the result of women's socialization to be homemakers (Ragins & Sundstrom, 1989). The theory is that women who deviate from this traditional path try to lessen their own role conflict and to appease their family and friends by choosing an occupation or specialty that is traditionally feminine. It is equally, if not more, probable that women are chaneled into appropriately feminine positions by many organizations. As some feminist analyses of homemaking have indicated, one aspect of that particular job is subordination (Palmer, 1989). Relative subordination also seems to characterize many female-typed occupations and specialties outside the home; in fact, relative subordination may be one of the necessary characteristics for a job to be defined as feminine. It is hardly surprising, then, that the jobs and specialties in which women cluster are low in power and influence.

One contributor to occupational segregation by sex is the scarcity of women in mathematical, scientific, and technical fields. Men outnumber women almost two to one among American university graduates in computer and information sciences (Snyder, 1987). In an era when the workplace is increasingly dominated by the use of sophisticated information technology, women as a group will lose power and become increasingly segregated if they do not master some aspects of this technology (Lips & Frantzve, 1990). Computers in the workplace also present an impetus toward occupational segregation in another way: Secretarial workers, the vast majority of whom are women, increasingly find their tasks computerized; they become virtually chained to their computers. Jobs that once involved a combination of typing, filing, going to other offices to deliver or collect documents, searching in the files for particular items now are condensed into sets of tasks that can all be performed at the keyboard in front of the video display terminal. The result is more social segregation for secretaries, less opportunity for making organizational contacts that might lead to job mobility—and a whole new breed of "repetitive motion"-based occupational injuries.

GENDER AND MARGINALITY OR CENTRALITY AT WORK

Tokens in the Workplace

Given the segregation by sex in the workplace, it is inevitable that women or men who move into gender-nontraditional fields will often find themselves as tokens—sole, or almost sole, representatives of their sex in a particular office, level of management, committee, or job category. Women are more likely than men to face this situation, since the number of men entering female-typed fields is actually declining (Blau & Ferber, 1985). The occupant of a token's position is unusually visible, and visibility is ordinarily a potential source of power. Yet, for people in token positions, visibility is likely to be a handicap, a source of vulnerability rather than power. Tokens tend to be perceived as members of the outgroup that they represent rather than as individuals. There is a tendency for others to interpret their actions as either typical outgroup behavior or unusual behavior *for that group* (Kanter, 1977). Their mistakes tend to be magnified into generalities ("Her presentation in that meeting was weak. Didn't I tell you a woman wouldn't be able to handle this account?"); and their successes tend to be discounted ("For a woman, her negotiating strategy was incredibly tough. Someone must have helped her with it").

Aware of their visibility, tokens tend to be self-conscious, to have difficulty being their normal competent selves under the watchful eyes of the dominant group. Research suggests that tokens face the unhappy prospect of both performing less well than usual and having their performance noticed and remembered more than usual by others.

Are Women Outsiders in a Male-Defined Workplace?

Some workplaces have been male-dominated for so long that women who enter them find their personal and collective effectiveness limited by the resentment of male workers, by the attitude that they are intruders, or by a system of rules and norms that keeps them, in numerous small and large ways, as outsiders. The lack of institutional acceptance of women may be manifested in obvious ways, such as the reported comment of one university president that the English department, which housed six females out of a total of 20 faculty members, had become a "damn matriarchy" (University loses appeal in bias case, 1989). More frequently, however, the exclusion of women is subtle enough that many people find it difficult to put their finger on how it is happening.

In many workplaces, male dominance provides structural barriers to gender equality. The first line of impediments to gaining powerful positions is faced by women in the recruitment process. When the most powerful positions in an organization are held by men, for example, recruitment practices tend to favor men. Information about job openings is passed along through the old boys network, and men are given more informal help in finding information about job openings (Hill, 1980). Sometimes men are actively recruited in preference to women. Even when organizations are trying to recruit women to fill affirmative action quotas, they may target them for positions that have impressive titles but very little power (Kanter, 1983).

Position power   Once inside the workplace, women face a variety of conditions that tend to keep their status marginal, to make them look, feel, and act like outsiders, and to limit their power. In business organizations, women are disproportionately employed in people-oriented departments, such as personnel or public relations, rather than in the more powerful production and marketing departments. Since an individual's power in an organization flows partly from the power of that individual's department, the clustering of women in low-power departments keeps them at a disadvantage (Ragins & Sundstrom, 1989). A woman who is offered the highest ranking position in the lowest-ranking department is not likely to be on her way to the top of the company.

While recruitment and hiring policies may lead women into positions with limited power, there are other ways in which women's position power is limited: A relatively powerful position may lose power when it is occupied by a woman. Research shows that men are more likely than women to get the power and prestige associated with a given position (Powell & Jacobs, 1983; Wolf & Fligstein, 1979). Whatever the combination of reasons, women as a group clearly hold less position power in business organizations than do men. In practical terms, this means that they have less discretion in planning and implementing programs, less visibility in the results of their work, and less involvement in activities relevant to the organization's central concerns (Kanter, 1983).

It also means that they simply have less authority over others. One large-scale survey found that one quarter of male employees had authority over others' pay and promotions, whereas only one tenth of female employees had similar authority (Hill, 1980). Another large study found that men had more authority over others in general than women did, that traditionally male-occupied positions had greater authority than did female-occupied positions, and that gender differences in authority were best predicted by the policies and practices of employers rather than by the qualifications or behaviors of the employees (Wolf & Fligstein, 1979). Other studies paint a similarly dismal picture for women. Kanter's (1977) case study of a single corporation showed that women's sources of power were more limited than men's in three important ways: Women had less access to supplies, materials, and money; less access to information in the organization; and less assurance of support for their decisions from important people in their organizations.

A woman may hope to augment her organizational power through promotion into a more powerful position. However, the evidence suggests that women need to be wary of *meaning* of promotions. Women can apparently receive more promotions than men and still end up lower in rank and power. A study of 217 male and 78 female managers showed that the female managers were promoted at a faster rate than their male counterparts, but they remained lower in rank (Tsui & Gutek, 1984). It appears that women may be promoted in order to appease them with the appearance of power and to satisfy affirmative action guidelines, but that the actual effect of promotions for women may be small in many cases.

The "mommy track"?   Although the previous discussion suggests that women are already on a special career track—a slow one, filled with organizational obstacles—there have been recent calls to recognize differences among women by allowing them to follow different paths to organizational success. Advocacy of this strategy came from Felice Schwartz (1989) in a widely read *Harvard Business Review* article that argued there are two basic types of female managers: those who put their career first and those who put a high priority on family goals. Schwartz argued that companies need the contributions of both kinds of women and should accommodate them by establishing separate "career-primary" and "career-and-family" tracks. Journalists quickly dubbed the career-and-family track the "mommy track"—thus, perhaps unintentionally, laying bare the way family concerns are trivialized in relation to work in our success-oriented society.

Schwartz's dual-track suggestion derives from her perception that the policies and practices of male corporate culture are not supportive to women who wish to have children. To avoid heavy costs associated with women's career interruptions and turnover, companies must create more flexible systems for career-and-family women. She argues that career-primary women should be treated just like male employees on the "fast" track, but that career-and-family women should be able to decide to progress more slowly without suffering the stereotype that they are uncommitted to their jobs. The latter women should have access to parental leave, flextime, shared jobs, part-time work, and work at home.

Few people argue with Schwartz that male-led corporations make life difficult for anyone who wants to combine career and family. However, many take issue with her focus on women as the only ones experiencing a conflict between these two areas of responsibility. The provision of two tracks for women but only a single one for men implies that it is and will be only women who may need or wish to deemphasize career in favor of family when their children are young. Schwartz's strategy, which may look at first blush like a reasonable and overdue accommodation to women, will actually function to keep women locked into the current vision of their roles, as the group that has the main responsibility for childcare. The dual-track strategy implies that career-and-family women are deviants (albeit deviants that must be tolerated and accommodated) from the approved corporate norms; nowhere does it question those norms or imply that anything about the *normal* career track should be changed. Thus, even this approach, which purports to be a solution to the tensions that exist between women employees and a male-dominated workplace, ultimately has the effect of defining most women as outsiders who do not fit the normal patterns of the (male-defined) workplace. It does not point the way toward female-male equality in the workplace.

Women as "fair game"   One sign that women are regarded as outsiders at work is the extent to which they are considered fair game for harassment. Since the issue from which the insider-outsider dimension springs is sex/gender, much of the harassment directed at reminding women that they do not belong is sexual in tone. In such environments, women are kept on the outside by being constantly reminded that they are viewed in terms of their gender and sexuality. They are viewed, not as colleagues, but as sex objects or as barely tolerated representatives of an unwanted group.

In some universities, engineering students publish newspapers in which they make a point of being sexually insulting to women. The female minority in these faculties is supposed to take the sexist humor in fun, but the message is very clear that engineers are men, that women do not belong in these faculties. Similarly, women in the military report encountering a pervasive attitude that they are unwelcome—an attitude that is sometimes expressed as general hostility and sometimes as sexual harassment. As Cpl. Linda Wynn, a dog-handler for the Marine Corps security police, said of her assignment to the Beaufort, South Carolina, Air Station: "When I was first put here, nobody wanted me—including the supervisor. They made it real clear. They wouldn't talk to me—they would pretend I wasn't here. . . . If it weren't for the dog I wouldn't have survived" (Moore, 1989b). Petty Officer Karen Bolton, standing in the food line on the first day of her assignment to a training aircraft carrier, overheard a male sailor say of her: "That's the new piece of meat."

Women in the military, like those in other institutions that are strongly and unapologetically male-dominated, report that it is necessary to develop survival techniques in the face of their male colleagues' general meanness and relentless references to them as sex objects. Some women ignore the comments or pretend they don't hear them. Others try to become one of the boys by laughing at sexist jokes and simply tolerating a certain amount of harassment. Still others challenge the offenders, either face-to-face or through channels for complaints. The latter strategy is the one that is most conducive to a personal sense of effectiveness, and it may even work to reduce the problem. Yet, as long as institutions do not make a concerted effort to prevent harassment, individual working women have to keep fighting the same battles over and over again, wasting their power on issues that should be beside the point.

LEADERSHIP AND INTERPERSONAL POWER IN THE WORKPLACE

The preceding discussions of stereotypes and of organizational structure provide some of the reasons for the difficulty of achieving equal power for women and men in the workplace. Yet these broad, sometimes impersonal, factors exert their influence through the medium of interpersonal behavior. How does interpersonal behavior in the workplace support or challenge the imbalance of power between women and men?

Power Begets Power

Experts on power in organizations argue that "power begets power"—that each increase in power for an individual sets the stage for the acquisition of still more power (Ragins & Sundstrom, 1989). This process depends partly on the perception by others that the individual is increasing in power, since much of the essence of power lies in others' willingness to recognize and accede to it. Here, too, women are at a disadvantage: Their powerful behavior may not be perceived as such. For example, increased visibility is one way of gaining organizational power. However, in male-dominated workplaces, women's visibility may be associated with their minority status; they may find their highly visible successes chalked up to luck or favoritism, their highly visible failures taken as evidence that "a woman can't do the job." A woman in a male-dominated organization may experience visibility as a handicap and may work hard at being *in*visible, at not drawing attention to herself as a special case in the organization. Similarly, while many people gain organizational power by taking charge and showing effective management in critical situations, such behavior by women may not always produce positive reactions in others. A woman manager who acts in a directive and authoritative way may be seen as unfeminine and may encounter resentment and sabotage by her subordinates.

Many studies of small-group behavior have shown a positive connection between the amount of verbal participation and emergent leadership (Stein & Heller, 1979). Simply put, people who talk a lot in the group are more likely to become leaders—whether participation is allowed to occur spontaneously or is manipulated by the experimenters. Even when people suggest the identical solution to an assigned problem in different groups, their leadership ratings by other group members are not identical; rather, their leadership ratings are linked to how much they talk (Ginter & Lindskold, 1975).

Although talking in itself is important in establishing leadership, certain kinds of talk are especially important. Task leadership behaviors, such as asking questions, helping to set up structures and procedures for the group, giving information and opinions, and identifying and solving problems, are especially important in attaining leadership. Why? Talking in a group, especially task-oriented talking, represents a successful exertion of influence—even if that influence involves only getting others to listen. It may be that a high degree of visibility, brought about by high participation, leads group members to attribute competence and self-assurance to the individual, giving that person a base of expert power.

Given the above information, it should be a simple matter for women to improve their leadership chances relative to men by just speaking up. It should be, but it is not. Studies indicate that in mixed-sex groups men talk more than women, women are more likely to yield to a man's opinion than vice versa, and a higher proportion of men's verbal behavior than women's is task-related (Lockheed & Hall, 1976). As discussed in Chapter 6, part of the explanation for this pattern is that men tend to interrupt women and to ignore topics of conversation raised by them, and women may, either in anticipation of or in response to this pattern, venture fewer comments. However, if expectations are changed by giving the women prior experience in the task assigned to the group, then women show greatly increased verbal behaviors in subsequent mixed-sex groups.

Differing Styles

In general ways, women's and men's interactional styles in our culture appear to differ, with women's emphasizing communication and men's emphasizing dominance relatively more. This difference, which appears early in childhood and continues into adulthood, may make cross-sex interactions especially hard on women (Maccoby, 1990). If this observation is carried into the organizational context, it suggests reasons beyond ascribed status for women's lower levels of verbal participation in mixed-sex working groups. Women may be more likely than men to find the competitive undercurrents of task-related interactions in organizations distasteful, frustrating, and wearing; men, on the other hand, may be more likely than women to find them stimulating and enjoyable. In a mixed-sex working group, women may feel that their efforts to communicate are wasted and may feel unwilling to speak merely in order to keep a high profile. Men may feel quite comfortable with the verbal jockeying for attention that sometimes characterizes task- or decision-oriented discussions. In terms of leadership emerging from group discussions, the odds are sometimes doubly stacked against women.

Nonverbal behaviors, too, are related to the acquisition of leadership status. When people were shown videotapes without sound of pairs of actors in conversation, the nonverbal behavior rather than sex of the actors influenced judgments of status. Women or men who used high-status or dominant nonverbal behaviors (smiled less, initiated more touching, acted more relaxed) were seen as higher in status than women or men who used low-status nonverbal behaviors (McKenna & Denmark, cited in Denmark, 1977). However, real-world interactions sometimes make it more difficult for women than for men to use high-status behaviors, since they must overcome an initial assumption by others that they are low in status. A female manager may be mistaken for a secretary, or a female professor may be mistaken for a student—simply because women in high-status positions are still statistical rarities. Furthermore, even when women engage in high-status behaviors, the effect is not always as power-enhancing as it is for men. Some research shows that persons who sit at the head of the table are more likely to emerge as leaders and that high-status persons are more likely than low-status persons to choose this seating position. However, for women in mixed-sex groups, sitting at the head of the table is *not* associated with being perceived as a leader (Porter & Geis, 1981).

Subsequent research has repeatedly demonstrated the existence of very strong perceptual biases against viewing women as leaders. In one study, college students were exposed through a combination of video-tapes and direct observation to a series of authority models that were all male, all female, or a mixture of male and female. Only in the all-female authority model condition did women and men participants receive equal leadership recognition (Geis, Boston, & Hoffman, 1985). The reluctance to see women as leaders does seem to be a product of generalized social expectations for men and women: As shown below, if those expectations are changed, women will be perceived more readily as leaders.

A study that exposed students to videotaped reenactments of television commercials in which either men or women took on the role of authority showed that it was role more than sex that determined the students' evaluations of the actors (Geis, Brown, Jennings, & Corrado-Taylor, 1984). An important aspect of the scenarios was that in each case the actor in the role of authority interacted with an actor of the other sex who was subordinate and communicated acceptance of her or his authority. The authors conclude that showing women in high-status roles *with the social support of coparticipants* may be a means of breaking gender stereotypes.

EQUALIZING POWER? AFFIRMATIVE ACTION AND PAY EQUITY

It appears that men's and women's power in the workplace derives from multiple sources: personal qualities, interpersonal behaviors, organizational structures and policies, societal attitudes. It is also clear that the male-female balance of power is asymmetrical: Men, as a group, simply have more. Finally, it seems likely that gender-related power differences in the workplace compound over the duration of individual careers, beginning with pre-employment training and education, continuing through the recruitment and selection process, and solidifying with each career transition (Ragins & Sundstrom, 1989).

Female-male inequalities in the workplace have become a matter of common concern: Opinion surveys show that most North Americans favor sexual equity at work (Tougas & Veilleux, 1989). Yet, the solutions are not as apparent as the problem is; the very terms "affirmative action" and "pay equity" are guaranteed to raise many people's blood pressure. The problem is compounded by the gap between workers' perceptions of their own situation and that of their group.

Perception (or Denial) of Discrimination

Many researchers have found among female workers a strong perception that women as a group are the victims of discrimination (Colwill &
Josephson, 1983; Crosby, 1982; Tougas & Veilleux, 1988). Less common
is the finding that female workers see themselves as being personally
victimized by discrimination. In one landmark study of a diverse sample
of female and male workers in Newton, Massachusetts, researchers were
surprised to find that the employed women displayed a strong sense of
group deprivation—a sense of dissatisfaction about the treatment of employed women in general—but they displayed little parallel sense of
personal deprivation (Crosby, 1982). This despite that by all objective
measures taken in the study, these women were certainly the victims of
discrimination.

Male and female workers in the sample, equivalent in terms of job
prestige, family situation, age, education, hours worked per week, and
commitment to their jobs, were far from equivalent on one important
outcome measure: their salaries. The average salary for men in high-
prestige jobs was $9000 per year higher than that for their female
counterparts; for males in low-prestige jobs the salary advantage was
$5000. Yet, the women workers were as likely as the men to feel satisfied
with their jobs, to agree that they received what they deserved from their
jobs, to feel little sense of grievance about their jobs.

How can these women's contentment be explained? Crosby (1984)
suggests three overlapping possibilities. First, the women's responses
may reflect a basic strategy of politeness in refusing to complain about
their individual situation while at the same time remaining loyal to their
group. Second, the responses may reflect the obvious difficulty of inferring
discrimination from one's own individual treatment without knowledge
of the relevant comparison information. Most of these women were
probably not aware of the discrepancies between men's and women's
salaries, or of how their own situation fit into the entire picture for female
and male workers. Third, the women may be reluctant to claim discrimination because discrimination implies the existence of a villain some-
where—and they do not want to lay blame on their supervisor or employer,
especially if that person has been personally supportive.

Clearly, there are both cognitive and social factors that inhibit individual members of a disadvantaged group from recognizing and/or acknowledging the unfairness of their personal situation, even when they
are aware of discrimination against their group. In some cases, individual
women do acknowledge personal discrimination. In Colwill and Josephson's
(1983) study of government workers, female workers attributed some of
their personal career limitations to sex discrimination in recruiting,

promotions, training, discipline, and distribution of assignments. One explanation for the greater willingness of some individuals than others to acknowledge personal discrimination may be the extent to which they identify with their deprived group, although this relationship has not been investigated. What has been investigated is the relationship among group identification, the experience of collective relative deprivation, and support for programs designed to remove the injustice.

Support for Affirmative Action

Some women, like the members of other groups adversely affected by the way power and the resources on which it is based are distributed, can recognize that their group is deprived relative to others—but at the same time not be particularly upset about that recognition. One way individuals can do this is by dissociating themselves from their group; in other words, by refusing to identify with it. Research shows that people who identify strongly with their group are the most upset and dissatisfied when they perceive that group to be collectively deprived (Guimond & Dube-Simard, 1983).

Even when women identify strongly with women as a group and feel a strong sense of dissatisfaction over women's collective deprivation relative to men, they may not be supportive of remedial programs such as affirmative action. The women participating in one study declared themselves ready to assert their discontent by denouncing sex discrimination in their workplace and by participating in a group intended to improve women's position in the work force, yet they were reluctant to endorse affirmative action (Tougas, Dube, & Veilleux, 1987). The researchers were puzzled by this seeming inconsistency, but they soon developed a possible explanation for it, based on procedural justice theory. According to this theory, people value justice, and this value affects the kinds of collective actions they are willing to advocate. Even when people are aware of an injustice, such as sex discrimination, and even when it affects them directly, they are unwilling to accept a means of correcting that injustice that itself seems unfair. Thus, the researchers reasoned, the willingness of women who feel discontent about their collective relative deprivation to endorse an affirmative action program should depend on the perceived fairness of that program.

In a second study, in a sample of French-Canadian employed women, strong identification with women was associated with feelings of collective relative deprivation, which in turn were associated with support for affirmative action policies *if those policies were not based on preferential treatment for women* (Tougas & Veilleux, 1988). In this study, half of the respondents were provided with a description of an affirmative action policy that emphasized preferential treatment of women in order to increase the percentage of women in higher-level job categories. The other half were given a description of an affirmative action policy that relied on eliminating discriminatory administrative practices and targeting women for special assistance in planning and preparing for career moves. Only the latter program found support among the women studied. These findings agree with those of Colwill and Josephson (1983), who found that discontented female employees were more favorable toward programs that emphasized on-the-job training and support for career development than toward those that stressed preferential hiring or promotion of women.

What about men's support for affirmative action programs? Their support is crucial, since they often hold the powerful positions that allow them to either smooth the way or make the road rocky for such programs. Like women, men too are influenced by group identification, by perception of and dissatisfaction with discrimination against women, and by the particular procedures used in affirmative action programs. For men, strong identification with men as a group is negatively related to the perception that women are discriminated against and to dissatisfaction with that state of affairs. Among men who are dissatisfied with the way women are treated, the procedures specified by an affirmative action program are critical to their support for that program and its goals. These concerned men also prefer programs in which the main objective is to eliminate systematic barriers over those that emphasize preferential treatment of women (Tougas & Veilleux, 1989). These findings underline the importance of choosing affirmative action procedures carefully and of making these procedures known to those whose support is desired.

It is understandable that men, who may feel threatened and cheated of opportunities if women are given preferential treatment, prefer affirmative action programs that do not entail such treatment. Why, though, are women so squeamish about accepting preferential treatment in the face of so many years of past discrimination? Perhaps the answer is that all that history has had an effect: Women have been taught to be generally less self-confident in their abilities than men have, and so they especially need to feel, when they are hired or promoted, that their competence is the basis for that decision.

Support for this hypothesis comes from a laboratory study in which female and male undergraduates were selected as task leaders either on the basis of merit or preferentially on the basis of their sex (Heilman, Simon, & Repper, 1987). Women's, but not men's, self-perceptions and self-evaluations were negatively affected by the sex-based preferential selection method in comparison to the merit-based method. When selected on the basis of their sex, women devalued their leadership performance, took less credit for successes, characterized themselves as more deficient in general leadership skills, and reported less interest in continuing as leader. It appears that women, having more doubts about their competence than men do to begin with, are especially vulnerable to the adverse effects of nonwork-related preferential selection. Men seem not to be plagued by self-doubts about their performance when selected for a job simply because they are men.

CONCLUSION: GENDER, EXCLUSION, AND MARGINALITY

Since the Industrial Revolution, the public world of work has been defined as a male world, although women have always worked—as domestics, as agricultural workers, as miners, as textile makers. In the organizations and institutions of this century, women have been allowed into the bottom ranks to perform support functions and have been gradually inching their way upward. After years of overt exclusion from positions of power and authority in the workplace, women are now represented in a few such positions, but in general the exclusion persists.

Unlike the overt and unapologetic discrimination of the past, today's mechanisms of exclusion are often a little more subtle: The leadership role is described as a better match to the masculine than to the feminine stereotype; the informal information network in an organization bypasses the new female manager; the new female lieutenant is surrounded by a wall of unfriendliness. For some women pioneers in traditionally male jobs, the message seems to be "We can't keep you out—but we can make you want to leave."

The workplace continues to be defined to fit the traditional male life pattern, despite the increase in the number of employers offering such female-oriented benefits as daycare and flexible work schedules. As the controversy over the "mommy track" demonstrates, women are expected to adjust their lives and their styles to the traditional workplace patterns or accept second-class status; men are expected to put their careers first and leave family concerns primarily to women. Not surprisingly in such a workplace atmosphere, women often feel and appear marginal. Men, by contrast, are more central and powerful in the workplace, but perhaps at a cost to their family relationships, their health, their general well-being.

Women have proven over and over again their competence to handle virtually any job in the workforce; men have proven over and over again their lack of infallibility. Yet, the patterns of exclusion and marginality persist, and relatively few women reach positions of power and authority at work. Is there any room for optimism here? Some signs of hope come from how much the conditions of women in the workforce have changed over the past half-century. Sex discrimination and sexual harassment are now grounds for legal complaint. Women cannot be fired because they get married or get pregnant. Women have, at least theoretically, the same opportunities for education and training as men. Women are routinely portrayed on television as doctors, lawyers, executives—and men are portrayed as fathers. Perhaps, very gradually, stereotypes will change and the patterns of exclusion will be replaced by patterns of acceptance. However, the problem with which this chapter began, the problem of the assignment of primary household and childcare responsibilities to women, remains—despite the best efforts of a significant minority of men who *do* do their share. Women and men will not have equal power in the workplace until they have equal responsibilities outside the workplace.

In Chapter Ten, we examine the relationship between power and gender in an area that affects both home and work: politics.

Gender, Power, and Politics

I n November, 1988, Arizona voters in the general election were given the opportunity to choose, among other things, whether or not to remove the requirement that holders of state offices must be male. Admittedly, the vote seemed to be little more than a formality, given that the state's chief executive at the time, Governor Rose Mofford, was clearly not male. Yet the male-only requirement was still officially in place—and nearly one-fifth of those voting apparently liked it that way, voting not to repeal it (Propositions, 1988).

The outcome of the Arizona vote on Proposition 103 was never really in doubt, and no campaigning to repeal or to preserve the male-only requirement was done. Yet, that a male-only requirement for state office lingered on the books until so recently, that it had to be voted out instead of simply being removed as discriminatory, and that 19% of the voters voted not to remove it, may give pause to those who believe that the days of male-female equality are at hand in the political realm.

Of course, politics is more than voting, more than individuals' running for or holding elective office. Politics is, in many respects, a story of individual alliances and group influence. It involves, fundamentally, the development and maintenance of an individual's sense of identification with a group, the growth, through many such identifications, of a group's sense of power, and the effective organization of that power toward goals that are beneficial to the group. We need to understand how and why men continue to predominate over women in the political realm. Why, for instance, after the 1988 general elections in both the United States

179

and Canada were there still only two women members of the United States Senate; only 27 (about 6.2%) female members of the House of Representatives; only 39 (about 13.6%) female members of the Canadian House of Commons? Why has sex equality legislation such as the Equal Rights Amendment languished for decades? To understand, we must examine individuals' identification with their sex/gender group, factors related to the perception of justice or injustice in the relations between sex/gender groups, and group organization and behavior in the service of political goals.

GROUP IDENTIFICATION AND THE GROWTH OF POLITICAL AWARENESS

Women as a Minority Group?

Social psychologists discovered long ago that members of randomly formed groups would quickly develop strong positive feelings and stereotypes about their own group (the "ingroup"). Furthermore, if another group, an "outgroup," were placed in competition with the ingroup, strong negative stereotypes and feelings of hostility developed between the groups (Sherif & Sherif, 1956). A substantial body of research shows that being classified as group members, even without competition or conflict, leads to ingroup identification and stereotyping (Brewer, 1979). In other words, even without any supporting evidence, people who are randomly assigned to groups tend to form positive stereotypes about their own group and to develop feelings of ethnocentrism, the notion that one's own group is more important and better than other groups. Apparently, we humans have a strong tendency to identify with the groups to which we belong and to seek to make that identity positive by exalting our own group at the expense of others. If such ingroup–outgroup feelings can be generated in nearly identical groups whose membership is determined by mere chance, how much more likely it is that readily distinguishable groups—such as women and men—should develop similar feelings.

If all groups were equally advantaged and equally connected to the bases of power, this human tendency to bolster one's own group identity would be divisive and promotive of intergroup hostility and rivalry. It would not, on the other hand, necessarily imply the domination of one group by another. But what if one finds oneself a member of a group that is manifestly less powerful, less advantaged, than others? How comfortable is it to identify with a group that holds a socially inferior position? Can one form a positive social identity around membership in such a group?

These questions take us to the heart of the politics of sex and gender, since women, historically laboring under the stereotype of female inferiority, confront these very questions with respect to their sex/gender group.

Are women a minority group? Certainly not numerically, as they make up 51% of the human population. Yet, as noted 40 years ago by Helen Hacker (1951), in an analysis that is still disturbingly current, the formal and informal discrimination against women makes their position comparable in some ways to that of minority racial and ethnic groups. The negative stereotyping of and discrimination against women is amply documented. The psychology of membership in the group "women" shares many elements with the psychology of membership in any minority group.

Members of groups that are negatively valued by society, that are the targets of negative stereotyping or discrimination, have a difficult time developing the positive ingroup and negative outgroup biases that come so easily to more advantaged groups. It has long been observed that members of socially devalued or less powerful groups tend to opt for one of two solutions to the dilemma described here: acceptance of a negative social identity or rejection of identification with their own group (Allport, 1954).

Acceptance of a negative social identity means internalizing the negative stereotypes about one's own group. For women, it can mean agreeing that they, as women, are less capable, logical, strong-willed, etc., than men. When individual women internalize these stereotypes, they accept inferiority and powerlessness. They also feel, as individuals, little motivation to emphasize their group identity as women—except perhaps as an excuse for avoiding masculine-stereotyped tasks. It is very difficult for a group to rally, to organize, especially to organize for change, around a negative identity.

Sometimes women will opt for the second solution, rejection of identification with their own group. In this case, women accept the negative stereotypes of femininity for other women but not for themselves. They may say that they do not enjoy the company of other women and may give low priority to female friendships. If they succeed in a male-dominated career, they may encourage the view that they are exceptions, with more talent than the average woman, and discourage other women from aspiring to similar success. Female politicians may repudiate involvement in women's issues in an attempt to disengage themselves from the low-status group and blend in with the dominant group.

It is necessary to recognize here that despite talk of women and men as monolithic groups, each of these groups is made up of many distinct subgroups, each of which may form a group identity relative to the larger sex/gender group. Black women, lesbian women, Jewish women, disabled women, for example, may identify more strongly with their specific group than with women in general. In fact, group identification is not necessarily bounded by sex or gender at all; many individuals may, for example, find their race, nationality, or religion to be a stronger dimension of their social identity than gender. Since group identification turns out to be a crucial precursor of political action on behalf of one's group, and each of us is potentially a member of many groups, the group identifications that we choose as primary are extremely important to our politics.

Members of most minority groups experience some difficulty in forming a strong, positive identification with their groups because of the negative social identity attached to those groups. Despite their large numbers, women face many pressures against forming a strong identification with their group, and those pressures do not stem only from the negative stereotypes attached to femininity. Women's situation as a minority group is unique in more than that they are not numerically a minority. There is more frequent and more intimate contact between females and males than between most minority and majority groups. Marriage and cohabitation, and the accompanying strong emotional bonds that form between individual women and men, serve to dilute feelings of sex/gender group identification. Women and men are more personally interdependent than are members of most minority and majority groups; for most individuals, sex separation or segregation is not practical or desirable.

Of course, members of a minority or socially devalued group are not doomed to the choice between two bad alternatives: accepting a negative identity or rejecting their group. The alternative is to challenge the negative identity assigned to one's group. Before that can happen, however, group members must awaken to the injustice of their situation. As a well-worn movement catch-phrase puts it, their "consciousness must be raised."

The Perception of Justice

Social psychologists have long argued that people are motivated to see their social relationships as fair and their social world as just (Lerner, 1970; Walster & Walster, 1975). This motivation apparently makes us reluctant to question a situation, such as the political predominance of European-American males, in which one group dominates another. When people see a situation, even a possibly unfair situation, as a given, they tend to justify it—literally to make it just—by the way they think about it. Thus, for example, Lerner's research (1970; 1974) shows that people who see a victim being hurt or punished for no apparent reason resolve their own discomfort by manufacturing reasons why the victim might have deserved the punishment. In some instances, the more apparently blameless the victim, the more she or he is described as a bad, weak, or stupid person.

A general motivation to see the world as just may provide a partial explanation for the frequent unwillingness to perceive injustice in the subordination of women. Historically and currently, apologists for male dominance have manufactured comprehensive lists of feminine qualities that are said to make women undeserving of or unfit for equal status with men: Women have smaller brains, not enough testosterone, too many raging female hormones, not enough team spirit, too much emotion, not enough moral sensitivity, too much sensitivity to context. The lists are fanciful, changeable, often including "facts" that have long been discredited, always grasping at every indication of gender difference as a sign of female inferiority. The persistent emergence of such lists bespeaks a strong need to rationalize the inequality between the sexes.

It is not only the need to see justice in the world, but also the distribution of power, that makes female-male inequality appear normal, natural, and right. Walster and Walster (1975) argue that the persons with the most power in a community tend not only to gain control over community resources but also to develop a social philosophy that supports their right to monopolize these resources. This philosophy is eventually accepted by the entire community as a justification for the status quo; if the entire group accepts the status quo, everyone avoids the discomfort of participating in a relationship experienced as inequitable or unfair. Their research suggests that both exploiters and victims can and frequently do convince themselves that the most unbalanced of exchanges is perfectly fair (e.g. Walster, Berscheid, & Walster, 1973). It appears that the ideology of dominance is self-perpetuating: the more power a group obtains, the more its members can convince themselves and others that such power is deserved and stems from superiority.

So where does consciousness-raising come in? Where, in the face of these powerful social forces toward acceptance of a negative social identity, toward rationalizing and accepting the status quo, is there room for an awakening of the sense of *in*justice?

POLITICAL CONSCIOUSNESS

Two qualities characterize women who say they support programs to improve women's status: a sense of identification with women as a group, and a belief that women have been and are being treated unfairly (Tougas

& Veilleux, 1989). Political consciousness, and, ultimately, political action, is directly rooted in the twin foundations of group identification and the perception of justice. It is likely that the two factors interact and are mutually reinforcing: The stronger and more positive the group identification the more likely it is that members of the group will see an unjust system, rather than any internal failings of their own, as the cause of difficulties they encounter. Similarly, the more external sources of injustice against them a group is able to identify, the more they are able to enhance their own image and identity by blaming failures on outside forces and by noting that their successes have been won despite adverse conditions. It is no accident that many young African-Americans find strength in rap lyrics emphasizing that it has taken "millions" of others to hold them back.

We have already noted that it is very difficult for individuals to form a satisfactory group identification with a group that is devalued according to dominant social stereotypes. A person can respond to membership in a negatively valued social group by accepting the negative social identity that comes with group membership; but such acceptance is linked to low self-esteem and is not conducive to the liking, respect, and admiration for other group members that lead to strong group identification (Brown, 1986).

Other strategies involve fleeing the group: trying to deny membership in the group or "passing" (as in gays passing for straight, blacks passing for white), or trying to "exit," or change, groups altogether (as in changing citizenship or religious affiliation, or changing socioeconomic class through upward mobility). The alternative to such acceptance or escape strategies is social action: to try to change the negative group identity to a positive one, a strategy known as "voice" (Tajfel, 1981). The latter strategy is the most positive in terms of the group's welfare, but its success requires the efforts of more than one, or even a few, isolated individuals. It would seem to require the kind of collective effort that implies at least elementary political awareness and action—yet, it is said that political awareness and action are built on positive group identification. The apparent chicken-and-egg quality to this analysis illustrates that what is going on in the growth of political consciousness is not a simple linear process: It is a series of mutually reinforcing cycles of group change. The process may appear to be triggered by a single incident or a single individual who helps the group to break through a threshold of acceptance into active questioning: for African-Americans Rosa Parks' refusal to give up her seat on the bus to a white man; for North American women, Betty Friedan's incisive examination of the "problem that has no name"; for Poles, Lech Walesa's stubborn defiance of the order to return to work. Such an individual trigger is crucial—but the time must be right.

Two centuries before Betty Friedan there was Abigail Adams, and in the intervening years many persuasive voices—Margaret Fuller, Nellie McClung, Elizabeth Cady Stanton, Virginia Woolf, Antoinette Brown Blackwell, Emma Goldman—have been raised in criticism of traditionally defined femininity: Yet rarely were so many women so ready to listen before Betty Friedan.

Political scientist Ethel Klein (1984) notes that there are three stages to the rise of political consciousness. These stages are nourished by a social context that sweeps the group in question into profound life change. In the first stage, group members affiliate with one another, form strong group bonds, and recognize common experiences and problems. In the second, group members reject the traditional group image for a more favorable and more powerful alternative image and ideal. In the third, group members become aware that they cannot solve their problems or achieve their new ideals simply by working harder; rather, their problems are rooted in social institutions and a system of social inequality. Despite Klein's characterization of these processes as "stages," they are not distinct, separate, and linear but overlapping and expanding. For example, the rejection of traditional group stereotypes in the second stage may lead in turn to the further strengthening of the group bonds characteristic of the first stage.

For women, the growth of political consciousness has included deliberate attempts to build positive group identification. One of the most common manifestations of the emerging women's liberation movement in the 1960s was the rise of the consciousness-raising or C-R group. Such groups were sponsored by fledgling women's centers or simply emerged informally as female friends met and began to discuss their lives in relation to new insights about the position of women offered in writings such as Betty Friedan's (1963) *The Feminine Mystique*. The groups provided a forum where women could explore their situation together and form the mutually supportive relationships necessary for the growth of a more positive social identity and collective action to change their situation. Today, many of these functions are subsumed by groups with more formal names and organizations: women's caucuses in professional organizations and political parties, women's networks, women's studies classes.

Yet, the large-scale questioning of traditional stereotypes about women would not necessarily emerge at any random time and place in history, no matter how strongly women banded together. In the latter half of this century, the processes of women's politicization have been helped along by rapid social change that profoundly affected women's lives: the increasing availability of reliable contraception, the necessity for women to spend a greater proportion of their lives in the paid workforce, the increasing divorce rate, the lengthening of the average lifespan, and a media explosion that has made all of the other changes visible and discussable as they happened. Large-scale social changes were occurring when earlier feminists articulated their concerns, but clearly the combination of circumstances was not quite right. One of the most interesting questions about the feminist movement, and about social movements in general, concerns just what constitutes the right time and place for the emergence of collective action to challenge the status quo.

One theory of social identity (Tajfel, 1981; 1982) spells out four variables that are thought to be crucial to whether members of a negatively valued group will find their collective power and voice and try to elevate their group rather than flee it or accept the negativity.

The first is the possibility of personal movement out of the group. Except in extreme circumstances, women cannot leave their female sex or gender identity behind, nor is it practical or desirable for the majority of them to pass for men. So, such personal movement in search of a more positive identity is excluded—making social action more likely.

The second variable, sharpness of group boundary, also works against individual action in the case of female and male groups. Fuzzy group boundaries make individual action, such as escape, easier. A consideration of these two variables shows that women as a group, if experiencing a negative social identity, face a choice between acceptance of that identity or finding a new collective voice.

It is the third and fourth variables, which are concerned with the perception of the social system, that influence group members in the direction of acceptance of or challenge to their group identity. The shape of these latter two variables helps to determine whether or not the time is right to inspire collective action. One is the perceived legitimacy of that system. As discussed in earlier chapters, perceived legitimacy provides a basis of interpersonal power for individuals. We now see that it provides a similar source of power for dominant groups. As long as everyone agrees there is a good reason for the subordination of or discrimination against women, there is little impetus toward social action to enhance women's social identity or status. However, if the legitimacy of the system begins to be questioned—if, for instance, some vocal individuals point out that the unequal treatment of women and men is inconsistent with generally accepted values of fairness—there is suddenly increased scope for women to develop a new voice. For example, the "male only" admissions policies of American military academies went unquestioned for decades because such exclusionary practices were believed necessary to the academies' legitimate purpose of producing "educated and honorable men" who would be "citizen-soldiers," "prepared for leadership in the board room or on the battlefield" (Henderson & Baker, 1990, p. B7). In the face of the sex desegregation of the military and the passage of laws prohibiting sex discrimination in public educational institutions, the legitimacy of the no-women policy has begun to be perceived as threadbare, and the thoughtless bravado embodied in the male cadets' defiant slogan "Better dead than coed" is unlikely to bolster that legitimacy.

The final variable is the perceived security of the social system—its invulnerability to challenge. Such security has both physical and mental aspects (Brown, 1986). A system is physically secure if it is backed by overwhelming military might or if the dominant group controls most of the wealth. The cognitive, or mental, aspects of security are less tangible but equally real. They involve the inability of the subordinate group to imagine that things could be different. Writers, artists, orators, scientists— all can play an important role in breaching the cognitive security of a social system by posing previously unthinkable questions, by helping to provide the tools and the inspiration for imagining a different social arrangement. In recent years writers of feminist science fiction have created imagined worlds of gender equality; historians have unearthed the stories of women who accomplished things that everyone had thought impossible for a woman; psychologists have carried out research that demolished stereotypes of immutable female-male differences—all with the result of allowing visions of previously unimagined possibilities for the pattern of gender relations.

In the early days of the women's movement, when the main goal was female suffrage—the vote for women—women challenged the notion that they were not competent to vote or that it was unladylike for them to sully their hands with politics. They made this challenge largely in the context of accepting the legitimacy of the distinctions between feminine and masculine roles (Klein, 1984). In fact, many of the arguments made for women's suffrage rested on the idea that women, who were naturally more high-minded than men, would use the vote to clean up social problems such as alcoholism, make society a safer, more virtuous place, and preserve the sanctity of the home. Many (though not all) early 20th-century suffragists sought the vote, not in the interests of female-male equality, but in order to become society's housekeepers.

In the United States, women won the right to vote in federal elections in 1920—after "56 referendum campaigns, 480 efforts to get state legislatures to allow suffrage referenda, 47 campaigns at state constitutional conventions for suffrage, 277 attempts to include woman suffrage in state party programs, and 19 campaigns to get the Nineteenth Amendment through Congress" (Klein, 1984, p. 16). Clearly, a massive organizational effort was required to reach this conclusion. However, perhaps because the suffrage movement required few chinks in the perceived legitimacy of a social system that placed men in charge of the public sphere and women in charge of home and family issues, the winning of the vote was viewed by many women as the end of the struggle rather than as a new beginning. Women had formed a strong, positive, group identification and had organized effectively for social change, but their perception of the injustice of their position relative to men was confined to a narrow range of issues. Even though women had experienced the power of collective action, most apparently did not dream of challenging the basic premises of a system of male leadership. In fact, when the National Women's Party drafted the Equal Rights Amendment in 1923, other women's organizations such as the Women's Bureau and the League of Women Voters testified against the amendment in congressional hearings on the grounds that the biological differences between the sexes necessitated different social and economic roles for women and men (Klein, 1984). Apparently, most women continued to view the social system as legitimate and either could not or would not challenge the security of that system by imagining that things could be different.

Political Action

As women won the right to vote in various countries, the stage was set for them to make a large impact on the political life of those countries. Yet, for anyone who expected major changes as a result of female suffrage, the early results were disappointing. In the United States, it became obvious during the first few elections after suffrage that women were not voting as a block—and that most women were not voting at all. However, the political experience that women had gained in the struggle for the vote and the potential political clout embodied in the vote gave women new sources of power relative to men. These new resources were not always used to women's best advantage, but their impact is evident over the years since women began the struggle for suffrage.

Gender Differences and Similarities in Political Participation

Voting   Despite the seriousness of the struggle for women's suffrage, there were many American women who failed to use the vote once it was won. Only a third of the eligible women actually voted in their first Presidential election in 1920, and the voter turnout among women remained 20% to 30% below that of men throughout that decade. As recently as 1960, voter participation was 11% lower among women than men (Klein, 1984). These gender differences were largest among groups, such as immigrants, rural dwellers, Southerners, and the poor, who adhered more strongly to traditional gender roles.

By 1968, women's voting turnout caught up with men's in the United States. Similarly, in other countries where women had been enfranchised, gender differences in voting rates diminished over the years and have now disappeared in many countries. Cross-national data show that it is usual for recently enfranchised women to have low voter turnout rates, but, over time, women develop the habit of voting and new generations of women participate as a matter of course. One study of 14 nations shows that the strongest predictor of gender differences in voter turnout is the proportion of pre-franchise generation women in a country's population (Christy, 1987).

One of the expectations of those who campaigned for women's suffrage was that women would use the power of the vote to change things in their favor. In other words, women were expected to vote differently than men. During the first few years after the passage of the Nineteenth Amendment in the United States, Congress responded to pressure from women's groups by approving a health care education bill for mothers, a consumer protection bill, and other pieces of legislation aimed particularly at women's interests. With the vote, women as a group had acquired a power resource that was potentially devastating to politicians depending on votes for re-election. In anticipation of the women's use of this new source of power, the politicians rushed to pass legislation that would endear them to the new voters. However, the initial flurry of support for "women's issues" soon faded as it became apparent that sex was less strongly related to voting choice than were party affiliation, religion, class, and ethnicity (Klein, 1984). Women either did not view their best interests as different from those of men, trusted the promises of male politicians who said they would look after women's interests, or put their own collective interests aside when they made voting choices.

It is only in recent years that politicians have again begun to be concerned about the women's vote. As late as the 1976 United States Presidential election, Jimmy Carter, who had a far better record than his rival Gerald Ford on supporting women's rights, did not bother to emphasize this difference in his campaign—leaving most of the electorate to perceive that the two candidates were equally supportive of women's rights (Klein, 1984). However, during recent elections in the United States and Canada, the phrase "gender gap" has been much bandied about, and politicians have taken care to court their female constituents by espousing such issues as childcare. The 1980 United States elections, which gave voters a choice between a Republican candidate who opposed the Equal Rights Amendment and favored a constitutional amendment banning abortion and a Democratic candidate who supported (albeit weakly) both the ERA and abortion rights, demonstrated that feminist concerns could and did influence women's vote more than men's. While

55% of male voters chose Reagan, only 47% of female voters did so. Moreover, the candidates' positions on female/male equality were a much stronger determinant of women's than men's voting choices. Of the men who agreed with Carter on gender equality and supported the ERA, 35% voted for Carter. Of the women holding these same positions, however, an impressive 59% gave Carter their vote (Klein, 1984).

The woman's vote has now emerged as a force to be reckoned with. It is related less closely to party loyalty and more closely to particular issues than is the man's vote. In the United States, women have tended to vote to support their rights when those rights were an issue between candidates (Klein, 1984), although not always by a large enough margin for their candidate to prevail. In the 1988 Presidential election, men's, particularly white men's, support for winner George Bush was considerably stronger than women's (White males propel Bush into office, 1988). Interestingly, though, American women and men apparently differ far less in their perceptions of what is good for them and for the country than do African-American and white voters. Women and men differed only 7 to 8 percentage points in their support for Bush; Blacks and Whites differed by a whopping 47 percentage points. Blacks voted 86% to 12% for Michael Dukakis (Portrait of the electorate, 1988). Although the gender gap is significant (even 1 or 2 percentage points can make a difference to the outcome of an election), it is clear that women and men often do not make their sex/gender group concerns as primary as other concerns.

Political office   Around the world, the percentage of women holding high political office is low. Among current and past heads of state, only a few female names are familiar: Margaret Thatcher of Great Britain, the late Indira Gandhi of India, Vigdis Finnbogadottir of Iceland, Benazir Bhutto of Pakistan, Corazon Aquino of the Phillipines, Gro Bruntland, former prime minister of Norway. So uncommon are women in high political office that new firsts for them are still occurring: In January of 1990, Benazir Bhutto became the first world leader in modern times to give birth while in office.

The higher and more prestigious the political office, the less likely a woman is to hold it. Thus, women who aspire to or hold high political office are often isolated because of their sex and have to work hard at keeping their courage and sense of humor intact. Jeannette Rankin, the first woman to serve in the United States Congress, could have been speaking for all women in politics when she commented that, "the individual woman is required . . . a thousand times a day to choose either to accept her appointed role and thereby rescue her good disposition out of the wreckage of her self-respect, or else follow an independent line of behavior and rescue her self-respect out of the wreckage of her good disposition" (*Jeannette Rankin: First Lady in Congress*, by Hannah Josephson, quoted in Partnow, 1977, p. 430).

The reason for the scarcity of women in high political office does not lie in a lack of political interest among women. Studies of participation in election campaigns in Canada (Kay, n.d.) and in political organizations in the United States (Lee, 1977) show that women are as likely (if not more likely) to work for political causes or candidates as are men.

Women's underrepresentation in political office is more likely linked to discrimination at various levels of the political process. Studies of political parties in Canada show that women are less likely than men to be chosen for the strategic leadership tasks that provide stepping stones toward the expertise and support networks necessary to run for public office (Brodie & Vickers, 1982). When women do run for office, they are more likely than men to be hampered by a lack of funds. Finally, there are signs that voters, particularly male voters, discriminate against female candidates.

Public opinion surveys generally show that voters are not unwilling to support qualified female candidates for office; however, these surveys are subject to bias, since it is becoming less and less acceptable to admit that one would not vote for a woman. Moreover, evidence shows that elected women are viewed as having exceptionally positive attributes (Githens & Prestage, 1977). The latter finding suggests that women candidates may have to be better qualified than their male counterparts to achieve the same degree of success.

One laboratory study using simulated candidates and elections showed that both sex and physical attractiveness may have an impact on electability (Sigelman, Thomas, Sigelman, & Ribich, 1986). In this study, college students evaluated six challengers to an incumbent running for the office of mayor or county clerk. The challengers were portrayed as men and women of high, moderate, or low physical attractiveness. Male students participating in this study showed a clear pro-male bias. They discriminated against female candidates, seeing them as less qualified than male challengers, voting for them less often, and ranking them lower. Women did not show a reciprocal pro-female bias but were equally favorable to female and male candidates. They appeared to be, as the researchers noted, "equal opportunity" voters (Sigelman, et. al., p. 244).

Furthermore, the physical attractiveness of the simulated candidates played a different role for men and women. For male candidates, physical attractiveness was a clear asset. The physically attractive male candidates were seen as more masculine and received more support. For female candidates, however, beauty was not consistently either advantageous or disadvantageous—perhaps because beauty was associated with femininity, a quality not usually associated with political success. The results of this study suggest that sexism in electoral politics may flourish even though opinion surveys fail to detect it.

The impact of political participation   It is not only the vote and the right to stand for office that confers political power on a person or group. Political power is also won through the participatory activities of campaigning, lobbying, communicating with politicians and other voters. A group's lobbying clout is, of course, enhanced by the perceived number of votes it can mobilize, so enfranchisement is far from irrelevant. Voting, however, is not where a group's political power stops.

One demonstration of the impact of political participation without the vote is found in the winning of that vote. As noted earlier, that particular victory came after hundreds of political actions—referendum campaigns, petitions, demonstrations—to mobilize public opinion and to change the minds of elected politicians. The gaining of the vote did not mean that other types of political participation were no longer required or useful. In fact, as Ethel Klein (1984) has shown in research on American women's political activism, activism is a key to getting things accomplished. She charted feminist activism, as indicated by the number of events aimed at changing women's traditional status, against legislative success across the years from 1899 to 1980. Women's political efforts over this time period have encompassed a wide range of goals, generally aimed at gaining more control for women over their own lives. Legislative outcomes are measured by two indicators: the number of bills or joint resolutions concerned with women's status introduced in Congress (an indicator of women's access to political decision makers), and the number of bills actually passed into law (an indicator of women's influence on legislative decisions). The results can be seen in Figure 1.

Klein's data show, first, that women's access to the political agenda, as measured by the introduction of legislation, increased with time. She explains this relationship by noting the gradual increase in women's political expertise and organization that began during the struggle for suffrage. By 1965, the combined membership in three well-entrenched women's organizations—The League of Women Voters, Business and Professional Women Clubs, and the American Association of University Women—was close to half a million. The growth of a solidly based, experienced women's lobby gave women substantial access to the country's political elite. This access made women's legislation increasingly likely to be introduced by politicians, even during times such as the 1950s when mass activism by women was low.

Getting legislation introduced is one thing; getting it passed is another. The second thing that Klein's chart shows is that although many bills relating to women's status were introduced during the years covered

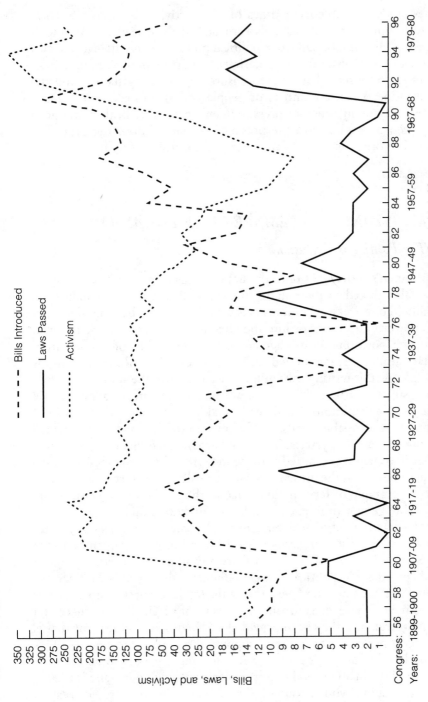

Figure 1   Reprinted by permission of the publishers from *Gender Politics* by Ethel Klein, Cambridge, Mass.: Harvard University Press, Copyright © 1984 by the President and Fellows of Harvard College.

in her study, it was during times of high activism by a visible, vocal women's movement that such bills were most likely to be passed. Women's successful wielding of collective political power has clearly involved two dimensions, both crucial: the gathering of expertise, money, connections, and other resources that help to ensure access to legislators; and the mobilization of large numbers of people willing to make a fuss about women's status in order to press women's concerns. Both dimensions have been necessary, and the presence of one without the other has resulted in disappointment for women in the realm of politics.

RESISTANCE TO FEMALE-MALE EQUALITY

The Politics of Exclusion

Women's movement onto the upper rungs of the political ladder is undeniably linked to their status in society. Resistance to female–male equality in one arena often translates into the de facto barring of women from powerful positions or into the effective disabling of those few who hold such positions in another arena. The exclusion of women from military academies, mentioned earlier, is an excellent illustration of this principle. At this writing, two military academies in the southern United States, supported by public funds, are under pressure to admit female students. The reaction of male cadets, along with generations of loyal alumni, to the possible intrusion of women onto their turf has resembled nothing so much as hysteria. The men have moaned that everything will change if women are admitted to the schools, that the spirit of brotherhood will disappear, that the presence of women will, in short, ruin everything. A better example of fervent adherence to the mythology of vast, insurmountable gender differences would be difficult to find.

The graduates of these determinedly all-male institutions—graduates who are apparently so unaccustomed to working with women that they panic at the thought of having to share a campus with them—go on to wield considerable political power. Graduates of Virginia Military Institute (VMI) can be found permeating the top levels of state government and business. These men are some of the state of Virginia's most successful and powerful, and they have provided VMI with an endowment that is the largest per capita of any state-supported school in the country. This brotherhood of power is not shy about making the assertion that maintenance of the brotherhood requires keeping women out—and it is clear that by keeping women out of the college they are also, in reality, excluding them from participation in the network of political power that controls much of the state. This situation is a clear example of the way that the impact of the exclusion of women can spread beyond the immediate situation to affect their broader political power.

The Politics of Legitimacy

Resistance to female-male equality in the political realm has come not only from men, but also from some women. During the American campaign for women's suffrage, a vocal anti-suffrage movement placed pressure on legislators to oppose the vote for women. The National Association Opposed to Woman Suffrage, while undeniably smaller than the cadre of women working for the vote, brought together an all-female executive board to lead the campaign to deny women the vote. These women expressed the opinion that it was not women's place to meddle in the affairs of politics, that the vote for women would distort the natural relationship between the sexes. Association president Alice Wadsworth wrote in a letter to Senator William Borah that giving women the vote "would be an endorsement of nagging *as a national policy*" (Wadsworth, 1917, p. 2). These women were not blind to the fact that women and men were treated differently under the law; they simply did not see that differential treatment as an injustice. They argued that differing rights and responsibilities were a natural, legitimate consequence of women's and men's differing natures, including women's childbearing capacity. They feared, perhaps, that women would lose more than they gained in the struggle for equal rights.

Resistance by women to political equality with men is not only a phenomenon of the past, although few women would now argue against having the vote. Women's organizations dedicated to the preservation of traditional gender roles (especially within the nuclear family) have emerged as political forces in several countries during the 1980s. In Australia, the founder of an anti-feminist group called Women Who Want to be Women, says that they "do not support the elimination of sexism" (Francis, quoted in Gray, 1985, p. 150). In Canada, a group called R.E.A.L. Women (Realistic, Equal, Active, for Life) claims that women are already equal with men, and they oppose government programs aimed at raising women's status. The motto that appears on their publications is "Women's rights but not at the expense of human rights." A determinedly vocal anti-feminist movement in the United States, including Phyllis Schafly's STOP-ERA and other groups such as Females Opposed to Equality (FOE) and Happiness of Motherhood Eternal (HOME), helped to block the ratification of the Equal Rights Amendment in the 1970s and is currently allied with other conservative groups working to limit access to legal abortion.

These organizations do not accept the existence of sex discrimination or structured inequality between women and men; they argue that women simply *choose* to work at low-paying, part-time jobs, or not to run for political office. They oppose affirmative action, the provision of daycare for children, and other changes that they see as threatening to the nuclear family and to women's role as nurturers of children. Besides their belief that the most legitimate role for women lies in the bearing and nurturing of children, members of these groups also seem to share a strong discomfort with the idea of "special privileges" for women. They take the position that it is unfair and offensive to pay special attention to the status of women, to have special programs targeted at improving women's education or occupational advancement or political opportunities. Their sense of injustice is aroused, not by the notion that women have been or are being given fewer opportunities than men, but rather by their perception that the feminist insistence on female-male equality actually represents the granting of "more than equal" opportunities for women. They believe that women and men *have* equal opportunities, and that the smaller numbers of women in political office, in executive positions, in educational administrative positions, simply reflect gender differences in ability and motivation.

Their analysis ignores or denies the existence of the gender-related power structure about which this book is written: the automatically higher status granted to males in interpersonal interactions, the greater control by men than women of most resources on which power is based, the self-perpetuating psychology of dominance and submission. A feminist perspective, on the other hand, holds that ignoring the gender power structure will not make it go away; rather, only a clear-eyed assessment of it will allow for its gradual dismantling. The two groups may not be far apart in their concern for justice and their desire for a society that is structured according to principles that are morally correct, but their perceptions of exactly what justice entails for female-male relationships are worlds apart.

CONCLUSION: VOTES AND VOICE

Even though women outnumber men, they have been psychologically a minority group in many respects. Because they have been devalued relative to men, women have had some trouble forming the strong, positive, group identification necessary for political action. Furthermore, sex/gender group identification is diluted by the strong emotional and economic bonds that form between individual women and men, and by the use of other dimensions, such as race or nationality, as primary sources of social identity. The growth of the feminist movement is a sign, however, that many women have identified strongly and positively with women as a group.

The movement to improve the status of women has been rooted in the twin factors of group identification and the perception that women have been treated unjustly relative to men. The movement has grown as more and more women found their voices and challenged the injustices they perceived. In the early part of this century, the injustices many women perceived were limited to women's exclusion from suffrage and from electoral politics. Perhaps for this reason, the winning of the vote for women did not immediately cause big changes in women's status. The modern feminist movement, on the other hand, views many more aspects of gender power relations as unjust and attempts to use political influence to move society in the direction of female-male equality on many fronts. A "gender gap" in voting patterns indicates that a significant number of women now view their interests as diverging to some extent from those of men.

Some women are still organizing to oppose the feminist movement, claiming that there is no great injustice in the ways that women and men are treated. Often, individuals do not view their own personal experiences as related to the structure of interrelationships between their own group and another. Indeed, as noted in this chapter, there is a very strong tendency to rationalize the status quo and to interpret outcomes as fair. However, the major premise of this book has been that there *is* structured inequality in the power relationships between women and men, and the main task of this book has been to make that structure visible and comprehensible. The more visible that structure is, the more often people will be able to use their political power to change it.

Epilogue: The Future

Much of the women's movement has been about forming a strong, positive, social identity for women. The formation of this collective identity has given women a basis for knowing that many of their difficulties are politically rather than personally based. The sense of injustice that has grown out of this knowledge has given women the impetus to organize for change—and organize they have.

Against the background of a social power structure based on an assumption of male authority, women have found their voice on many levels. They have had to find it, impelled by changes in their lives so drastic that simple acquiescence to the traditional gender power structure has become unworkable—and intolerable. These changes—the economic necessity of many years in the workforce for most women, the rising divorce rate, a lengthening lifespan, more reliable contraception, the economic and ethical pressures against having large families—have motivated women to redefine their position in society. Since women and men do not, for the most part, lead separate lives, and since the two gender roles are defined, to some extent, in relation to each other, men must also reshape their expectations and their behavior. The changes are in the direction of increasing equality of power between women and men, and they are occurring at personal, interpersonal, social, and political levels.

Opinion surveys indicate an increasing recognition that women and men deserve equal access to education and employment, that responsibility for childcare cannot be left solely to individual women, that husbands have no right to abuse their wives. Women have moved into the workforce

198

and into traditionally male jobs in significant numbers. Some efforts are being made to reevaluate women's traditional jobs in terms of their real economic worth. Women's political participation has increased dramatically. There are signs that this general movement in the direction of female–male equality will continue and that, indeed, it is regarded as inevitable by many people. For instance, the great majority of women and men surveyed expected that by the year 2000 all adult women will be in the workforce (*The 1980 Virginia Slims American women's opinion poll,* 1980). Across many countries, female–male equality in political activity is increasing, even when other indicators of women's status show no definite progress (Christy, 1987). It appears, on the face of it, that the movement toward sexual equality is inexorable, with little potential for reversal.

It is true enough that much has changed in personal and political gender relations. Rising expectations, once unleashed, are difficult to contain; they tend to push the process of change in the hoped-for direction. Rights, once won, are difficult to rescind—but not, as Margaret Atwood illustrates in her chilling novel about the subordination of women, *The Handmaid's Tale,* impossible. Despite strong social trends toward equality between women and men, equality is far from being a reality. Women still suffer enormous economic discrimination. They bear a disproportionate burden of childcare and household responsibilities. They are as a group respected less than men. They are forced to adjust to institutions shaped by the values and perspectives of men and run, for the most part, by men. Their political presence has increased, but it comes nowhere near proportional representation: Television news footage of important national or international meetings, summits, or high-level conferences often features only groups of men—shaking hands, making deals, signing agreements, smiling for the cameras.

Significant numbers of women and men have begun to understand the organization of social and economic power that underlies the automatic attribution of authority to men, the social and interpersonal patterns of male dominance and female deference. Many women and some men have struggled to change the way power is organized along gender lines, but that struggle is far from finished. Before it is finished it will have to address the very difficult problems inherent in the practice, as opposed to the idea, of female–male equality. It is easy to say that women and men should have equal access to economic benefits; it is more difficult to create a society where this equality is a reality. If all the women who wanted to were able simply to join the ranks of men holding well-paid positions in the workforce, the problem would not be solved unless other major social adjustments also occurred. Serious provisions for childcare would have to be made. Levels of social stress might well rise as more

people devoted more time to their jobs and had less time for relaxa-
tion, for socializing, and for such necessary maintenance activities as
shopping, cleaning, and personal business (and no one to help them with
these activities). The important communal values of relationship, of
nurturance, of devoting time to the care of others, which women in the
traditional homemaker role have protected and enacted by their lifestyle,
might be lost.

The above concerns are not minor ones. Neither are they justifica-
tions for leaving the gender imbalance of power as it is. Some restructuring of the workplace and of the family is inevitable, and it is not a
process to be left in the hands of either women or men alone. It will take
ferocious creativity to do the restructuring so as to arrive at a society
where both female–male equality and important communal values are
protected, where the economic structure is designed with consideration
for the needs of female *and* male employees and their families. Nothing
is more certain than that such a goal will never be reached if women are
the only ones who change.

References

Abramson, Lyn Y., Seligman, Martin E. P., & Teasdale, John D. (1978). Learned helplessness in humans: Critique and reformulation. *Journal of Abnormal Psychology*, *87*, 49–74.

Adams, K. A., & Landers, A. D. (1978). Sex differences in dominance behavior. *Sex Roles*, *4* (2), 215–223.

Alic, Margaret (1986). *Hypatia's heritage: A history of women in science from antiquity through the nineteenth century*. Boston: Beacon Press.

Allen, Paula Gunn (1986). *The sacred hoop: Recovering the feminine in American Indian traditions*. Boston: Beacon Press.

Allport, Gordon W. (1954). *The nature of prejudice*. Reading, Mass.: Addison-Wesley.

Archer, John (1971). Sex differences in emotional behaviour: A reply to Gray and Buffery. *Acta Psychologica*, *35*, 415–429.

Aries, Elizabeth J. (1976). Interaction patterns and themes of male, female, and mixed groups. *Small Group Behavior*, *7* (1), 7–18.

Aries, Elizabeth J. (1982). Verbal and nonverbal behavior in single-sex and mixed-sex groups: Are traditional sex roles changing? *Psychological Reports*, *51*, 127–134.

Aries, Elizabeth J., Gold, Conrad, & Weigel, Russell H. (1983). Dispositional and situational influences on dominance behavior in small groups. *Journal of Personality and Social Psychology*, *44* (4), 779–786.

Atwood, Margaret (1986). *The handmaid's tale*. Boston: Houghton Mifflin.

Bahr, Stephen J. (1974). Effects on power and division of labor in the family. In L. W. Hoffman & F. I. Nye (Eds.), *Working mothers* (pp. 167–185). San Francisco: Jossey-Bass.

Bart, Pauline (1980, March). How to say no to Storaska and survive. Paper presented at the National Conference on Feminist Psychology, Santa Monica.

Barusch, Amanda Smith (1988). Power dynamics in the aging family: A preliminary statement. *Journal of Gerontological Social Work, 11* (3/4), 43–55.

Becker, Joseph R. (1981). Differential treatment of females and males in mathematics classes. *Journal for Research in Mathematics Education, 12,* 40–53.

Belenky, Mary F., Clinchy, Blythe M., Goldberger, Nancy R., & Tarule, Jill M. (1986). *Women's ways of knowing.* New York: Basic Books.

Belk, Sharyn S., Snell, William E., Garcia-Falconi, Renan, Hernandez-Sanchez, Julita E., Hargrove, Linda, & Holtzman, Wayne H. (1988). Power strategy use in the intimate relationships of women and men from Mexico and the United States. *Personality and Social Psychology Bulletin, 14* (3), 439–447.

Bem, Sandra L. (1974). The measurement of psychological androgyny. *Journal of Consulting and Clinical Psychology, 42,* 155–162.

Berardo, Donna H., Shehan, C. L., & Leslie, Gerald R. (1987). A residue of tradition: Jobs, careers, and spouses' time in housework. *Journal of Marriage and the Family, 49,* 381–390.

Berger, Joseph, Rosenholtz, Susan J., & Zelditch, Morris, Jr. (1980). Status organizing processes. *Annual Review of Sociology, 6,* 479–508.

Berger, Joseph, Wagner, David G., & Zelditch, Morris, Jr. (1985). Introduction: Expectation states theory: Review and assessment. In Joseph Berger & Morris Zelditch, Jr. (Eds.), *Status, rewards, and influence: How expectations organize behavior* (pp. 1–72). San Francisco: Jossey-Bass.

Bernard, Jessie (1972). *The future of marriage.* New York: World.

Bernard, Jessie (1981). The good provider role: Its rise and fall. *American Psychologist, 36* (1), 1–12.

Blau, Francine D., & Ferber, M. A. (1985) Women in the labor market: The last twenty years. In L. Larwood, A. H. Stromberg, & B. A. Gutek (Eds.), *Women and work. Vol I: An annual review* (pp. 19–49). Beverly Hills, CA: Sage.

Blau, Francine D., & Winkler, Anne E. (1989). Women in the labor force: An overview. In Jo Freeman (Ed.), *Women: A feminist perspective* (Fourth Edition), pp. 265–286.

Block, Jeanne H. (1984). *Sex role identity and ego development.* San Francisco: Jossey-Bass.

Blood, Robert O., Jr. (1963). The husband-wife relationship. In F. I. Nye & L. W. Hoffman (Eds.), *The employed mother in America* (pp. 282–305). Chicago: Rand McNally.

Blood, Robert O., Jr., & Wolfe, D. M. (1960). *Husbands and wives.* New York: Free Press.

Blumberg, R. (1984). A general theory of gender stratification. In R. Collins (Ed.), *Sociological theory 1984* (pp. 23–101). San Francisco: Jossey-Bass.

Blumstein, Phillip, & Schwartz, Pepper (1983). *American couples.* New York: Morrow.

Bond, John R., & Vinacke, William E. (1961). Coalitions in mixed-sex triads. *Sociometry, 24,* 61–75.

Booth, Rachel Z., Vinograd-Bausell, Carole R., & Harper, Doreen C. (1984). Social power and gender among college students. *Psychological Reports, 55* (1), 243–246.

Bowman, G. E., Wortney, B. N., & Greyser, S. H. (1965). Are women executives people? *Harvard Business Review, 43* (4), 164–178.

Brehm, Jack W. (1966). *A theory of psychological reactance.* New York: Academic Press.

Brewer, Marilyn B. (1979). In-group bias in the minimal intergroup situation: A cognitive-motivational analysis. *Psychological Bulletin, 86,* 307–324.

Briere, John, & Malamuth, Neal (1983). Self-reported likelihood of sexually aggressive behavior: Attitudinal versus sexual explanations. *Journal of Research in Personality, 17,* 315–323.

Brodie, M. Janine, & Vickers, Jill McCalla (1982). *Canadian women in politics: An overview.* Ottawa, Ontario: Canadian Research Institute for the Advancement of Women.

Bronstein, Phyllis (1984). Differences in mothers' and fathers' behaviors toward children: A cross-cultural comparison. *Developmental Psychology, 20* (6), 995–1003.

Brophy, J. (1985). Interactions of male and female students with male and female teachers. In L. C. Wilkinson & C. B. Marrett (Eds.), *Gender influences in classroom interaction* (pp. 115–142). Orlando, FL: Academic Press.

Broverman, Inge K., Vogel, Susan R., Broverman, Donald M., Clarkson, Frank E., & Rosenkrantz, Paul S. (1972). Sex-role stereotypes: A current appraisal. *Journal of Social Issues, 28,* 59–78.

Brown, Roger (1986). *Social psychology: The second edition.* New York: The Free Press.

Brownmiller, Susan (1975). *Against our will.* New York: Bantam Books.

Campbell, Joseph (1959). *The masks of God: Primitive mythology.* New York: Viking.

Campbell, Joseph (with Bill Moyers) 1988. *The power of myth.* New York: Doubleday.

Cann, Carleton (1979, March). Sex role and social identity: Achievement and power. Paper presented at the National Conference on Feminist Psychology, Dallas.

Carbonell, Joyce L. (1984). Sex roles and leadership revisited. *Journal of Applied Psychology, 53,* 377–382.

Carles, Elena M., & Carver, Charles S. (1979). Effects of person salience versus role salience on reward allocations in a dyad. *Journal of Personality and Social Psychology, 37,* 433–446.

Cartwright, Dorwin W., & Zander, Alvin (Eds.). (1968). *Group dynamics: Research and theory* (3rd edition). New York: Harper & Row.

Centers, R., Raven, B. H., & Rodrigues, A. (1971). Conjugal power structure: A re-examination. *American Sociological Review, 36,* 264–278.

Chira, Susan (1988). Working women find slow progress in Japan. *The New York Times,* December 4, p. Y13.

Chodorow, Nancy (1978). *The reproduction of mothering: Psychoanalysis and the sociology of gender.* Berkeley, CA: University of California Press.

Christie, Agatha (1977). *Agatha Christie: An autobiography.* London: William Collins.

Christy, Carol A. (1987). *Sex differences in political participation: Processes of change in fourteen nations.* New York: Praeger.

Cixous, Helene & Clement, Catherine (1975). *The newly born woman.* Translated by Betsy Wing. Minneapolis: University of Minnesota Press.

Clark, Lorenne, & Lewis, Debra (1977). *Rape: The price of coercive sexuality.* Toronto: The Women's Press.

Coltrane, Scott (1988). Father-child relationships and the status of women: A cross-cultural study. *American Journal of Sociology, 93* (5), 1060–1095.

Colwill, Nina L., & Josephson, Wendy L. (1983). Attitudes toward equal opportunity in employment: The case of one Canadian government department. *Business Quarterly, 48* (1), 87–93.

Colwill, Nina L., & Lips, Hilary M. (1988). Corporate love: The pitfalls of workplace romance. *Business Quarterly, 53* (1), 89–91.

Comas-Diaz, Lillian (1988). Mainland Puerto Rican women: A sociocultural approach. *Journal of Community Psychology, 16*, 21–31.

Cooney, Rosemary S., Rogler, Lloyd H., Hurrell, Rosemaire, & Ortiz, Vilma (1982). Decision making in intergenerational Puerto Rican families. *Journal of Marriage and the Family*, August, 621–631.

Coontz, Stephanie, & Henderson, Peta (1986). *Women's work, men's property.* London: Verso.

Cowan, Gloria, Lee, Carole, Levy, Daniella, & Snyder, Debra (1988). Dominance and inequality in X-rated videocassettes. *Psychology of Women Quarterly, 12* (3), 299–312.

Cronin, Constance (1977). Illusion and reality in Sicily. In A. Schlegel (Ed.), *Sexual stratification: A cross-cultural view* (pp. 67–93). New York: Columbia University Press.

Crosby, Faye J. (1982). *Relative deprivation and working women.* New York: Oxford University Press.

Crosby, Faye J. (1984). The denial of personal discrimination. *American Behavioral Scientist, 27* (3), 371–386.

Daly, Mary (1973). *Beyond God the father: Toward a philosophy of women's liberation.* Boston: Beacon Press.

Daly, Mary (1978). *Gyn/Ecology: The metaethics of radical feminism.* Boston: Beacon Press.

Davis, Elizabeth Gould (1971). *The first sex.* New York: Putnam.

Deaux, Kay, & Emswiller, T. (1974). Explanations of successful performance: What is skill for the male is luck for the female. *Journal of Personality and Social Psychology, 29*, 80–85.

Deaux, Kay, & Lewis, Laurie (1984). Structure of gender stereotypes: Interrelationships among components and gender label. *Journal of Personality and Social Psychology, 46* (5), 991–1004.

de Beauvoir, Simone (1952). *The Second Sex.* New York: Alfred E. Knopf.

DeJarnett, Sandra, & Raven, Bertram H. (1981). The balance, bases, and modes of interpersonal power in Black couples: The role of sex and socioeconomic circumstances. *The Journal of Black Psychology, 7* (2), 51–66.

Demare, Dano (1985). *The effects of erotic and sexually violent mass media on attitudes toward women and rape.* Unpublished Honours thesis, University of Winnipeg, Winnipeg, Manitoba.

Demare, Dano, Briere, John, & Lips, Hilary M. (1988). Violent pornography and self-reported likelihood of sexual aggression. *Journal of Research in Personality, 22,* 140–153.

Denmark, Florence L. (1977). Styles of leadership. *Psychology of Women Quarterly, 2* (2), 99–113.

Denzin, Norman K. (1984). Toward a phenomenology of domestic family violence. *American Journal of Sociology, 90* (3), 483–513.

Derrida, Jacques (1978). *Writing and difference.* Chicago: University of Chicago Press.

Dexter, C. R. (1985). Women and the exercise of power in organizations: From ascribed to achieved status. In L. Larwood, A. H. Stromberg, & B. A. Gutek (Eds.), *Women and work. Vol. 1: An annual review* (pp. 239–258). Beverly Hills, CA: Sage.

Diamond, John (1989, February). Episcopalians install the first woman bishop. *Arizona Daily Star,* February 12, pp. 1A, 2A.

Dinnerstein, Dorothy (1976). *The mermaid and the minotaur: Sexual arrangements and human malaise.* New York: Harper & Row.

Divale, William, & Harris, Marvin (1976). Population, warfare, and the male supremacist complex. *American Anthropologist, 78,* 521–538.

Dobash, R. E., & Dobash, R. P. (1979). *Violence against wives.* New York: Free Press.

Donnerstein, Edward, & Barrett, Gerald (1978). Effects of erotic stimuli on male aggression toward females. *Journal of Personality and Social Psychology, 36,* 180–188.

Douglas, Mary (1987). *How institutions think.* Syracuse: Syracuse University Press.

Downs, James F. (1972). *The Navaho.* New York: Holt, Rinehart & Winston.

Dweck, Carol S. (1986). Motivational processes affecting learning. *American Psychologist, 41* (10), 1040–1048.

Dweck, Carol S., Davidson, William, Nelson, Sharon, & Enna, Bradley (1978). Sex differences in learned helplessness: II. The contingencies of evaluative feedback in the classroom and III. An experimental analysis. *Developmental Psychology, 14,* 268–276.

Dworkin, Andrea (1974). *Woman Hating.* New York: Dutton.

Eakins, Barbara W., & Eakins, R. Gene (1976). *Sex differences in human communication.* Boston: Houghton Mifflin.

Edelman, Murray S., & Omark, Donald R. (1973). Dominance hierarchies in young children. *Social Science Information, 12* (1), 103–110.

Edwards, John R., & Williams, John E. (1980). Sex-trait stereotypes among young children and young adults: Canadian findings and cross-national comparisons. *Canadian Journal of Behavioural Science, 12,* 210–220.

Ehrenreich, Barbara, & English, Deirdre (1973). *Witches, midwives and nurses: A history of women healers.* Old Westbury, NY: Feminist Press.

Entwisle, Doris R., Alexander, Karl L., Pallas, Aaron M., & Cadigan, Doris (1987). The emergent academic self-image of first-graders: Its response to social structure. *Child Development, 58,* 1190–1206.

Eron, Leonard (1980). Prescription for reduction of aggression. *American Psychologist, 35,* 244–252.

Etaugh, Claire, & Brown, B. (1975). Perceiving the causes of success and failure of male and female performers. *Developmental Psychology, 11,* 103.

Falbo, Toni, & Peplau, L. Anne (1980). Power strategies in intimate relationships. *Journal of Personality and Social Psychology, 38,* 618–628.

Fedigan, Linda M. (1982). *Primate paradigms: Sex roles and social bonds.* Montreal: Eden Press.

Feldman, H. (1967). *The Ghanian family in transition.* Ithaca, NY: Winneba Training College and Cornell University.

Fish, Stanley (1980). *Is there a text in this class?: The authority of interpretive communities.* Cambridge, Mass.: Harvard University Press.

Ford, Maureen R., & Lowery, Carol R. (1986). Gender differences in moral reasoning: A comparison of justice and care orientations. *Journal of Personality and Social Psychology, 50* (4), 777–783.

Fox, G. L. (1973). Another look at the comparative resources model: Assessing the balance of power in Turkish marriages. *Journal of Marriage and the Family, 35,* 718–730.

Fox, Mary Frank, & Hesse-Biber, Sharlene (1984). *Women at work.* Mountain View, CA: Mayfield.

Frankel, Marc T., & Rollins, Howard A., Jr. (1983). Does mother know best? Mothers and fathers interacting with preschool sons and daughters. *Developmental Psychology, 19* (5), 694–702.

Freeman, Jo (1973). The tyranny of structurelessness. *Ms., 2*(1), 76–78, 86–89.

French, John R. P., Jr., & Raven, Bertram (1959). The bases of social power. In D. Cartwright (Ed.), *Studies in social power.* Ann Arbor, MI: University of Michigan.

Friedan, Betty (1963). *The Feminine Mystique.* New York: Dell.

Friedl, Ernestine (1967). The position of women: Appearance and reality. *Anthropological Quarterly, 40,* 97–108.

Frieze, Irene H. (1986, August). The female victim: Rape, wife battering, and incest. American Psychological Association Master Lecture, presented at the annual meeting of the American Psychological Association, Washington, DC.

Frieze, Irene H. (1975). Women's expectations for and causal attributions of success and failure. In M. Mednick, S. Tangri, & L. Hoffman (Eds.), *Women and Achievement.* New York: Wiley.

Frieze, Irene H. (1983). Causes and consequences of marital rape. *Signs, 8,* 532–553.

Frieze, Irene H., & Ramsey, Steve (1976). Nonverbal maintenance of traditional sex roles. *Journal of Social Issues, 32* (3), 133–142.

Gager, Nancy, & Schurr, Cathleen (1976). *Sexual assault: Confronting rape in America.* New York: Grosset & Dunlap.

Geis, Florence L., Boston, Martha B., & Hoffman, Nadine (1985). Sex of authority role models and achievement by men and women: Leadership performance and recognition. *Journal of Personality and Social Psychology, 49* (3), 636–653.

Geis, Florence L., Brown, Virginia, Jennings, Joyce, & Corrado-Taylor, Denise (1984). Sex vs. status in sex-associated stereotypes. *Sex Roles, 11* (9/10), 771–785.

Gerson, Kathleen (1986). What do women want from men? Men's influence on women's work and family choices. *American Behavioral Scientist, 29* (5), 619–634.

Gilligan, Carol (1982). *In a Different Voice: Psychological Theory and Women's Development*. Cambridge, MA: Harvard University Press.

Ginsberg, George L., Frosch, William A., & Shapiro, Theodore (1972). The new impotence. *Archives of General Psychiatry, 26* (3), 218–220.

Ginter, G., & Lindskold, S. (1975). Rate of participation and expertise as factors influencing leader choice. *Journal of Personality and Social Psychology, 32,* 1085–1089.

Githens, Marianne, & Prestage, Jewel (1977). Introduction. In M. Githens & J. Prestage (Eds.), *A portrait of marginality* (pp. 1–10). New York: Longman.

Glass, Becky L., & Stollee, Margaret K. (1987). Family law in Soviet Russia, 1917–1945. *Journal of Marriage and the Family, 49,* 893–902.

Goffman, Erving (1967). *Interaction ritual.* Garden City, NY: Doubleday.

Gold, Dolores, Crombie, Gail, & Nobel, Sally (1987). Relations between teachers' judgments of girls' and boys' compliance and intellectual competence. *Sex Roles, 16* (7/8), 351–358.

Gold, Martin (1958). Power in the classroom. *Sociometry, 21,* 50–60.

Gray, Charlotte (1985, March). R.E.A.L. Women: The traditionalists take on the feminists. *Chatelaine,* pp. 57ff.

Gray-Little, Bernadette, & Burks, Nancy (1983). Power and satisfaction in marriage: A review and critique. *Psychological Bulletin, 93,* 513–538.

Greer, Germaine (1977). Seduction is a four-letter word. In E. S. Morrison & V. Borosage (Eds.), *Human sexuality.* Mountain View, CA: Mayfield.

Gross, Alan (1978). The male role and heterosexual behavior. *Journal of Social Issues, 34* (1), 87–107.

Guimond, Serge, & Dube-Simard, Lise (1983). Relative deprivation theory and the Quebec nationalist movement: The cognitive-emotion distinction and the personal-group deprivation issue. *Journal of Personality and Social Psychology, 44* (3), 526–535.

Gutek, Barbara, & Nakamura, Charles (1983). Gender roles and sexuality in the world of work. In E. R. Allgeier & N. B. McCormick (Eds.), *Changing boundaries: Gender roles and sexual behavior.* Mountain View, CA: Mayfield.

Gysels, Monique, & Vogels, Mary (1982). Belgian husbands and wives: Equal in patrimonial matters? *International Journal of the Sociology of Law, 10,* 205–216.

Haavind, Hanne (1984). Love and power in marriage. In Harriet Holter (Ed.), *Patriarchy in a welfare society* (pp. 136–235). Oslo, Norway: Universitetsforlaget.

Hacker, Helen M. (1951). Women as a minority group. *Social Forces, 30,* 60–69.

Hall, Edward T. (1966). *The hidden dimension.* New York: Doubleday.

Hall, K. R. L., & Mayer, B. (1967). Social interactions in a group of captive patas monkeys (*Erythrocebus patas*). *Folia Primatologica, 5,* 213–236.

Halley, Lorelei (1980). Old country survivals in the new: An essay on some aspects of Yugoslav-American family structure and dynamics. *The Journal of Psychological Anthropology, 3*, 119–131.

Halpern, Sue (1989, May). AIDS: Rethinking the risk. *Ms., 17* (11), 80–87.

Hariton, Barbara E., & Singer, Jerome L. (1974). Women's fantasies during sexual intercourse: Normative and theoretical implications. *Journal of Consulting and Clinical Psychology, 43*, 313–322.

Harlan, A., & Weiss, C. L. (1982). Sex differences in factors affecting managerial career advancement. In P. A. Wallace (Ed.), *Women in the workplace* (pp. 59–96). Boston, MA: Auburn House.

Harrison, J. (1963). *Mythology*. New York: Harcourt Brace.

Heilman, Madeline E., Simon, Michael E., & Repper, David P. (1987). Intentionally favored, unintentionally harmed? Impact of sex-based preferential selection on self-perceptions and self-evaluations. *Journal of Applied Psychology, 72* (1), 62–68.

Heisenberg, Werner (1972). The representation of nature in contemporary physics. In S. Sears & G. Lord (Eds.), *The discontinuous universe*. New York: Basic Books.

Henderson, Nell, & Baker, Peter (1990). For VMI cadets, it's still 'better dead than coed'. *The Washington Post*, Friday, February 2, pp. B1, B7.

Hendrick, Susan, Hendrick, Clyde, Slapion-Foote, Michelle J., & Foote, Franklin H. (1985). Gender differences in sexual attitudes. *Journal of Personality and Social Psychology, 48* (6), 1630–1642.

Henley, Nancy M. (1973). Status and sex: Some touching observations. *Bulletin of the Psychonomic Society, 2*, 91–93.

Henley, Nancy M. (1977). *Body politics: Power, sex, and nonverbal communication*. Englewood Cliffs, NJ: Prentice-Hall.

Henriques, Julian, Holloway, Wendy, Unwin, Cathy, Venn, Couze, & Walkerdine, Valerie (1984). *Changing the subject: Psychology, social relations and subjectivity*. London: Methuen.

Herek, Gregory M. (1988). Heterosexuals' attitudes toward lesbians and gay men: Correlates and gender differences. *Journal of Sex Research, 25* (4), 451–477.

Herman, Dianne (1979). The rape culture. In Jo Freeman (Ed.), *Women: A feminist perspective* (Second Edition), (pp. 41–63). Palo Alto, CA: Mayfield.

Herman, Judith L. (1981). *Father-daughter incest*. Cambridge, MA: Harvard University Press.

Heslin, Richard, & Boss, Diane (1980). Nonverbal intimacy in airport arrival and departure. *Personality and Social Psychology Bulletin, 6*, 248–252.

Hill, M. S. (1980). Authority at work: How men and women differ. In G. J. Duncan & J. N. Morgan (Eds.), *Five thousand American families: Patterns of economic progress* (Vol 7, pp. 107–146). Ann Arbor: University of Michigan, Survey Research Center, Institute for Social Research.

Hite, Shere (1976). *The Hite report*. New York: Dell.

Hollos, Marida, & Leis, Philip E. (1985). "The hand that rocks the cradle rules the world": Family interaction and decision making in a Portuguese rural community. *Ethos, 13* (4), 340–357.

Homans, George C. (1974). *Social behavior: The elementary forms.* New York: Harcourt Brace Jovanovich.

Hornaday, Ann (1988, November). Who makes what—the inside scoop on the wages of some. *Ms., 17* (5), 60–62.

Howard, Judith A., Blumstein, Phillip, & Schwartz, Pepper (1986). Sex, power, and influence tactics in intimate relationships. *Journal of Personality and Social Psychology, 51* (1), 102–109.

Hoyenga, Katharine B., & Hoyenga, Kermit T. (1979). *The question of sex differences.* Boston: Little, Brown.

Hrdy, Sarah B. (1981). *The woman that never evolved.* Cambridge, MA: Harvard University Press.

Hughes, Everett C. (1945). Dilemmas and contradictions of status. *American Journal of Sociology, 50,* 353–354.

Irigaray, Luce (1977). *Ce sexe qui n'en est pas un.* Paris: Minuit.

Irvine, Jacqueline Jordan (1985). Teacher communication patterns as related to the race and sex of the student. *Journal of Educational Research, 78* (6), 338–345.

Irvine, Jacqueline Jordan (1986). Teacher-student interactions:Effects of student race, sex, and grade level. *Journal of Educational Psychology, 78* (1), 14–21.

Jacklin, Carol Nagy, & Maccoby, Eleanor Emmons (1978). Social behavior at thirty-three months in same-sex and mixed-sex dyads. *Child Development, 49,* 557–569.

Janeway, Elizabeth (1981). *Powers of the weak.* New York: Morrow Quill Paperbacks.

Johnson, Paula (1974, May). Social power and sex role stereotypes. Paper presented at the meeting of the Western Psychological Association, San Francisco.

Johnson, Paula (1976). Women and power: Toward a theory of effectiveness. *Journal of Social Issues, 32* (3), 99–110.

Jones, Diane C. (1983). Power structures and perceptions of power holders in same-sex groups of young children. *Women and Politics, 3,* 147–164.

Jones, Diane C. (1984). Dominance and affiliation as factors in the social organization of same-sex groups of elementary school children. *Ethology and Sociobiology, 5* (3), 193–202.

Judge says lawyer used female wiles (1988). *Arizona Daily Star,* December 11, p. 16A.

Kahn, Arnold S., & Gaeddert, William P. (1985). From theories of equity to theories of justice: The liberating consequences of studying women. In Virginia E. O'Leary, Rhoda Kesler Unger, & Barbara Strudler Wallston (Eds.), *Women, gender, and social psychology.* Hillsdale, NJ: Lawrence Erlbaum Associates (pp. 129–148).

Kanter, Rosabeth Moss (1977). *Men and women of the corporation.* New York: Basic Books.

Kanter, Rosabeth Moss (1983). Women managers: Moving up in a high tech society. In J. Farley (Ed.), *The woman in management: Career and family issues* (pp. 21–37). Ithaca, NY: ILR Press.

Kay, Barry J. (n.d.). *Gender and political activity in Canada: Evidence from the 1984 national election study.* Working paper # 8692, Department of Political Science, Wilfrid Laurier University, Waterloo, Ontario, Canada N2L 3C5.

Kennedy, Carol W., & Camden, Carl (1983). Interruptions and nonverbal gender differences. *Journal of Nonverbal Behavior, 8* (2), 91–108.

Kimball, Meredith M. (1989). A new perspective on women's math achievement. *Psychological Bulletin, 105* (2), 198–214.

Kipnis, David (1972). Does power corrupt? *Journal of Personality and Social Psychology, 24,* 33–41.

Kipnis, David, Castell, Patricia J., Gergen, Mary, & Mauch, Donna (1976). Metamorphic effects of power. *Journal of Applied Psychology, 61,* 127–135.

Kleiman, Carol (1989). A penny a year for female workers. *The Washington Post,* October 1, p. H3.

Klein, Ethel (1984). *Gender politics.* Cambridge, MA: Harvard University Press.

Kohlberg, Lawrence (1984). *The psychology of moral development.* San Francisco: Harper & Row.

Komarovsky, Mira (1935). *The unemployed man and his family.* New York: Dryden.

Komarovsky, Mira (1976). *Dilemmas of masculinity: A study of college youth.* New York: Norton.

Komorita, Samuel S., & Moore, Danny (1976). Theories and processes of coalition formation. *Journal of Personality and Social Psychology, 33,* 371–381.

Koss, Mary P., Gidycz, C. A., & Wisniewski, N. (1987). The scope of rape: Incidence and prevalence of sexual aggression and victimization in a national sample of higher education students. *Journal of Consulting and Clinical Psychology, 55,* 162–170.

Koss, Mary P. (1989, January). Is there a rape epidemic? Paper presented at the annual national meeting of the American Association for the Advancement of Science, San Francisco.

Lacey, H. M. (1979). Control, perceived, control, and the methodological role of cognitive constructs. In L. C. Perlmuter & R. A. Monty (Eds.), *Choice and perceived control.* Hillsdale, NJ: Lawrence Erlbaum.

Lancaster, Jane B. (1976). Sex roles in primate societies. In M. S. Teitelbaum (Ed.), *Sex differences: Social and biological perspectives* (pp. 22–61). New York: Anchor Press.

Lancaster, Jane B. (1984). Introduction. In Meredith F. Small (Ed.), *Female primates: Studies by Women Primatologists* (pp. 1–10). New York: Alan R. Liss, Inc.

Lance, Kathryn (1978). *Getting strong: A woman's guide to realizing her physical potential.* Indianapolis, IN: Bobbs-Merrill.

Leacock, Eleanor (1986). Women, power and authority. In L. Dube, E. Leacock, & S. Ardener (Eds.), *Visibility and power* (pp. 107–135). Delhi: Oxford University Press.

Lee, Marcia Manning (1977). Toward understanding why few women hold political office. In Marianne Githens & Jewel Prestage (Eds.), *A portrait of marginality* (pp. 118–138). New York: Longman.

Lerner, Melvin J. (1970). The desire for justice and reactions to victims. In J. Macaulay & L. Berkowitz (Eds.), *Altruism and helping behavior*. New York: Academic Press.

Lerner, Melvin J. (1974). Social psychology of justice and interpersonal attraction. In T. Huston (Ed.), *Foundations of interpersonal attraction*. New York: Academic Press.

Levin, R. J., & Levin, A. (1975, October). The *Redbook* report on premarital and extramarital sex. *Redbook*, p. 38.

Linz, Daniel, Donnerstein, Edward, & Penrod, Steven (1984). The effects of multiple exposures to filmed violence against women. *Journal of Communication, 34*, 130–147.

Lipman-Blumen, Jean (1984). *Gender roles and power*. Englewood Cliffs, NJ: Prentice-Hall.

Lips, Hilary M. (1981). *Women, men, and the psychology of power*. Englewood Cliffs, NJ: Prentice-Hall.

Lips, Hilary M. (1985). Gender and the sense of power: Where are we and where are we going? *International Journal of Women's Studies, 8* (5), 483–489.

Lips, Hilary M., & Frantzve, Jerri (1990, June). Computers in the workplace: Power and dependence issues for women and men. Paper presented at the annual convention of the Canadian Psychological Association, Ottawa.

Lockheed, Marlaine E. (1985). Sex and social influence: A meta-analysis guided by theory. In Joseph Berger & Morris Zelditch, Jr. (Eds.), *Status, rewards, and influence: How expectations organize behavior* (pp. 406–429). San Francisco: Jossey-Bass.

Lockheed, Marlaine E. & Hall, Katherine P. (1976). Conceptualizing sex as a status characteristic: Applications to leadership training strategies. *Journal of Social Issues, 32* (3), 111–124.

Lockwood, Daniel (1980) *Prison sexual violence*. New York: Elsevier.

London, Ira (1974). Frigidity, sensitivity and sexual roles. In Joseph Pleck & Jack Sawyer (Eds.), *Men and masculinity*. Englewood Cliffs, NJ: Prentice-Hall.

Lord, R. G., Foti, R. J., & Phillips, J. S. (1982). A theory of leadership categorization. In J. G. Hunt, U. Sekaram, & C. A. Schriesheim (eds.), *Leadership: Beyond establishment views*. Carbondale: Southern Illinois University Press.

Maccoby, Eleanor E. (1990). Gender and relationships: A developmental account. *American Psychologist, 45* (4), 513–520.

Maccoby, Eleanor E., & Jacklin, Carol N. (1974). *The psychology of sex differences*. Stanford, CA: Stanford University Press.

MacCormack, C. P. (1977). Biological events and cultural control. *Signs, 3* (1), 93–100.

MacKinnon, Catherine (1987). *Feminism unmodified: Discourses on life and law*. Cambridge, Mass.: Harvard University Press.

Mahony, Pat (1983). How Alice's chin really came to be pressed against her foot: Sexist processes of interaction in mixed-sex classrooms. *Women's Studies International Forum, 6* (1), 107–115.

Major, Brenda, & Heslin, Richard (1982). Perceptions of cross-sex and same-sex nonreciprocal touch: It is better to give than to receive. *Journal of Nonverbal Behavior, 6* (3), 148–162.

Malamuth, Neal M. (1981a). Rape fantasies as a function of exposure to violent sexual stimuli. *Archives of Sexual Behavior, 10,* 33–47.

Malamuth, Neal M. (1981b). Rape proclivity among males. *Journal of Social Issues, 37* (4), 138–157.

Malamuth, Neal M. (1984). Aggression against women: Cultural and individual causes. In N.M. Malamuth & E. Donnerstein (Eds.), *Pornography and sexual aggression.* New York: Academic Press.

Malamuth, Neal M., & Check, James V. P. (1981, September). *The effects of exposure to aggressive pornography: Rape proclivity, sexual arousal and beliefs in rape myths.* Paper presented at the Annual Meeting of the American Psychological Association, Los Angeles.

Malamuth, Neal M., Haber, Scott, & Feshbach, Seymour (1980). Testing hypotheses regarding rape: Exposure and sexual violence, sex differences and the "normality" of rapists. *Journal of Research in Personality, 14* (1), 121–137.

Malamuth, Neal M., & Spinner, Barry (1980). A longitudinal content analysis of sexual violence in the best-selling erotic magazines. *Journal of Sex Research, 16* (3), 226–237.

Marks, John B. (1957). Interests and leadership among adolescents. *Journal of Genetic Psychology, 91,* 163–172,

Marshall, Jon C., & Bannon, Susan (1988). Race and sex equity in computer advertising. *Journal of Research on Computing in Education, 21* (1), 15–27.

Maslow, Abraham H. (1971). *The farther reaches of human nature.* Harmondsworth, England: Penguin Books.

Mason, A., & Blankenship, V. (1987). Power and affiliation motivation, stress, and abuse in intimate relationships. *Journal of Personality and Social Psychology, 52,* 203–210.

McCance, Dawne (1987). Ethics in postmodern perspective. *Studies in Religion/ Sciences Religieuses, 16* (4), 421–430.

McClelland, David C. (1975). *Power: The inner experience.* New York: Irvington.

McClelland, David C., Davis, William N., Kalin, Rudolf, & Wanner, Eric (1972). *The drinking man.* New York: Free Press.

McCloskey, Laura (1989) Personal communication.

McClung, Nellie (1915). *In times like these.* New York: D. Appleton & Company.

McDermott, Robert J., Hawkins, Michele J., Moore, John R., & Cittadino, Susan K. (1987). AIDS awareness and information sources among selected university students. *Journal of American College Health, 35* (5), 222–228.

McHugh, Marilyn, Duquin, M. E., & Frieze, Irene H. (1977). Beliefs about success and failure: Attribution and the female athlete. In C. A. Oglesby (Ed.), *Women and sport: From myth to reality.* Philadelphia: Lea & Febiger.

Meeker, B. F., & Weitzel-O'Neill, P. A. (1977). Sex roles and interpersonal behavior in task-oriented groups. *American Sociological Review, 42,* 91–105.

Meese, Elizabeth (1986). *Crossing the double-cross: The practice of feminist criticism.* Chapel Hill, NC: University of North Carolina Press.

Megargee, Edwin (1969). Influence of sex roles on the manifestation of leadership. *Journal of Applied Psychology, 52,* 377–382.

Mehrabian, Albert (1972). *Nonverbal communication.* Chicago: Aldine-Atherton.

Midelfort, H. C. Erik (1972). *Witch hunting in southwestern Germany 1562–1684, the social and intellectual foundations.* Stanford, CA: Stanford University Press.

Mikalachki, D. M. , & Mikalachki, A. (1985). Women in business—Going for broke. *Business Quarterly, 50* (2), 25–32.

Miller, Jean Baker (1977). *Toward a new psychology of women.* Boston: Beacon Press.

Minton, Henry L. (1967). Power as a personality construct. In B. A. Maher (Ed.), *Progress in experimental personality research* (Vol. 4). New York: Academic Press.

Moglen, Helen (1983). Power and empowerment. *Women's Studies International Forum, 6* (2), 131–134.

Monagle, Katie (1989, May). Nice girls do. *Ms., 17* (11), 50, 52.

Moore, Molly (1989a). Women in the military: Combat ban undercuts significant advances. *The Washington Post,* September 24, pp. A1, A16–A17.

Moore, Molly (1989b). Sexual harassment. Attitudes of male-oriented culture persist despite high-level efforts. *The Washington Post,* September 25, p. A9.

Moore, Molly (1989c). Women in the military: Canadians face physical—not legal—barriers. *The Washington Post,* September 26, p. A1, A18–A19.

Morin, Stephen F., & Garfinkle, Ellen M. (1978). Male homophobia. *Journal of Social Issues, 34* (1), 29–47.

Morris, N. M., & Sison, B. S. (1974). Correlates of female powerlessness: Parity methods of birth control, pregnancy. *Journal of Marriage and the Family, 36,* 708–712.

Murray, Henry A. (1937). Techniques for a systematic investigation of fantasy. *Journal of Psychology, 3,* 115–143.

Navy women find obstacles on way to top (1988). *Tucson Citizen,* November 28, p. 14A.

Nieva, Veronica F., & Gutek, Barbara A. (1981). *Women and work: A psychological perspective.* New York: Praeger.

Nolen-Hoeksma, Susan (1987). Sex differences in unipolar depression: Evidence and theory. *Psychological Bulletin, 101* (2), 259–282.

Nyquist, Linda, & Spence, Janet (1986). Effects of dispositional dominance and sex role expectations on leadership behaviors. *Journal of Personality and Social Psychology, 50* (1), 377–382.

O'Kelly, Charlotte G., & Carney, Larry S. (1986). *Women and men in society: Cross-cultural perspectives on gender stratification.* Belmont, CA: Wadsworth.

Omark, Donald R., & Edelman, Murray S. (1975). A comparison of status hierarchies in young children: An ethological approach. *Social Science Information, 14* (5), 87–107.

Osgood, Charles E., Suci, George J., & Tannenbaum, Percy H. (1957). *The measurement of meaning.* Urbana, Ill.: University of Illinois Press.

Pagelow, M. D. (1984). *Family violence.* New York: Praeger.

Paikoff, Roberta L., & Savin-Williams, Ritch C. (1983). An exploratory study of dominance interactions among adolescent females at a summer camp. *Journal of Youth and Adolescence, 12,* 419–433.

Palmer, Phyllis (1989). Housework is real work: How feminist theory has de- and re-constructed the meaning of work. Lecture presented to the Southwest Institute for Research on Women, University of Arizona, February 17.

Parker, Ian (1989). Discourse and power. In John Shotter & Kenneth Gergen (Eds.), *Texts of identity* (pp. 56–69). London: Sage Publications.

Parlee, Mary Brown (1979). Conversational politics. *Psychology Today, 12* (12), 48–49, 51–52, 55–56.

Parsons, T., & Bales, R. F. (1955). *Family, socialization, and interaction process.* Glencoe, IL: Free Press.

Partnow, Elaine (1977). *The quotable woman* (Vol. I). Los Angeles: Pinnacle Books.

Person, Ethel M. (1986). Male sexuality and power. *Psychoanalytic Inquiry, 6* (1), 3–25.

Peters, Tom (1989). Firms may be dancing last macho tango. *The Arizona Daily Star,* April 4, p. 1C.

Piercy, Marge (1976). *Woman at the edge of time.* New York: Fawcett Crest.

Porter, N., & Geis, Florence (1981). Women and nonverbal leadership cues: When seeing is not believing. In Clara Mayo & Nancy Henley (Eds.), *Gender and nonverbal behavior* (pp. 39–59). New York: Springer-Verlag.

Portrait of the electorate (1988). *The New York Times,* November 10, p. A16.

Powell, B., & Jacobs, J. A. (1983). Sex and consensus in occupational prestige ratings. *Sociology and Social Research, 67,* 393–404.

Priest, R. F., & Wilhelm, P. G. (1974). Sex, marital status and self-actualization as factors in the appreciation of sexist jokes. *The Journal of Social Psychology, 92,* 245–249.

Propositions (Nov. 9, 1988). *The Tucson Citizen,* p. 8A.

Puner, M. (1974). Will you still love me? *Human Behavior, 3* (6), 42–48.

Putnam, L., & Heinen, J. S. (1976, Summer). Women in management: The fallacy of the trait approach. *MSU Business Topics,* pp. 47–53.

Rabin, Joan S. (1986). Adaptation across the life span: Evolution, future shock, and sex roles. In J. D. Sinnott, *Sex roles and aging: Theory and research from a systems perspective* (pp. 25–34). Basel: Karger.

Ragins, Belle Rose, & Sundstrom, Eric (1989). Gender and power in organizations: A longitudinal perspective. *Psychological Bulletin, 105* (1), 51–88.

Random House Dictionary (1980). New York: Random House.

Raven, Bertram H. (1965). Social influence and power. In I. D. Steiner & M. Fishbein (Eds.), *Current studies in social psychology.* New York: Holt, Rinehart & Winston.

Raven, Bertram H., Centers, R., & Rodrigues, A. (1975). The bases of conjugal power. In R. E. Cromwell & D. H. Olson (Eds.), *Power in families* (pp. 217–232). New York: Wiley.

Raymond, Janice (1978). Women's history and transcendence. In F. H. Littell (Ed.), *Religious liberty in the crossfire of creeds.* Philadelphia: Ecumenical Press.

Rich, Adrienne (1976). *Of woman born.* New York: Norton.

Rodin, Judith, & Janis, Irving (1979). The social power of health-care practicioners as agents of change. *Journal of Social Issues, 35* (1), 60–81.

Rodman, H. (1972). Marital power and the theory of resources in cultural context. *Journal of Comparative Family Studies, 3,* 50–69.

Rogers, Susan (1975). Female forms of power and the myth of male dominance: A model of female/male interaction in peasant society. *American Ethnologist, 2,* 759–792.

Romero, Gloria J., Castro, Felipe G., & Cervantes, Richard C. (1988). Latinas without work. Family, occupational, and economic stress following unemployment. *Psychology of Women Quarterly, 12* (3), 281–297.

Rosaldo, Michelle Z. (1974). Woman, culture and society: A theoretical overview. In Michelle Z. Rosaldo & Louise Lamphere (Eds.), *Woman, culture and society.* Stanford, CA: Stanford University Press, pp. 1–16.

Rosen, B., & Jerdee, T. H. (1978). Perceived sex differences in managerially relevant characteristics. *Sex Roles, 4,* 837–843.

Ross, Mark (1986). Female political participation. *American Anthropologist, 88,* 843–858.

Rothbart, Mary K., Hanley, Dean, & Albert, Marc. (1986) Gender differences in moral reasoning. *Sex Roles, 15* (11/12), 645–653.

Rubenstein, Carin (1983). The modern art of courtly love. *Psychology Today, 17* (2), pp. 40–41, 44–49.

Ruether, Rosemary R. (1975). *New woman, new earth: Sexist ideologies and human liberation.* New York: Seabury Press.

Ruether, Rosemary R. (1983). *Sexism and god-talk: Toward a feminist theology.* Boston: Beacon Press.

Russell, Diana E. H. (1975). *The politics of rape: The victim's perspective.* New York: Stein & Day.

Russell, Diana E. H. (1982). *Rape in marriage.* New York: Macmillan.

Russell, Diana E. H. (1984). *Sexual exploitation: Rape, child sexual abuse and workplace harassment.* Beverly Hills, CA: Sage.

Sacks, Harvey (1972). On the analyzability of stories by children. In J. Gumperz & D. Hymes (Eds.), *Directions in sociolinguistics.* New York: Holt, Rinehart & Winston.

Sadker, Myra, & Sadker, David (1985, March). Sexism in the schoolroom of the '80s. *Psychology Today, 17,* 640–646.

Safilios-Rothschild, Constantina (1969). Patterns of familial power and influence. *Sociological Focus, 2,* 7–19.

Safilios-Rothschild, Constantina (1976). A macro- and micro-examination of family power and love: An exchange model. *Journal of Marriage and the Family, 38,* 355–362.

Saldeen, Ake (1987/88). Sweden: Reforms of marriage, inheritance and cohabitation proposed. *Journal of Family Law, 26,* 197–205.

Sallot, Jeff (1989). Sexual equality remains elusive despite standards of Soviet history. *The Globe and Mail,* March 8, pp. A1, A9.

Sampson, Edward E. (1975). On justice as equality. *Journal of Social Issues, 31* (3), 45–64.

Sanday, Peggy R. (1981). *Female power and male dominance: On the origins of sexual inequality.* Cambridge: Cambridge University Press.

Schjelderup-Ebbe, T. (1922). Beitrage zur sozialpsychologie das haushuhns. *Z. Psychol., 88*, 225–252.

Schlozman, K. L. (1979). Women and unemployment: Assessing the biggest myths. In J. Freeman (Ed.), *Women: A feminist perspective* (2nd ed.). Mountain View, CA: Mayfield.

Schoenberger, Karl (1989). Korea's 'Henyo' divers: Master of the sea—but second class on land. *Los Angeles Times,* May 18, pp. 1, 12–13.

Schwartz, Felice N. (1989). Management women and the new facts of life. *Harvard Business Review, 89* (1), 65–76.

Seligman, Martin E. P. (1975). *Helplessness: On depression, development, and death.* San Francisco: Freeman.

Serbin, Lisa A., & O'Leary, K. Daniel (1975, December). How nursery schools teach girls to shut up. *Psychology Today, 9* (7), 56–58, 102–103.

Serbin, Lisa A., Sprafkin, Carol, Elman, Meryl, & Doyle, Anna-Beth (1982). The early development of sex-differentiated patterns of social influence. *Canadian Journal of Behavioural Science, 14* (4), 350–363.

Sherif, Carolyn Wood (1982). Needed concepts in the study of gender identity. *Psychology of Women Quarterly, 6* (4), 375–395.

Sherif, Muzafir, & Sherif, Carolyn Wood (1956). *Groups in harmony and tension.* New York: Harper.

Showalter, Elaine (1982). Feminist criticism in the wilderness. In Elizabeth Abel (Ed.), *Writing and sexual difference.* Chicago: University of Chicago Press.

Sigelman, Carol K., Thomas, Dan B., Sigelman, Lee, & Ribich, Frederick D. (1986). Gender, physical attractiveness, and electability: An experimental investigation of voter bias. *Journal of Applied Social Psychology, 16* (3), 229–248.

Silveira, J. (1972). Thoughts on the politics of touch. *Woman's Press, 1* (13).

Silverman. Wendy K. (1984). Self-, peer, and teacher judgments of dominance in eight- and 23-year-old children. *Journal of Genetic Psychology, 144* (2), 291–292.

Simic, Andrei (1983). Machismo and cryptomatriarchy: Power, affect, and authority in the contemporary Yugoslav family. *Ethos, 11* (1/2), 66–86.

Sinclair, Donna (1984, August). Promise of female power. *United Church Observer.*

Singer, M. (1976). Sexism and male sexuality. *Issues in Radical Therapy, 3*, 11–13.

Snodgrass, Sara E., & Rosenthal, Robert (1984). Effects of sex of subordinate and romantic attachment status upon self-ratings of dominance. *Journal of Personality and Social Psychology, 52* (4), 355–371.

Snyder, T. D. (1987). *Digest of education statistics 1987.* Center of Education Statistics. Washington DC: U.S. Government Printing Office.

Starhawk (1982). *Dreaming the dark: Magic, sex and politics.* Boston: Beacon Press.

Stein, R. T., & Heller, T. (1979). An empirical analysis of the correlations between leadership status and participation rates reported in the literature. *Journal of Personality and Social Psychology, 37* (11), 1993–2002.

Stevens, Evelyn P. (1973). *Marianismo:* the other face of *machismo* in Latin America. In Ann Pescatello (Ed.), *Female and male in Latin America* (pp. 89–101). Pittsburgh: University of Pittsburgh Press.

Stewart, Abigail J. (1975). *Longitudinal prediction from personality to life outcomes among college-educated women.* Unpublished doctoral dissertation, Harvard University.

Stewart, Abigail J., & Rubin, Zick (1974). The power motive in the dating couple. *Journal of Personality and Social Psychology, 34,* 305–309.

Stewart, Abigail J., & Winter, David G. (1976). Arousal of the power motive in women. *Journal of Consulting and Clinical Psychology, 44* (3), 495–496.

Stockard, Jean & Johnson, Miriam (1979). The social origins of male dominance. *Sex Roles, 5* (2), 199–218.

Straus, Murray A., Gelles, Richard J., & Steinmetz, Suzanne K. (1980). *Behind closed doors: Violence in the American family.* Garden City, NY: Doubleday.

Tajfel, H. (1981). *Human groups and social categories.* Cambridge, England: Cambridge University Press.

Tajfel, H. (1982). *Social identity and intergroup relations.* Cambridge, England: Cambridge University Press.

Tangri, Sandra, Burt, Martha R., & Johnson, Lawrence B. (1982). Sexual harassment at work: Three explanatory models. *Journal of Social Issues, 38* (4), 33–54.

Thibaut, John, & Kelley, Harold H. (1959). *The social psychology of groups.* New York: Wiley.

Tiger, Lionel & Fox, Robin (1971). *The imperial animal.* New York: Holt, Rinehart & Winston.

Top banker lauds affirmative action (1988). *Arizona Daily Star,* December 11, p. 16A.

Tougas, Francine, Dube, Lise, & Veilleux, France (1987). Privation relative et programmes d'action positive. *Canadian Journal of Behavioral Science, 19* (2), 167–176.

Tougas, Francine, & Veilleux, France (1988). The influence of identification, collective relative deprivation and procedure of implementation on women's responses to affirmative action: A causal modeling approach. *Canadian Journal of Behavioral Science, 20* (1), 16–29.

Tougas, Francine, & Veilleux, France (1989). Who likes affirmative action: Attitudinal processes among men and women. In F. A. Blanchard & Faye Crosby (Eds.), *Affirmative action in perspective.* Boston: Springer-Verlag.

Touhey, John C. (1974). Effects of additional women professionals on rating of occupational prestige and desirability. *Journal of Personality and Social Psychology, 29,* 86–89.

Tsui, A. S., & Gutek, Barbara A. (1984). A role set analysis of gender differences in performance, affective relationships, and career success of industrial middle managers. *Academy of Management Journal, 27,* 619–635.

Uleman, James S. (1966). A new TAT measure of the need for power. Unpublished doctoral dissertation, Harvard University.

University loses appeal in bias case (1989). *The Washington Post,* December 9, p. A7.

U. S. Department of Commerce, Bureau of the Census (1989). *Statistical Abstract of the United States,* 109th Edition. Washington D.C.: U. S. Government Printing Office.

Veroff, Joseph (1957). Development and validation of a projective measure of power motivation. *Journal of Abnormal and Social Psychology, 54,* 1–8.

Vickers, Jill M. (1988, March). Women and power: Four questions in search of a theory. Keynote address to the Canadian Advisory Council on the Status of Women's Symposium on Women and Power, Ottawa.

Vinacke, William E. (1959). Sex roles in a three-person game. *Sociometry, 22,* 343–360.

The 1980 Virginia Slims American women's opinion poll (1980). New York: Roper Organization.

Wadsworth, Alice H. (1917). Letter to William E. Borah, December 11. William Edgar Borah papers, Manuscript Division, Library of Congress, Washington, D.C.

Walker, Lenore E. (1979). *The battered woman.* New York: Harper & Row.

Wallace, Phyllis (1980). *Black women in the labor force.* Cambridge, MA: M.I.T. Press.

Waller, Willard (1938). *The family: A dynamic interpretation.* New York: Dryden.

Walster, Elaine, Berscheid, Ellen, & Walster, George W. (1973). New directions in equity research. *Journal of Personality and Social Psychology, 25,* 151–176.

Walster, Elaine, & Walster, George W. (1975). Equity and social justice. *Journal of Social Issues, 31* (3), 21–43.

Washburn, S. L., Jay, P. C., & Lancaster, Jane B. (1965). Field studies of Old World monkeys and apes. *Science, 150,* 1541–1547.

Weiner, Bernard, Frieze, Irene H., Kukla, Andy, Reed, Linda, Rest, Stanley & Rosenbaum, Robert M. (1971). *Perceiving the causes of success and failure.* New York: General Learning Press.

Weissman, Myrna, & Klerman, Gerald (1977). Sex differences and the epidemiology of depression. *Archives of General Psychiatry, 34,* 98–111.

Weitzman, Lenore J. (1985). *The divorce revolution: The unexpected consequences for women and children in America.* New York: Free Press.

West, Candace (1984). When the doctor is a "lady": Power, status and gender in physician-patient encounters. *Symbolic Interaction, 7* (1), 87–106.

White males propel Bush into office, exit polls show (1988). *Tucson Citizen,* November 9, p. 1A.

Whiting, Beatrice B., & Whiting, John W. M. (1975). *Children of six cultures: A psycho- cultural analysis.* Cambridge, MA: Harvard University Press.

Whitten, Patricia L. (1984). Competition among female vervet monkeys. In Meredith F. Small (Ed.), *Female primates: Studies by women primatologists* (pp. 127–140). New York: Alan R. Liss, Inc.

Wiemer, Annegret J. (1987). Foreign l(anguish), mother tongue: concepts of language in contemporary feminist science fiction. *Women's Studies, 14,* 163–173.

Wiest, Raymond E. (1983) Male migration, machismo, and conjugal roles: Implications for fertility control in a Mexican municipio. *Journal of Comparative Family Studies, 14* (2), 167–181.

Wilsnack, Sharon (1974). The effects of social drinking on women's fantasy. *Journal of Personality, 42,* 243–261.

Winter, David G. (1967). Power motivation in thought and action. Unpublished doctoral dissertation, Harvard University.

Winter, David G. (1973). *The power motive.* New York: Free Press.

Winter, David G. (1988). The power motive in women—and men. *Journal of Personality and Social Psychology, 54* (3), 510–519.

Winter, David G., & Barenbaum, Nicole B. (1985). Responsibility and the power motive in women and men. *Journal of Personality, 53* (2), 335–355.

Winter, David G., & Stewart, Abigail J. (1978). The power motive. In H. London & J. E. Exner (Eds.), *Dimensions of personality.* New York: Wiley.

Winter, David G., Stewart, Abigail J., & McClelland, David C. (1977). Husband's motives and wife's career level. *Journal of Personality and Social Psychology, 35,* 159–166.

Wolf, W. C., & Fligstein, N. D. (1979). Sex and authority in the workplace: The causes of sexual inequality. *American Sociological Review, 44,* 235–252.

Yankelovich D., Skelly, & White (1980). Surveys conducted for the American Council on Life Insurance, 1973–1978. Reported in *Public Opinion,* December-January, p. 34.

Zellman, Gail L., & Goodchilds, Jacqueline D. (1983). Becoming sexual in adolescence. In Elizabeth Rice Allgeier & Naomi B. McCormick (Eds.), *Changing boundaries: Gender roles and sexual behavior* (pp. 49–63). Mountain View, CA: Mayfield.

Zimmerman, Don H., & West, Candace (1975). Sex roles, interruptions and silence in conversation. In Barrie Thorne & Nancy Henley (Eds.), *Language and sex: Difference and dominance* (pp. 105–129). Rowley, MA: Newbury House.

Subject Index

Author Index

240

6634